LEADERSHIP

EDDIE JONES

WITH DONALD McRAE

LEADERSHIP

Lessons From My Life in Rugby

MACMILLAN

First published 2021 by Macmillan
an imprint of Pan Macmillan
The Smithson, 6 Briset Street, London EC1M 5NR
EU representative: Macmillan Publishers Ireland Ltd, 1st Floor,
The Liffey Trust Centre, 117–126 Sheriff Street Upper,
Dublin 1, D01 YC43
Associated companies throughout the world
www.panmacmillan.com

ISBN 978-1-5290-7215-0 HB
ISBN 978-1-5290-7216-7 TPB

1 3 5 7 9 8 6 4 2

A CIP catalogue record for this book is available from the British Library.

Typeset in Warnock Pro by Jouve (UK), Milton Keynes
Printed and bound by CPI Group (UK) Ltd, Croydon, CR0 4YY

Visit **www.panmacmillan.com** to read more about all our books
and to buy them. You will also find features, author interviews and
news of any author events, and you can sign up for e-newsletters
so that you're always first to hear about our new releases.

For my father – who always gave me such guidance and support

CONTENTS

Prologue: Inside the Bubble   1

STAGE 1: VISION

1   Setting the Vision   7
2   Character over Cover Drive   31
3   Clarity Is the New Clever   53
4   The Glue of Knowledge   77

STAGE 2: BUILD

5   Growth Mondays   99
6   Disciplined Thinking and Emotional Journeys   117
7   Conflict Is Healthy   137
8   Finding the Access Point   155

STAGE 3: EXPERIMENT

9   Review Constantly   175
10   The 3 Per Cent Reminder   191
11   Other Voices   209
12   A Close Examination   227

STAGE 4: WIN [OVERCOME FAILURE]

13   The Science of Learning   247
14   Red Teaming Transformation   261
15   A Clean Sweep   277
16   Chemistry and Diversity   295

STAGE 5: REBUILD

17   The Cycle Continues   315

Acknowledgements   337
Picture Acknowledgements   339
Index   341

LEADERSHIP – THE CYCLE OF SUCCESS

- Building a high-performing team is a cycle of endeavour. The journey will have a clear start but does not stop

- High-performing teams require continuous improvement and a regular refresh or rebuild

- The cycle requires leadership – leadership with values, methods, tools and above all communication

- At every stage of the cycle, leadership will apply strategic, operational and tactical thinking

- A successful leader will ebb and flow between each level of thinking, recognizing and applying the right level for each situation

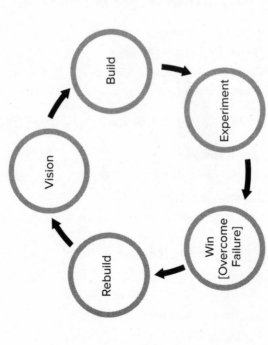

LEADERSHIP VALUES TO BE APPLIED

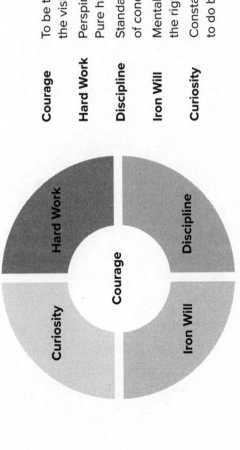

Courage   To be the best, to achieve the vision

Hard Work   Perspiration vs. inspiration. Pure hard graft

Discipline   Standards, applying the code of conduct

Iron Will   Mental toughness, displayed at the right times

Curiosity   Constant hunger to learn more, to do better

PROLOGUE:
INSIDE THE BUBBLE

This is a book about leadership inside the usually secretive bubble of a high-performance environment. It is built around my work as the head coach of the England rugby team, but I hope it will appeal to anyone interested in methods of leadership, learning and growth, whether they are working in sport or business, education or the arts, politics or the media, or any field where an organization faces immense challenges and stimulating opportunities.

It is written primarily for people intrigued by leadership and coaching, but my interests and influences are as varied as a career which has seen me work as the national coach of Australia, South Africa, Japan and England. I have coached at four World Cups, reaching the final three times and with a winner's gold medal tucked away in a box somewhere, but I am also proud of my work in the amateur club game with Randwick in Sydney, in Super Rugby with the Brumbies, and in club rugby in Japan and the English Premiership. As a leader I am shaped, too, by my past experiences as a schoolteacher and a principal and by my personal life as a son, a brother, a husband and a father. The family, just like a school, is also a team and an entity which is always evolving and hopefully strengthening.

So the ideas and principles in the ensuing pages are not limited to sport. They are not applicable only to business either, even though I have learnt so much from corporate leaders, whether as a part-time consultant to Goldman Sachs in Tokyo or while talking to inspiring men like Tadashi Yanai, the founder and head of

Uniqlo, the casual clothing company which he started from nothing in Japan and built up to its current global worth in excess of $45 billion. The leadership strategies and techniques discussed in the book can be utilized in most areas of life.

They are told through the prism of rugby, with stories of the past and the present helping to clarify and explain the lessons I have absorbed over 25 years as a professional coach. I write in detail about my work in Australia, South Africa and Japan, but the focus is on my current role with England. I have concentrated on the last two years from the World Cup in 2019 to the tumultuous back-to-back seasons we have just endured in 2020–1. This has been a period of great highs and difficult lows.

We reached the World Cup final and won the Six Nations and the Autumn Nations Cup. But we also encountered problems both inside and outside the squad and within our leadership group. As a consequence, we endured a difficult Six Nations in 2021, losing three out of five matches and finishing fifth. Of course this is unacceptable to me, to the players and to any passionate supporter of the England team.

But here, in these pages, I do not shy away from the troubles we have endured. They are illuminating and instructive. Show me a coach or a leader who has worked only in a successful environment and I will know that he or she have only been in the job for a very short time. They won't have learnt much and they won't have many lessons to offer you. I want to learn from people who have been exposed to adversity, who have had to reflect and adapt and who have emerged from the struggle feeling even more robust and fiercely competitive.

So this book is also informed by everything I have absorbed during my constant dialogue with leading coaches around the world. One of the privileges of my position is that I am able to talk in detail about leadership with men such as Sir Alex Ferguson and Arsène Wenger, Pep Guardiola and Gareth Southgate, while also participating in frequent coaching forums with colleagues from across the globe.

Some readers will be surprised to learn how my work with England has been sharpened by conversations with Ron Adams, the 73-year-old assistant coach of the National Basketball Association's Golden State Warriors. Ron has been the indispensable truth-teller to head coach Steve Kerr during three championship-winning campaigns. I have also learnt new ideas by studying the stunning rise of the Gonzaga Bulldogs, a hugely successful college basketball team from one of the smallest universities in America. Each day is a new opportunity for me to listen and to learn.

Every team, organization, company, coach and individual person can learn from the simple five-step cycle of leadership which drives my work and this book. The last two years have been the most intense and testing of my coaching career. The long shadow of Covid has stalked everything we have done and I have been stretched and examined as a leader like never before. But it's all part of the ceaseless cycle of leadership.

I believe I have grown and matured as a coach while relying on the building blocks of:

- Strategy

- People

- Operation

- Management

We have been through five stages of the leadership cycle:

- Vision

- Build

- Experiment

- Win [Overcome Failure]

- Rebuild

In each stage I have relied on the three Ms where I have strived to:

- Manage people

- Mine for conflict

- Map where we are in the cycle

The vision, structure and culture of our work is dependent on the quality of people we can call upon with England. We have some exceptional players and people but, above all else, they are human beings. There has been complexity and conflict. We have been undermined by a possible sense of entitlement, and a subtle denting of the desire which took us all the way to the World Cup final. I will outline the steps we are taking to remedy this situation as we move through the leadership cycle.

We constantly reflect and review, and rely on the insights provided by fresh sets of eyes from experts in divergent fields who assess our camp with independent clarity. This summer we were revitalized and refreshed. A new chemistry emerged and so we turn to the next two years before the 2023 World Cup is held in France with renewed belief and purpose.

The cycle of leadership is relentless and demanding. But it is always absorbing and fascinating. It covers areas of preparation and communication, growth and development, identity and cohesion. Mistakes are made and errors are rectified. Games are won and lost, players come and go, but the leadership cycle keeps whirring and churning because there is never perfection – only the steady pursuit of improvement.

I hope you will enjoy reading about the lessons we have learnt, both with England and my other teams over the past quarter of a century. I also hope they might be of practical interest to you and even pertinent to your own work and life.

STAGE 1: VISION

1. Setting the Vision
[STRATEGY]

- Always start with the end in mind
- Set the principles
- Establish the values
- Understand the climate
- Know the environment

2. Character over Cover Drive
[PEOPLE]

- Put the right people around you
- Build togetherness
- Identify the quick wins and the big changes required
- Plan the transformation

3. Clarity Is the New Clever
[OPERATION]

- Assess everything
- Provide the clarity – the code of operation, the expectations of delivery
- Translate the vision into achievable goals

4. The Glue of Knowledge
[MANAGEMENT]

- Understand the groups, understand the individuals
- Understand the gaps – in capability, values and belief
- Align the vision to individual journeys

1

SETTING THE VISION

ALWAYS START WITH THE END IN MIND

I faced another test of leadership, and of character, in the dark and uncertain days of November 2019. As the English winter rolled relentlessly towards us, I was still hurting. We had gone from playing arguably the best game of rugby that England had ever produced, in beating New Zealand, to losing the World Cup final a week later against South Africa. The nature of our defeat on 2 November felt every bit as painful as the 32–12 margin of defeat suggested. But just seven days earlier we had come close to sporting perfection.

Rugby, like life itself, is an imperfect business. The basics of the game are simple enough as it is based on courage and daring, cohesion and commitment, but rugby's ever-shifting laws and patterns make it a complicated sport. I have always said it is far harder to pursue the elusive idea of perfection in rugby than in games like football or basketball. But on 26 October 2019, at a pulsating Yokohama Stadium in Japan, we blew away the All Blacks, who had started the tournament – and our World Cup semi-final – as typically heavy favourites.

England dominated the match from the get-go and, on this occasion, the 19–7 margin of victory did not tell the full story. If we had taken our chance for one more try, and had kept out New Zealand for their solitary score, we would have pretty much played the perfect game of rugby. It's a quest that has intrigued me for 25 years as a professional coach, and while working in the Test arena for 175 international matches with Australia, South Africa, Japan and England. We had not been perfect against the All Blacks but the performance and a World Cup semi-final win went a long way to justifying four years of rigorous planning and hard work.

I focused on the next match, the one which mattered most, that very same night. There was only one fleeting private moment early the following week when I allowed the thought to flit across my mind: 'What will I do if we win the World Cup?' It hung there, tantalizingly, as I wondered if I would simply want to return with England to try and win the tournament again in 2023. Or would I feel it was time to do something totally different in coaching?

The memory is vivid. I was alone in my room in the Tokyo Hilton but, after ten seconds, I shut down the pointless speculation. I had a word with myself: 'Mate, you're getting way ahead of yourself. We've got a huge match ahead.' I can honestly say that I did not think about winning the World Cup again all week. I concentrated on the team and the task ahead.

The World Cup is a reminder that constant winning is abnormal. Twenty teams play in the tournament and only one emerges as the winner. For 19 teams it's normal to lose in the end. Only one team is going to be abnormal. So you're always striving to be abnormal and it's incredibly difficult. People might expect that, before we beat the All Blacks, I would have made a defining, tub-thumping speech of leadership to inspire an exceptional performance. I was, instead, pretty low-key and measured that evening.

But, three days earlier, on the Wednesday, I felt we weren't quite there in training. We weren't sharp enough for the All Blacks. So I did something different that evening. I brought a samurai sword into the team room. It was impressive and authentic and I had spent a fair amount of money on it from an antique shop in Tokyo. I also brought in some kiwi fruit. You could say it was cheesy, rather than fruity, but I used the samurai sword to scythe them in two. The blade was so sharp that the kiwi fruits split apart in an instant.

'There you go, boys,' I said. 'See how we do it now?'

The players were laughing but a few of them shot me a look as if to say, 'Shit, this guy is nuts.' I still walked around the room with the samurai sword and made them all feel the deadly blade.

From there we developed the idea of facing down the Haka in a V formation with Owen Farrell at the head of it. We also had a very rigorous meeting with the players' leadership group the next morning and I pointed out some of the minor problems. The players addressed them and got it right. We won the game.

If we had lost, people would have been entitled to say: 'How stupid was all that stuff with the samurai sword?' But it makes a good story and we can say we brought out the sword and a small tray of kiwi fruit before one of England's most famous victories.

We faced a different challenge in the week of the final. Pretty much everyone outside of South Africa expected us to win. We knew this truth, but understanding the consequences is much harder to fathom. Sometimes I feel like people only really understand a situation once they've experienced it. It's a bit like having a baby. Before the birth you are given so much advice from people who are already parents. But until the baby arrives you cannot really understand what is involved.

In the week of the final we spent a lot of time telling the players that the Springboks were going to come at them with ferocious intent. We reminded them that South African rugby players tend to dislike the English and so they would dredge up even more emotion. We spoke about the fact that the Boks were also trying to do something special for South Africa as a country. They were being captained for the first time by a black player, the inspiring Siya Kolisi, and they were coached by a canny Afrikaner, Rassie Erasmus, who is very smart when planning for decisive games. We didn't underestimate any of these factors but, until they had been through the experience of facing a fired-up Springbok team in a World Cup final, it was hard for the players to understand what was coming.

South Africa had taken a different route to the final. They had lost their first game in Japan when they were beaten comprehensively by New Zealand. It concentrated their minds because they knew that if they lost another game they were on their way home. No other team had lost a group game and gone on to win the World Cup and so they also understood they had to make history. England, in contrast, won every game up until the final. The Springboks scraped into the final after beating Wales by the narrowest of margins. They had been under immense pressure since the very first game. But it actually strengthened South Africa. Having been so strong until the final we learnt that in the World Cup it's more the mental strain, rather than the physical exertion, that fatigues you.

I made a decision to keep the week fairly normal in terms of training. We stuck to the same routine which had served us so well against Argentina, Australia and New Zealand in the previous three games. The week went pretty well and then, travelling to the ground on the day of the final, we got caught in traffic. Of course we had rehearsed for this eventuality and gone through a mock drill in the past when you arrive late for a game. So we were prepared, but I'm sure one or two players were still unsettled by the fact it happened on World Cup final day.

A couple of minutes into the final something far more disconcerting happened: Kyle Sinckler and Maro Itoje collided as they went to tackle the Springbok wing Makazole Mapimpi. Kyle was knocked out. He was eventually able to stand up and walk slowly from the field but his World Cup final was over. We had lost one of our key men, our in-form tighthead prop, and we would soon buckle under the sustained might of the Springbok scrum.

We were under the pump in the first 20 minutes, and my lasting regret is that I didn't make the two early substitutions we needed to change the momentum of the game. But to take off a couple of players after 20 minutes in a World Cup final was a huge call. I have done it before in the international arena – when I withdrew Luther Burrell after 20 minutes and changed the course of a Test match against Australia in Brisbane in 2016. But I chose not to do anything so radical against South Africa.

Perhaps I was guilty of making the wrong decision simply because it was the World Cup final rather than addressing the actual game slipping away in front of my very eyes. If I had been bolder as a leader we would have had a better chance of becoming world champions that night.

Neil Craig is our head of high performance, but that's a meaningless title which doesn't come close to explaining his value to me and the squad. He is here to tell the truth and, also, to help me coach the coaches. Neil is an expert in communication and leadership and he had a conversation in Melbourne with Corinne Reid, a psychologist, after the World Cup. Corinne had worked with our players and she had done a lot of good work with the squad before she returned to Australia to take up an academic post. Neil told Corinne we'd had a very good tournament until the final. 'What were the problems?' she asked, before adding, 'You surely know that there were problems?' Neil couldn't quite articulate a clear answer and I think that played on his mind.

Corinne had always encouraged us to understand that healthy conflict is crucial in high-performance activity. She had reminded us to look for problems in victory. This is a crucial lesson in the science of learning in elite sport. Get real if you think everything is rosy just because you won. Don't be naïve – particularly if you're leading a squad of 31 highly motivated guys wanting to play rugby and win the World Cup. So many things will be happening under the surface that you can't see. So you need to monitor conflict.

The longer we're in this game the more we know that if everything seems to be operating beautifully, and no issues are being raised by anyone, your antenna should be twitching. Your best and healthiest environment is when items are being tabled that need to be fixed. Such a situation means that people are pointing out what's not going well, or what they're having trouble with, and you then have a chance to rectify them before your next big challenge. You need to be far more wary when it seems as if everything is perfect and nothing needs to be examined. Neil and I believe now that we fell into that illusion in the week of the final.

He thinks we should have generated more conflict in the camp. Neil has a point because, deep down, he and I were a little anxious about the final and the players would have been the same. We could have brought it to the surface in a stark way instead of cruising along as if this was just another match. Perhaps we should have spoken about that in more direct terms. We could have dug into the reality that the win over New Zealand had created so much more expectation externally as well as internally. The final was a very different game with much greater consequences.

Neil believes we should have put those facts on the table to get different players' points of view as to how we would handle the changed circumstances. A group of us could have sat down together and perhaps a player who was feeling more anxious than normal might have been surprised to hear Neil talking about how he was on edge. It could have generated an open and healthy discussion about conflicted feelings and suddenly that one particular player would realize that he was far from the only one in camp with those intense emotions. It's natural to experience them in World Cup final week. We can never know, but maybe getting more out in the open could have shifted our mindset before we played South Africa.

Neil argues that it was all too smooth and too good to be true. He says he should have told himself, 'Get real, Neil. This is the game that decides the best team in the world. Of course our boys are going to be anxious. So let's get fucking serious about everything we're discussing here.' He believes we should have rattled the cage and let out all the conflict swirling inside everyone.

But there is not just one right way to prepare for a final. So much depends on the mentality of your group. We need to understand what the players need and so I continue to work hard to be more accurate in this area. But there is always an element of rolling the dice when you approach the peak of a high-performance goal. We could have delved into the psychology of the team that week and unearthed some issues that were clearly there. It could have made the team stronger but, equally, it could have weakened us. I've seen it happen both ways. There were things I saw that week which I could have attended to right there and then. It might have fixed us, but I could also have made the problem worse. You always run the risk because these are not black-and-white situations. There is so much grey nuance as you make a very complex call of judgement.

On the Wednesday, we trained pretty well. The players looked strong and focused, but I could have nitpicked over a couple of things. I might have made the matter worse by doing so, or I could have made it better. I decided to accentuate the positives and stick to the usual pattern of our training week.

Other coaches sometimes choose to do things differently. Before a different World Cup knockout match, a head coach decided to rattle the cage. He had developed a very strong system of play and his squad followed the same pre-game routine before every match. It had worked for many years, but then, in this particular World Cup week, the coach made them do two extra walk-throughs of various moves to iron out any problems. Some of their leading players were saying, 'What the fuck is going on here? What's wrong with us?' If your most experienced players are having such thoughts, what might their younger teammates be thinking? 'The coach doesn't trust us any more. There's something wrong here.'

Their team went into the game and got pounded. The coach had rolled the dice, deciding that some issues needed to be brought to the surface so he could try to fix them. Maybe he got it wrong, but these are the judgements you make all the time. You can be smart after the event but, before the game, you never really know for certain which is the best approach. But the key point to remember is that you can never expect to find that everything is just right. There are always problems.

You've always got to be mining for those problems and making sure that you develop a solution-based culture. Players and staff shouldn't see any problem as being terminal. They need to see it as an opportunity to provide a solution. We didn't have enough people who thought in solution-based terms. They were more conditioned to see a problem as a threat – and, most of all, a threat to their levels of comfort.

The bottom line remained that we didn't have enough ex-perience – both of such a massive occasion, but also of what it takes to beat two excellent teams who play the game in totally different ways. We shocked New Zealand with our attack and our intensity, but we failed to adapt to the far greater physicality and set-piece concentration that South Africa bring to a Test. Our flexibility and versatility were not effective enough. Over the course of the whole tournament, you could probably make an argument that England were the best and most consistent team. But we were just off the mark when it mattered most. All of us, coaches and players, need to take responsibility for that. But sometimes you have got to acknowledge it's just not your day.

Defeat was crushing. We believed that the boys were ready to fulfil the vision I had set out for them when I took charge of Eng-land in November 2015. Winning the World Cup in Japan had always been the end result we had in mind. It was our vision for England and we had worked backwards from that imagined goal and created the culture, the environment and the sheer belief that made it a realistic aim. There had been challenges along the way, with a few bumpy spells on the road to Japan, but the objec-tive was always clear.

We had a fantastic group of players whose talent was matched by their willingness to learn and their determination to improve. We became a tight and ambitious outfit primed to become world champions – until we ran into South Africa.

The Springboks were better than England on the night of the final. They were more aggressive, more clinical, more powerful and, most of all, more convinced that the World Cup belonged to them. The big difference was that South Africa lifted themselves at least two levels above their patchy win over Wales the week before. They were exceptional against us.

We watched them lift the trophy and dance around with delight and all we could do was wonder what we might have done differently. But there was not much point. The dream of 2019 had died. I was unsure whether I should bury it even deeper by preparing to walk away.

We flew from Tokyo to London and, while I said most of the right things, and tried to shrug and smile when asked how I felt, I was bereft. I felt just as empty as I had done 16 years earlier when I had coached Australia to the World Cup final in Sydney – where we had lost in extra time to England and that famous Jonny Wilkinson drop goal in November 2003.

I had made the mistake of staying on as the Wallabies' head coach because I thought I could set a new vision and start a new cycle of success for Australian rugby. The vision made sense but I made too many mistakes over the next two years. It was partly down to sheer fatigue. I was burnt out by the job. Even before I was sacked in 2005, I knew it would have been better for both Australian rugby and myself if we had made a clean break after the final.

England was different. Months before we left for Japan I had signed a new contract to remain as head coach until 2021. While the Rugby Football Union (RFU) wanted me to take England to the next World Cup in 2023, I needed to work out if I had the necessary desire to complete another four-year cycle.

Over the years I had analysed the aftermath of every rugby World Cup and the picture was clear. The losing team in the final almost always suffered a bad blip as they struggled to get over the disappointment. Most World Cup final coaches, with the exception of New Zealand's Steve Hansen, disappeared from the Test arena or failed to replicate the same success.

I had a World Cup winner's medal from 2007, after I spent a three-month spell as a technical consultant to South Africa when the Boks won the tournament under Jake White. So, while I had been involved in three World Cup finals, I knew how immensely difficult it was to sustain success.

All those thoughts tumbled through my mind, which still felt a little scrambled during that long and draining November. The easy option was to see out my contract and help England prepare the way for a new coaching regime. I would be professional and dedicated and oversee the transition before I began a new rugby adventure of my own in 2021. Secondly, I knew it would be wrong to renege on my agreement and walk out on England before then. They had given me a fascinating and unexpected opportunity by appointing me as head coach in 2015.

The third option seemed uncertain. Could I really lift myself and England and have an almighty crack at another four years? How would I even go about such a task? Was it a crazy idea? Or could I achieve even more this time around than I had done in the first cycle where I started with a 17-Test winning streak and a Grand Slam on the way to the World Cup final?

I thought about it for a few days, on my own, and it helped to use the values, principles and methods which run through this book. They are worth repeating, for I believe they apply to so many aspects of leadership, in sport, business, education, and most other fields of work.

- Building another high-performing team would demand a ceaseless cycle of activity

- England would need continuous improvement

- There would be a rigorous process of rebuilding and refreshing

- I would have to apply strategic, transformational, operational and managerial thinking

- It would require me to criss-cross between each level of thinking, while also applying tactical insights and crystal-clear communication with my assistant coaches and the players, so that we could grow in every stage of this consuming cycle

- I would need to draw on all my years of leadership experience – and mine the lessons of both victory and defeat

As I wrote down these notes I also underlined this key point as I thought how I would begin the cycle:

ALWAYS START WITH THE END IN MIND

It doesn't matter if you are the CEO of a giant corporation, the head of a school department, the coach of a sports team or just the leader in any activity which you love. You've always got to know where you're going. Your final goal, your mission, provides the map to help you reach your destination.

But if you are still clouded in your thinking, and your ending remains fuzzy in your own mind, you might as well abandon the journey. Otherwise you will go round in circles and keep hitting dead ends. There are only so many U-turns you can make before those who follow you become demotivated.

You should always start with the vision of your end goal and work backwards to your starting point. It is like climbing down a ladder step by methodical step but, once your strategy is in place, you will be able to forge ahead as a unit. Your foundation will be steeped in clarity and precision. It will take time and effort, as everything worth doing in life does, but it will also be immensely rewarding as you accumulate knowledge.

Many people fall into the trap of not saying where they want to go. And if you fail to spell out your final destination as a leader, then the focus of everyone in your company or team will drift.

You become lost and, inevitably, you will lose deals and games, people and profits. But if you always have the end in mind, you will have the vision to guide you each difficult step of the way.

At the highest level of business or sport, the competition is searing and the challenges are profound. To overcome the opposition and move beyond the obstacles, you need to have a voracious ambition to improve every day. If you lose that relentless desire, the restless feeling within you, then it's time for you to step aside as a leader.

As soon as you start questioning yourself in these terms you're pretty much shot. I think you're on the way out if you say to yourself: 'We're in a good position so why should I get up and work really hard again today? Why don't I give myself a little break? I reckon I've earnt it.' You probably deserve to do something else, but it's time then to admit you've had enough of leadership at this level. It's time for you to step aside.

There is no shame in making that choice. Instead, it's a sign of honour, and wisdom, to know when your race is run. You've reached the end point and it is the moment for someone else, with fresh energy and resolve, to drive your organization to a new destination. Of course it will happen to me, and probably in not too many years from now, but back in November 2019 it was suddenly obvious that I had not reached that point with England.

I was on board for the full four-year tilt at a new cycle as soon as I started thinking about how much I wanted to get back to it. I thought about the boss who walks the floor in his factory every day. Instead of staying in his office, out of sight, while having a peaceful cup of tea, he is walking the floor because he has that ceaseless desire to keep progressing. He needs to see whether people are doing their job properly and, if they're not, he will give them a push or a prod to remind them to give that little bit extra.

Most teams think they give 100 per cent, and they're probably close to doing that on the big occasion. But the missing extra few per cent make all the difference. I call it 'the discretionary effort', because it comes down to you and your desire to find that extra 5 or even 10 per cent that lies dormant within us all. The leaders who reach deep within themselves and unearth that extra ambition and desire are the ones who help their teams, or organizations, become great.

It was obvious I had the hunger to continue all the way to France in 2023. I was climbing aboard the train again and I was ready to drive it to the very end with renewed impetus.

But, before I told anyone, I needed to imagine the end point myself. I needed to set the vision.

I also reminded myself that no one knows the limits of what we can do. If we set the right vision for ourselves, we can push past the imagined boundaries and reach somewhere new.

There was no point regurgitating the same vision as before by telling everyone we were aiming to win the World Cup in 2023. That was less a vision than an echo of the original plan. Obviously that World Cup-winning aim would be at the heart of our endeavours, but we needed a new vision which would inspire the players.

The seed of an idea had begun to germinate. I have always been open to influences outside of sport, and the longer I have worked in coaching, the more that curiosity has grown. It is one of the reasons why, over the last seven years, I have acted as a part-time consultant on the Goldman Sachs board in Tokyo. Business people are often fascinated by elite sport and they are keen to extract any lessons we offer which can be used in their own companies. At the same time, in sport, we can learn so much from leaders in business and other fields. So my occasional meetings at Goldman Sachs were a reciprocal arrangement – and they have been of great benefit to me.

A prime example is that my work there led me to forge a friendship with Tadashi Yanai. He is a Japanese billionaire but, to me, being less interested in money, he is much more than that. Tadashi is a bold and original thinker who is relentless and courageous in his visionary way. He is the founder, owner and president of Fast Retailing, which is dominated by Uniqlo – the company he set up in 1984. Uniqlo now have about 2,500 stores around the world and Tadashi is considered the richest man in Japan. In 2021 his personal wealth was estimated at more than $45 billion. Personally, I love the story of how he became successful.

Tadashi's father owned a department store in western Japan. It was a small and modest company. When Tadashi eventually took over from his dad and began running the store, the business blew up in a few weeks. Every employee in his area quit because he was too brash. Tadashi was driven and he knew exactly what he wanted to do. But, as he tells the story to me now, he didn't have any emotional intelligence or even the basic capacity to work with people. He wanted to change everything his father had built up in order to make the old department store something new and very different. But it didn't work.

It was time for Tadashi to step back and think. Instead of tearing up a steady business, it became clear to him that he should set up his own department store. Rather than just attacking the business in a haphazard way, he also took the time to set out his vision.

Tadashi's dream was to become the biggest casual-clothes maker in the world. It is amusing because he was this young guy who had failed badly when taking over a little department store. Suddenly, he wanted to storm the fast-fashion market and become a worldwide force in the retail business. Once he had his vision in mind, he went after it with energy and enterprise. His first Uniqlo store opened in Hiroshima in 1984 and Tadashi was so successful that he began buying factories in Japan. He was so aggressive in driving his dream that it did not take him long to create a chain of shops.

He explains now that, at the same time, he learnt how to teach and how to lead. He had begun as a very autocratic leader, but the more lessons he absorbed, the more he morphed into a company owner who gave responsibility back to his workforce. But he and his staff always kept his vision in mind – which was to become the biggest casual-clothes brand in the world. They are closing in on the dream as they're now up to number three in the world of fast fashion. Only Zara, the Spanish company, and H&M, from Sweden, are ahead of Uniqlo.

I thought of Tadashi's bold vision, and the courage and drive of his character, as I set the vision for England in late November 2019. I had four years ahead of me and I wanted to emulate Tadashi in believing that there is no end of possibility to what we can do. I imagined a vision for England that would be far bigger than anything ever dreamt up in this rugby-playing country where extravagant ambition generally creates suspicion and doubt.

None of the cultural differences between me, the little bloke who looks half-Japanese while sounding like a full-on Aussie, and the English rugby establishment should ever get in the way. It still makes me laugh – the irony of an Australian coaching the England rugby team. It was one of the attractions for me in taking the job because I knew it would be difficult. I might be the first and the last Australian ever to coach England because our thought patterns, as sports people, are diametrically opposed.

In 2015 I had to be brave enough to change. I had to accept the traditions of England rugby while also being strategic enough to transform the mindset that clogged the game over here. I reined in my more abrasive characteristics while making some appropriate changes to English rugby.

I had done that for four years and we had been relatively successful. The bare statistics said I had the best rate of winning Test matches of any England coach in history. But, still, we had fallen just short of completing the World Cup dream.

It was time to dream even bigger. I had the end in mind, at the very start of this new cycle of activity, and I was convinced of the vision.

We would turn England into the world's greatest team.

The vision was set and, most excitingly of all, there was no finite finish line. Any coach and team can achieve short-term success. But the essence of greatness is sustained success. We would aim to keep improving and winning, climbing higher and higher, with a dream that included – and stretched beyond – winning the World Cup.

The end goal was clear. We would strive to become the best team in rugby history.

When you have established your vision, it is important to take four strategic steps:

- Set the principles

- Establish the values

- Understand the climate

- Know the environment

Throughout the book we will explore the principles and the values we need to apply to fulfil our vision but, for now, it is important to stress that courage is at the heart of all leadership. Hard work, discipline, mental toughness, humility, curiosity and integrity provide the bedrock of our principles and values, but they are redundant without the courage it takes to lead a vision.

In recent years I admired how Jürgen Klopp set the vision at Liverpool. It was a courageous vision which suited the mentality of the city. The way he walked into Liverpool was transformative because he immediately made everyone understand he was determined to drive them to somewhere special. I've not had the chance to meet Klopp, so I am not sure if he knows that the origin of the word 'coach' is Hungarian. It explains the nature of our job, which is to get the people we look after to the destination we have set for them.

Klopp has been such a success at Liverpool because he had the courage, as well as the determination and intelligence, to take the club, the city and its people to some incredible places. They won the Champions League and, after 30 years without being

England's champions, they finally lifted the Premier League title in 2020. But his bravery underpinned everything because the vision he set was bloody difficult to bring to life.

Many leaders don't have such courage. They want to be careful. They want to be comfortable. And if you're careful and comfortable, rather than brave, your vision will be limited.

I don't think you can learn how to generate this kind of courage. It's either inside you or it's not. There is no doubt that people who are not cut out for leadership can draw on deep reservoirs of courage. But the courage to set a deeply ambitious vision, and make people want to follow you towards its fulfilment, is distinctive. I think it often comes from our parents or from something that happened in our past lives that has exacerbated this need to lead.

Leadership is also driven by ego because, to have such courage, you need conviction and self-belief. You need to think: 'I can lead my team to this visionary place.' But leadership should never be dominated by your own motives. It's got to be about the motives of the organization you lead. Tadashi Yanai learnt this after his wayward start, and I hope that I, too, have absorbed this crucial lesson in balancing my own ego so that it becomes secondary to the needs of my team. Experience has helped so much in this regard.

It is not a contradiction of leadership to say that I now regard myself as a servant to the players.

When I decided to recommit fully to England, I knew I needed to step forward and give voice to a new vision. In the last cycle, from 2015 to 2019, we focused too much on the outcome of winning the World Cup.

Now we need to think in far more ambitious terms, because to win in 2023 we're going to have to be better than we were in 2019. So why not try to be the greatest rugby team of all time?

In this way we will focus more on the process of where we want to go – and concentrate on helping extend and encourage the players to think big. I want them to know that playing for

England will help them become the best they can possibly be over the next four years.

They're moving in the right direction. But it was telling when, in December 2020, various experts picked a World XV from the last ten years. Not one England player made the selection. I agreed, because I didn't think a single England player demanded inclusion for his performances between 2010 and 2020. But don't tell me there are not enough talented England players to make the cut. There are plenty with the potential but, clearly, there's still a big step ahead. I believe we can help them take that step.

To become the greatest team in the world, we need five or six of our players to establish themselves as the very best in their position. So we have made it a goal to change the whole way we talk about selection. Being picked for England isn't the pinnacle. You are only just starting on the road to improvement and finding out how good you can be in the coming years.

In the past, to many players, England selection almost capped your career. You had made it. Mission accomplished. But now we're saying: 'This is just an entrée, boys. You're just beginning your real career.' It's one of the many ways we try to have a psychological theme to get more out of the players.

I ask them to think about becoming the kind of team that people talk about in the years ahead. I describe a scene where you might get a bunch of blokes in a pub and, when they look back over a few drinks, we want them to say our England side was the greatest rugby team they ever saw. That's a simple aim we want to chase hard and make real.

I have learnt that, when giving voice to the vision, you need to drip-feed ideas and test reaction. So you drop thoughts into your conversations at various times. It's interesting to see how people respond, so that any idea you have becomes a collaborative process, because you've already tested it with your senior associates. Obviously you can do this in a formal way, but I always remember the technique of the ex-Australian prime minister, Paul Keating. He used very colourful language and often inspired people. He would test out ideas on his staff at all times to gauge their reaction. If the response was uncertain or unclear, he would consider fresh ways of presenting the idea or, perhaps, even shelving it.

It's so important to work really hard on your observations. This was the main lesson I gleaned from my time with Sir Alex Ferguson. He emphasized the significance of close observation in his work at Manchester United. It echoes the idea of walking the shop floor, because understanding the atmosphere of your workplace is such a vital skill. I know it's tiring to do this, and it's one of the reasons why some leaders avoid it. But the best leaders are always gauging the mood and canvassing people in their organization. They know that you need to understand the climate around your group and know the environment within which you are working.

I will always keep walking the floor.

When I set the vision for England on my arrival in 2015, it was a simple task. It seemed obvious to me that they were playing the wrong style. If you go back to Tadashi Yanai, he set a relatively pragmatic vision. His ambition to become a world leader was vast but his vision was focused. He did not try to emulate the most stylish designers at the high end of fashion. That would not have been practical for a young man whose first venture with a department store in Japan had failed. Tadashi cut his cloth to suit his skill set. He would concentrate on sensible design and good quality and get the basics right. From there he would build and transform and expand. His vision was smart, his planning was methodical and his operation was clinical. We just need to see where Uniqlo are now to know that he set the right vision for his company.

It might seem absurd to draw an analogy between fast fashion and the way in which England play Test rugby. But in 2015, after they had been humiliated and knocked out of the group stages of their home World Cup, I knew England needed to emulate that pragmatic but ruthless approach. You learn a lot about English rugby when you watch their clubs play in the Premiership. It's not attractive rugby, but it's hugely competitive, very traditional and relentlessly tough. That is the kind of game England's players are steeped in, so you cannot then expect them to cut loose and play Test rugby like New Zealand.

It was important to get England back on track by setting the right vision for them. We would play a style steeped in the honest values of English rugby and we would strive to win the 2019 World Cup. We came pretty close to fulfilling that vision. It helped that our objective was so clear. I also avoided making the mistake that is so tempting when you take over a floundering organization. Many new head coaches or CEOs try and solve all the issues that have caused the problems which led to the demise of their predecessor. But I steered clear of the deeper issues that lie at the fractured heart of English rugby. I did not try to sort out the mess between club and country. I remained laser-focused on my England squad and poured all my energy into welding them together into a tight-knit unit.

Twelve years earlier, when deciding to keep working with Australia in 2003, I spent more time addressing the operational side of the team than developing a new vision. I had become obsessed with winning the World Cup and that consumed my thinking in regard to our end goal. I was convinced that a radical change in our style of play would bring the vision to life. We wanted to redefine attacking rugby, and we needed to blend a running game into a kicking game to be successful. In that four-year period between World Cups, Australia went from a running game in 2003 to a tournament in 2007 which was dominated by the boot. At its very peak there were 95 kicks a game in that World Cup.

So we were on the right track and the playing formations of many teams now replicate the ideas we formulated with Australia in 2004. When we had Stephen Larkham at number 10, we were successful. But we fell away. The problem was less with the team, or even the vision, but more with me. I was still aggrieved at losing the 2003 final to England in such a close game. Foolishly, I thought about the 2007 tournament in France endlessly, rather than developing the best team I could over a four-year cycle. I allowed my World Cup obsession to get the better of me.

That bitter lesson taught me that, beyond strategy, you need to work even harder on the next three phases of leadership:

- Finding the right people

- Operation

- Management

I also understood, after my mistakes, that you need a selfless vision. It can't be about where you want to go as a leader. It's about where your organization needs to go. Those end goals are distinctly different. I just wasn't experienced enough as a leader to realize the difference in 2004 and 2005. So I was very lucky to have that South African experience which saw me join the Springboks before they became world champions in 2007. As a consultant I saw how a very good team operated, and I also identified a few errors which could be easily corrected.

Beyond the World Cup winners' medal I was given, it seemed far more important that I could use that wonderful experience and take Japan, a team with no expectations, to the World Cup in 2015. The success of Japan in that tournament set me up for the England job. But it was the four years I had building the Japanese players from total obscurity, to creating one of the greatest surprises in the history of sport, which enriched me the most as a leader.

My vision with Japan was clear-cut. They had won only one World Cup match in their entire history, against Zimbabwe. Apart from one draw, Japan had lost every other World Cup match by an average of 35 points. The absolute low had occurred when they conceded 145 points to New Zealand in 1995. When I took over as head coach in 2012, having spent the previous three years at Suntory in Tokyo, I set a bold vision for Japanese rugby.

We would aim to reach the World Cup quarter-finals in England in 2015.

Even my fellow coaches and the players thought I was crazy. But we nailed the areas of choosing the right people, operation and management, and I knew – on the eve of the tournament – that we had become a serious rugby team. It was why I was so embarrassed for Japan, and angry on behalf of my team, when we attended the 2015 opening ceremony. They depicted Japan as this nice little country that would host the 2019 tournament, but which had a team without a hope in Hades of winning a game. When it came to the 'highlights' section for Japan, the only footage they showed was that 145-point drubbing by the All Blacks 20 years before. I was furious.

However, I didn't go over the top. At the next team meeting I just touched on what we had seen and reset the vision which had driven our incredible growth over the previous three years. The players believed in the vision finally and they were very calm and very determined.

Japan's opening match of the World Cup against South Africa, the holders, turned out to be the second game of international rugby I've been involved in which came close to perfection. In a completely different way to England's defeat of New Zealand in 2019, we stunned the Springboks. We set the players a clear task before the game. Japan needed to be within a shout of victory at the 60-minute mark. If the game was still close after an hour, I believed the scoreboard would do the work for us. South Africa could struggle under pressure and we would take advantage. We were able to do that, and the way in which we won the game, at the death, going for the winning try rather than settling for a penalty to secure a draw, made it seem like a fairy tale. But our 34–32 victory was rooted in the vision we had set at the outset.

When we returned to Japan for the 2019 World Cup, the picture was very different. In the highlights reel at the opening ceremony, we saw four clips of Japan being triumphant. It showed us how far Japanese rugby had come. And then, of course, Japan made it all the way to the quarter-finals at their home World Cup. I felt I had played a significant part in that story by setting out the vision seven years earlier. It showed that if you dream big you can achieve something very special, and surprise those in the outside world.

England's mission, this vision, is also to create something special. We want the players in our squad to feel that they have an opportunity to create a legacy. When they come to write a great big book about the legacy of English rugby, we want it to start and end with all we have done on and off the field.

Coaching and leadership is a cyclical process. There is no end. As soon as you've achieved an end goal, you move on to the next vision. If you hang on to something, and say it is the best, you're mistaken. A team or a product can be the best in the world for a certain period. But nothing stands still and so, as the cycle continues, you need to produce a new vision.

What are Apple going to do with the iPhone? They might need to replace it in a few years with something very new. They had to downgrade the iPad to hasten the success of the iPhone. They had the courage to do this even though the iPad had been selling like hot cakes. Most of us had an iPad for a while. But Apple set themselves an even bigger vision with the iPhone.

It is the same with coaching an elite sports team. You can help them reach the World Cup final, and even win it, but you cannot stand still. You need to move on because there is no finish line when you are leading a team or an organization. I really believe you only cross your own finish line when you decide to walk away or retire. Until then you are in this endless cycle of activity.

Within the cycle you need to move ahead with a new quest. It always begins with your vision. And whenever you kick off a new phase in your leadership role, you must identify your goal and work backwards from that point. It is a simple but effective technique:

ALWAYS START WITH THE END IN MIND

- Set the vision

- Set the principles

- Establish the values

- Understand the climate

- Know the environment

- Keep walking the shop floor

2

CHARACTER OVER
COVER DRIVE

BUILD TOGETHERNESS WITH THE RIGHT PEOPLE
AROUND YOU

When I was appointed as Australia's head coach in 2001, the emotion of the moment was framed by a clear insight into the essential loneliness of leadership. Rod Macqueen, the man I replaced and the coach who had helped Australia win the World Cup in 1999, congratulated me and then added a telling sentence: 'You are now officially the loneliest man in Australia.'

Rod is a really intelligent bloke and I soon discovered the truth of his words. The head coach works in a lonely place. I'm sure it's the same with the CEO of any company, or the leader of most organizations – whether business or education, the military or politics. Leadership is a solitary existence, which is why, to overcome the isolation, you need to appoint the right people around you. They cannot take away the intense scrutiny you alone will feel when the job is at its most demanding – but they can ease the burden.

Sometimes you can be given a big job and you get burnt by it. You don't want to get too near the fire again. I think of Robbie Deans, who is one of the most brilliant coaches in world rugby. He coached the Crusaders to five Super Rugby titles, worked as an assistant coach of the All Blacks and then took over as head coach of Australia in 2008. Robbie was with Australia for five years. He started strongly, winning his first five Tests and thumping his

native New Zealand. But the job became complicated and difficult, and in the last couple of years it seemed as if Robbie was
constantly on the back foot. He was ridiculed in Australia, and the
fact that he was a Kiwi obviously didn't help. By the time the Wallabies had lost the series to the British and Irish Lions in 2013,
there was little option but for Robbie to resign.

The following April he accepted an offer to coach the Panasonic Wild Knights in Japan. Robbie has been there for the past
seven years. There is no sign of him moving back into a major job
in world rugby. I love Japanese rugby and I do a little consultancy
coaching with Suntory whenever I get a break from England. I
was also Suntory's head coach for three years, from 2009 to 2012,
so I understand the fascination of coaching in Japan. But you
cannot compare the odd big game between Panasonic and Suntory with the relentless white-heat intensity of Test rugby. It is
comfortable in Japan, whereas in the international arena it is
bruising and uncomfortable.

Wayne Smith is another brilliant coach who stepped away
from the cauldron of leadership at its highest level. He is one of
rugby's great coaches and an exceptional tactical thinker. We
came up against each other a few times – firstly when I was coaching the Brumbies in Canberra and Wayne was in charge of the
Crusaders in Canterbury. In his two years at Canterbury, the Crusaders won back-to-back Super 12 rugby titles in 1998 and 1999.
He then became the All Blacks' head coach for two years and
I coached against him in his final match in charge of New
Zealand.

Just as I began my career in international rugby, we played the
All Blacks twice in 2001. In my second Test as Australia's head
coach that August, I took the Wallabies to Dunedin to face
Smith's All Blacks. New Zealand had never lost at Carisbrook, or
the House of Pain, as it was called, and they were formidable.
Jonah Lomu scored a try for them in the second minute but we
held our nerve, played some tough rugby and won 23–15.

It was hardly disastrous for New Zealand but their press turned up the heat. Wayne is such an honest and good man that when they asked him if he was up to the job, he admitted he didn't know for sure. It was a truthful answer because none of us really know if we are going to be successful. So many intangibles and uncertainties can derail even a remarkable coach. But that moment of vulnerability was never forgotten. The pressure became scalding.

We went into the final game of the 2001 Tri-Nations with the competition in the balance. New Zealand had eight points and Australia had seven. South Africa, with six points, were out of the running, but the championship would be decided at Stadium Australia on 1 September in front of 90,978 fans.

It was a memorable Test. After dominating the first half, and building a 19–6 lead at the break, we were rocked by an immense comeback from Smith's team. They were 23–19 ahead and, after each side slotted a penalty, we needed a try in the dying minutes. We found it. Toutai Kefu rumbled over to help us win the match 29–26 and lift the Tri-Nations at my first attempt. It had been desperately close, but our victory, and New Zealand's defeat, cost Wayne his job.

He would never work as a head coach again in international rugby and, even though he was only 44, just three years older than me, it sounded as if Wayne knew it was all over. At the press conference after the game, he said: 'I'm an old dog. I'm out.'

Wayne returned to the All Blacks to work as an assistant coach to both Graham Henry and Steve Hansen as New Zealand won back-to-back World Cups in 2011 and 2015. He played a key role in their success, and found joy in being an assistant, but there must be some regret that he didn't get a longer crack in the head role. But perhaps Wayne didn't want to feel that fierce heat again. Maybe he had had enough of the loneliness you feel at the top. He has not worked as a coach since 2017, when he turned 60, which is a year younger than I am now in 2021.

I was thinking of Wayne Smith and Robbie Deans just days after England lost to Wales on 27 February in 2021's Six Nations. It was our second loss in the tournament, after a pretty shocking defeat at home to Scotland in the opening game. I can feel the heat. And it is a lonely heat: when you're the coach of a big team and you lose, everyone's at you. They are throwing some pretty big rocks my way because England were poor against Scotland. I can hear them bouncing off the windows. We then had two horrendous refereeing decisions go against us in the Welsh game, but that mattered less than the fact that we lost. That's how it is, and I have no problems with the criticism. In many ways I find this the most interesting time.

Some coaches find it really hard and it becomes even more difficult if their families suffer as a result of the criticism. I can imagine how tough it must have been for Wayne Smith's family in New Zealand when they lost twice in a row to Australia. It would have also been a hard experience for Robbie Deans's family to see him being dismissed in another country by people who have only an ounce of his knowledge.

When you're a leader in another field, and your organization is in a slump, you're going to receive most of the barbs and criticism. If your partner, your kids or your parents get hurt by the comments, then you're going to start thinking: 'Do I really want to do all this again? Do I really want to expose my family to this abuse?'

I'm lucky because my family don't allow the noise to affect them. My daughter Chelsea lives and works in Australia, while my wife Hiroko is not that interested in rugby and she knows I can look after myself. She also makes me laugh. Hiroko was still in Japan early on in this year's Six Nations and I sent her a text asking her what she would like for her birthday. She said: 'Just win.' She doesn't get embroiled in the doubt and negativity. Hiroko knows I love coaching and she gives me great support. It makes my position feel so much less lonely.

During the Six Nations, I had two fascinating meetings over Zoom with Ron Adams, the 73-year-old assistant coach of the Golden State Warriors. Ron is a deep thinker and a fantastic basketball coach who specializes in defence. As I mentioned in the

Prologue, Ron sees his role as being 'a truth-teller' – to Steve Kerr, the head coach, and to the other Golden State coaches and, most of all, to the young basketball players he inspires, despite being more than 50 years older than most of them.

I asked Ron who was the best coach he'd ever had. He said: 'Easy. My wife. She tells me what I'm good at and what I'm not good at. Supports me when I need support.' That sounded so familiar, and it makes me think that to be successful as a leader, particularly in coaching, which is such an emotionally charged environment, it is a massive help to have a settled home life.

I've been a professional coach for all but three of the 29 years Hiroko and I have been married. My wife doesn't want or expect me to talk about rugby. She doesn't follow rugby in the media and she doesn't want to be friends with the players' wives – even though she will always be happy to help them if they ask. In all those years she has only questioned my rugby judgement on two occasions, and both times she was dead right.

When I was coaching Australia, she asked me a pointed question about one of my staff: 'Why did you employ that coach?' she said bluntly.

I was surprised and replied: 'Why?'

Hiroko said: 'Can't you see? He's employed by his mother-in-law.'

She was right. He was not a strong coach and he ended up returning to work for his mother-in-law. Hiroko was also astute a second time when she made the right call about the character of another coach who worked for me. So my wife is probably the best judge, because she's got that pure instinct when gauging who is the right or the wrong fit as a person.

As a leader, your job will be a lot easier if you have a wise and calm partner at home. I would also suggest, and I am only half-joking here, that you should buy a dog if you're the boss at work. After a long week or a bad day at the office, the dog still loves you when you get home. You can rely on the dog to be happy to see your face again.

But of course the best way to negate the solitary nature of leadership, and to turn down the heat, is to build togetherness in your organization by choosing the right people to work with you. Recruiting the best staff can make or break you as a leader.

IT IS VITAL THAT YOU PUT THE RIGHT PEOPLE AROUND YOU

I have learnt over the years that it is never about liking your staff or getting on with them socially. Of course it's a bonus if that happens but it cannot be forced. All that really matters in terms of work are your professional and performance relationships. Can you work together professionally to improve the performance of the organization? Can you, in tandem, improve the people in the organization? Those are the points that count in elite sport and business.

Empathy and interpersonal skills have an important role to play, and if anyone around me is struggling with personal problems, it is important they should feel able to approach me to discuss them. I try to help with advice and suggest ways in which they might cope. There were a couple of occasions in this most recent Six Nations when someone on my staff as well as in the playing group opened up about difficulties away from rugby. They felt it was affecting their performances and it was good that they could come to me to discuss the situation.

Offering human support, however, is very different to liking everyone you appoint. There are numerous coaches I really like as people. I enjoy meeting up with them and talking about rugby and life, over a meal or a drink, but I wouldn't offer them a job. Conversely, most of the people I've really enjoyed working with professionally are not great friends of mine. We have had a fantastic working relationship, but the job is so consuming that I'm not on their list of people to see when they just want to relax.

People go on about great teams being great friends. Most of the time they're not that close. Great teams have great performance relationships rather than great friendships. Look at Sir Alex

Ferguson's revered Manchester United teams. Apart from a small group of four or five, none of them seem to be close. They don't talk to each other and they've got contrary views. But the job of a leader is to make sure there's enough cohesion in the group so they have positive working relationships.

If you are trying to bring in people you like, rather than the people you need, then you will not develop your organization. I always try and find people who know more than me in their specialist area. They might be very different to me, and we might have little in common socially, but they offer the balance to improve myself and the squad. That balance is always crucial when it comes to choosing the right people.

When I arrived in England in late 2015, I needed a nuts-and-bolts set-piece person to sort out my forward pack. That man was always going to be Steve Borthwick, who was such an invaluable ally when I coached Japan. I would put Steve in the top two of all the coaches I've appointed over the years. Ewen McKenzie, my teammate at Randwick in Sydney, who then worked with me at ACT Brumbies and when I took over the Wallabies, is my other standout assistant coach. He was with me for eight years. Ewen and Steve are both deep thinkers, pretty cerebral men, and they have a great capacity to analyse detail and then cut to the heart of a problem. They're driven, loyal and intelligent. It also helped that Steve had captained England from 2008 to 2010.

The other appointments soon fell into place because we needed to balance our staff. I turned 56 in January 2016 while Steve, who was then 37, is quite a serious man. So I needed someone gregarious and lively who could communicate easily with young players on their level. That man was Paul Gustard and he worked really well alongside Steve and myself.

No head coach can be popular for long because before every game he is upsetting half of the players in the dressing room who feel that he was wrong not to pick them for the starting XV. It just doesn't suit some people to take on that level of leadership.

Paul still chose to leave his role as England defence coach in

2018 so he could take the top job at Harlequins. I was happy to support his decision because it gave him a chance to discover if this was the kind of work he wanted. It didn't work out for Paul at Quins and he is back working as a very good assistant coach at Benetton in Italy.

The next person I brought in to the England set-up in 2016 was Neil Hatley. Steve looked after the lineout and Neil concentrated on our scrum. Neil is just a good guy. I call him a glue coach. These are coaches whose technical knowledge matters less than their ability to keep people together. Players like being with Neil and we added even more of that balance when I brought Scott Wisemantel – Wisey – in as our attack coach in 2017.

Scott's another glue person. He is upbeat and energetic, always fizzing with ideas, and the players enjoy being around him – just as they did when he worked as my backs coach with Japan. Scott's a blokey bloke, a very typical Australian; he's laidback and he doesn't take anything too seriously. We needed that injection of easy-going vitality because I knew Gustard was on his way. I replaced Gustard with John Mitchell, who then became my assistant coach.

John replaced Wayne Smith as head coach of the All Blacks. We have not discussed it in detail, but losing the 2003 World Cup semi-final to my Wallaby team cost John his job. He coached in South Africa for many years after that, and when he accepted the invitation to work with me in 2018 it marked a return for John – as he had been an assistant coach for England under Clive Woodward from 1997 to 2000. John is very serious, so bringing in Wisey gave us the right balance to keep building that togetherness which all great teams, and organizations, possess.

In choosing this group of people to help me take England all the way to the 2019 World Cup final, I also had to break the news to members of the previous regime that they would not be needed. It was no reflection on the coaching skills of Andy Farrell, Graham Rowntree and Mike Catt when I explained that I wanted a clean slate. They were all part of Stuart Lancaster's team and, while they had achieved plenty of positive results, the disappointment of the 2015 World Cup meant we would be better off with a totally new coaching staff.

Another simple but clear-cut decision after setting out the vision in 2015 was to change the leader of the squad. I chose Dylan Hartley as my captain because he had the courage, positivity and resolve to step forward. He would lead by example, because he was such a tough and abrasive player, but he would also use his intelligence and empathy to talk to the players and make them understand our principles and values. It felt important that Dylan hadn't been to the 2015 World Cup. He represented a new start.

Chris Robshaw lost the captaincy, but I did not cut him adrift. I felt he epitomized the most admirable qualities of English rugby. He was honest, resilient and hard working. Chris was not the man to lead my vision of winning the World Cup, but I sensed he would be an immensely valuable member of the team for the first few years of our transition. He proved me right and, backing Dylan all the way, he embraced our vision.

I was right to think that, whether in sport or business, you can demote a player or a staff member while finding a way to ensure they still feel important to the organization. So much depends on the character of the individual, because Chris could easily have sulked or downed tools because he lost the captaincy. But he quickly bought into my assurance that he had much to offer England. He and Dylan might be less gifted than some other leading international rugby players, but few can claim to have more character.

Justin Langer, Australia's current cricket coach, uses a lovely phrase when he says that he picks his teams on the same basis:

CHOOSE CHARACTER OVER COVER DRIVE

As a massive cricket fan, I'm just as much a sucker for an elegant cover drive as the next bloke in the stands. But all my experience in Test rugby has taught me that character – in the form of grit, dedication and the ability to perform under pressure – matters more than pure talent.

Some positions on the field or in business are different and, in such cases, knowledge and technical ability takes precedence. Then, the player or coach's interpersonal skills, and general characteristics, don't have to be as sharp. Yet, fundamentally, you need people who want to be good teammates and are prepared to put the work in for the benefit of the squad and not just themselves.

Coaching a team in elite sport has become more complex in the 2020s – I am sure the same applies in business – and so that simple saying of 'character over cover drive' has become even more important. It is the same when choosing the right people to work around you and when building togetherness in your squad. Some people might have occasionally brilliant technical insights or be spellbinding talkers – but they won't be as much of an asset to you as the coach who can balance your vision and add a consistency which will improve the overall organization.

Players are human beings and so they need different coaches that they can turn to at different times. Some days they need more analytical, hard-nosed coaching. On other days they need a cuddle and a chat about the universe. We try to get the right match for them and, on the whole, we have done pretty well with England.

It always helps if you have a trusted number two, or an ally, with whom you can share personal concerns and doubts. That vulnerability is often fleeting and so it is not always appropriate to express it to the other staff. I also don't think it helps the players much if they see you looking down or uncertain. But there are occasions when it can work.

After we lost to France in Paris in the opening game of the 2020 Six Nations, I said to the players: 'Boys, that was my fault. I didn't get you ready in the right way. I've let you down, and I apologize.'

I meant it, and I think the players respected that. It encourages an atmosphere of brutal honesty which can be hard to engender otherwise.

Vulnerability is such an important concept now in society. People are less judgemental if someone admits to feeling vulnerable or having made a mistake. But sport is still pretty old school – particularly in public. Imagine if, before England play France or New Zealand, the press ask me: 'Are you the right person for the job?' If I followed Wayne Smith's lead and said, 'I don't really know', I would be slaughtered. It's the same if you're leading a big financial institution. People expect you to exude certainty. I'm interested in the fact that it seems as if politicians can now show more vulnerability because people understand it. But, when it comes to sport or big business, leaders are still expected to show conviction above all else.

Most of the time it's best to address your loneliness or vulnerability in private. This is where Neil Craig offers so much, as a sounding board and as a quality thinker who also plays the part of, in Ron Adams's words, 'a truth-teller' for me as England's head coach. I can open up to him and ask for his honest advice.

Neil is steeped in Australian Rules Football, having excelled as a player and then even more so as coach for the Adelaide Crows from 2004 to 2011. It doesn't matter that Neil does not understand all the intricacies of rugby. His role is to observe me, as well as my fellow coaches and the players, and to talk honestly when he addresses the ways I express myself. Neil is here to tell the truth and, also, to help me coach the coaches. He is an expert in communication and leadership.

After all our key meetings, and following a team talk or a performance review, Neil and I will talk in robust detail. What could I have said or done differently? How did my fellow coaches or the players react? How can we engender more leadership among the staff and in the squad? Neil sees things that I miss, and it helps that he is also a very different character to me. He appears a much softer person and he has an empathy and emotional intelligence that dovetails well with my strengths and weaknesses. Neil is also older than me and so there is no need for deference. He tells me straight when I have got it right or wrong. You could call him my critical friend.

The contrast makes our partnership tick. If you're the kind of leader who regards yourself as a teacher, then you need a deputy who is big on detail. If you are a methodical leader then you need a more creative ally.

You usually want someone who is very different to you as your deputy and truth-teller. It's like filling in the circle. Most of us aren't the full circle. You want your number two to be the person who completes the circle for you. Once you get that right you will have come a long way to finding the balance and harmony you need to lead your team or company.

Neil Craig is definitely my truth-teller, rather than my number two. He knows me so well that he understands I am uncomfortable when I start feeling comfortable. Neil often says I have evolved as a head coach because I have learnt to become more tolerant. My standards remain as exacting as ever, but I know that not everyone works in the same way as I do. I am more willing, now, to give people a little more leeway as they do their work in their own way. It has been an important lesson of leadership for me.

We have a small, tight-knit staff. Many of the best people in English rugby are already working for their clubs. There are some great English coaches out there – and Shaun Edwards is an obvious example. He has done outstanding work with Wales and now with France. While I have been head coach, we've not had the chance to approach him with an offer to return to England. If that ever happens, he will provide incredible knowledge and dedication.

As long as my staff share our end vision, and buy into it totally, I don't care about anyone else. If they start to doubt this vision, then it's time for them to move on. They will show by their actions whether they want to be involved. If they don't, then we'll find someone else to replace them. It's not negotiable. Either you want to be a part of the vision or you don't.

Will Carling did not want to be part of the vision. He knocked me back in a reminder that sometimes, when you're striving to find the right people to join you, there are hurdles to overcome. You would have to be crazy to think that everyone you approach will be sold on the idea of working with you. There are some people you have to work hard to convince, and these are often the ones who are worth pursuing.

Will and I have, putting it mildly, very different backgrounds and contrasting experiences.

I grew up as part of a mixed-race family in a gritty working-class suburb of Sydney. My best mates were the Ella brothers – Mark, Glen and Gary – who came from a great Indigenous Australian family. As small boys they shared one mattress on the floor of their parents' bedroom. Gordon and May Ella, their parents, were wonderful people but they had a job on their hands, raising 12 kids in a two-bedroom house in a stark neighbourhood like La Perouse. There was no inside toilet. There was no hot water. But the Ella boys didn't mind. They were too busy playing sport with me and our mates outside. We had a sun-kissed childhood. As teenagers, the twins, Mark and Glen, looked like they were straight out of the Jackson Five with their huge afros. They ran, passed and scored tries like gods at Matraville High, our school, which lay in the shadow of the local prison.

Will's early years in England stood in stark contrast. He went to public school from the age of six and then joined the army, where he became an officer. He was only 22 years old when, in 1988, he became the youngest England rugby captain in history. Carling's England were a pragmatic bunch but, to the outside world, they seemed arrogant and unlikeable. Their young captain, who looked very self-assured and privileged, epitomized a team which won the Grand Slam and reached the 1991 World Cup final.

I was as guilty as the next bloke in reducing Carling to the stereotype of an English toff. I was delighted when Australia, under my mentor Bob Dwyer, beat his England team at Twickenham to win the World Cup. Four years later Jonah Lomu ran straight over Carling in Cape Town as he scored four tries and demolished England in the 1995 World Cup semi-final.

That was about the extent of my knowledge of Will Carling when I met him for the first time soon after I became England head coach. It was early in 2016 when Ian Ritchie, then the CEO of the RFU, took me out for dinner with Will and Martin Corry, another former England captain. Corry is part of the great old Leicester school where they don't deal in bullshit. I had spent six months as a player at Leicester, just as Martin Johnson was coming through, and I liked their no-nonsense brand of uncompromising rugby. It wasn't pretty but it was honest.

Carling had played instead for Harlequins – the traditional entertainers of English club rugby, with their colourful shirts and close ties to big business in the City. Quins were linked inextricably to London and the seemingly pampered south-east of England. Carling and Quins were made for each other.

But here is the surprise. Over the course of the evening I came to some very different conclusions about Will Carling. He was happy to take the piss out of himself and, rather than having an inflated sense of his achievements, he was open about his shortcomings as a very young leader. Will also preferred to talk about the game today, rather than hark back to the days when he was the king of English rugby.

A few years later I came to learn that, rather than being pampered by a soft life with a silver spoon, Will had suffered as a kid. I read about the ordeal he had been through at boarding school when, as that six-year-old boy, he curled into a ball at the bottom of his bed and cried himself to sleep every night. Unlike my own good fortune in having loving and supportive parents, Will's mum and dad expected him to just get on with the harsh loneliness of boarding-school life. It seemed to Will that his mother was more interested in status than in him as her son.

There was similar snobbery in the army. Will, as clear officer material, was meant to downplay the fact that his grandfather, whom he loved, had been a butcher. That class-driven madness riled him. It also meant that, far from being the dream choice as England captain for the RFU's committee men, Will was provocative and spiky.

It suddenly made sense that he had broken the old amateur rugby code when, in becoming England captain, he left his job at Mobil to play full time. People assumed he was lured by the commercial potential of leading England. But he simply wanted to concentrate on the demanding task of leadership at such a young age. The more I listened to him that evening, the more I remembered how it had been Will who had been stripped briefly of the captaincy, just three weeks before the 1995 World Cup, after he was caught on a television microphone dismissing the '57 old farts' in blazers who were suffocating the English game. Only the intervention of his teammates forced the RFU to reinstate him as England captain.

We met a few more times over the next two years, and it reinforced my belief that it's really important to maintain links with the past. I've always admired the way in which the All Blacks have forged a connection between their legacy and where they aspire to reach in the future. I felt Will could be the link with the past we needed.

He also understood the English rugby identity better than anyone I knew. It is hard for me, as an Australian, to get a firm grip on the nuances of the English national character. I found a way inside Japanese culture, but it was trickier to pinpoint a coherent English identity. Will, I was sure, would be able to penetrate this tangled web and reach the leadership group as I strove to sharpen our cohesion and identity.

I called him up in the autumn of 2018, not long after we had come through a tough season where we had lost five Tests in a row. I asked Will if he would come in and talk to my coaches about leadership. Will didn't jump at the offer. He said: 'Well, maybe, but let's meet for a coffee first. I'm not sure I can talk to them in the way you need.'

A couple of weeks later we met up and I surprised him. 'Mate,' I said, 'change of plan. Will you come and talk to the team?'

Will turned me down flat. 'Why?' I replied in surprise.

'I don't want to talk about how it was in my day,' Will said. 'I've got nothing relevant to say.'

I was disappointed because the more I had looked into Carling, and the more people I spoke to about him, the more I understood he could solve a blind spot in our organization. We lacked leaders. We needed cohesion. We needed a clearer identity. Will could help us.

If nothing else, I'm a persistent guy, and I refused to give in. I kept telling Will we needed him. England needed him. A lot of this was based on instinct, but that's what a leader needs – a gut feel when it comes to solving problems. And once your gut tells you something you need to follow it through. I refused to give in and, finally, Will relented.

'OK,' he said. 'I'll do one meeting and we'll see how it goes.'

He came in a couple of days after we had lost in agonizing circumstances to New Zealand at Twickenham. On 10 November 2018 the All Blacks won 16–15 – but only after a late Sam Underhill try for us had been overturned by the TMO. The boys had played well after a very hard year.

Will was more nervous addressing my players than he had been 30 years earlier when he first stood up as England captain to face his dubious new teammates. Will hated the idea that he would drone on about how rugby had been back in the 1990s, and so he poured huge effort into making his speech fresh and pertinent to the players. It left him feeling absolutely drained.

But I now had him on board and I wasn't about to let him get away. I felt he was just the right kind of mentor for my English players, while also offering a bridge to the past. 'Why didn't you call Rob or Johnno instead?' Will said of Rob Andrew and Martin Johnson.

'No, mate,' I said with a firm shake of my head. 'I've talked to enough people and they just say that you'll tell me to fuck off if I'm getting things wrong.'

Will liked that and he began laughing. 'Yeah, I will!' he said.

That kind of honesty is vital to any leader, and so I was relentless in persuading Will to join us. I did the same with Richard Hill, who was such a great player in England's 2003 World Cup-winning side. Richard became our team manager in 2019. Will and Richard maintain our bond with recent English rugby history.

All great teams have glue players. They're the unsung heroes who offer cohesion and togetherness. People might be surprised when I pick out Mark Wilson as one of England's definitive glue players. We all need a Wilson in our ranks because they give of themselves constantly. They're usually uncomplicated and are vital in balancing and unifying your squad.

I reckon neuroticism is one of the most important personality traits in elite sport. You need to have some neurotic players. They're always the most creative and the most brilliant. At the same time they're also the most difficult and troubled. Look at Shane Warne. He could be chaotic and wayward but, when he was playing cricket, he was the most disciplined athlete. Everything outside of cricket? He was a little wayward, wasn't he? I imagine Kevin Pietersen was the same. He was deemed to be difficult outside of cricket, but he still hit 23 Test centuries. You need players like that to give you greatness but, to balance the side and build a sense of togetherness, you have to put the right people around them.

You have to pick your glue guys – choosing character over cover drive. These stable personalities give everything of themselves to help their teammates shine. I like footballers in the mould of Jordan Henderson. Every game he plays for Liverpool he runs hard, does his job, gets on with the dirty work and lifts the players around him. It also helps that he is bright and enthusiastic. These glue guys keep you humming.

They can also be characters with an edge or a sense of originality. I have had plenty of those in my England squad. Owen Farrell's a glue guy. Competitive, tough, rolls his sleeves up, gets stuck in, leads by example. Jonny May's another glue person. He's unusual because he's got quite a unique personality – but he's not destructive. Jonny's got constructive habits and he is quirky and funny. Some players just don't need to be coached. Jonny is the perfect example. He only needs to be encouraged to keep being his best. Other players need reinforcement and to know you care about them.

It's a system that resembles a family. Some of your kids just get on with life, whereas other kids need to know their mum and dad are always looking out for them and acknowledging everything they do well. I see it in my own family. My middle sister just got on with life. She just did what she wanted and never worried about anything. My older sister and I were more formal and looked up to our parents. It's the same in any rugby team. Some guys just get on with it. Some guys you need to love a bit more. Some guys you need to be harder on. It's trying to find the right balance with each one to build that togetherness.

We are always a much better and happier squad when we've got Manu Tuilagi in camp and on the field. The players love him because he's a bright, bubbly, loving guy. He's very unassuming but on the field he's so powerful. And in camp he's the king of the coffee breaks and the chessboard. He beats everyone who takes him on, but the players gravitate towards him. A few years ago, when he was young and silly, he was apparently a disruptive presence. But those days are long gone. Getting married and having a baby teaches you lessons in responsibility and cohesion, and that is why Manu became the kind of player we love having around the place.

Courtney Lawes is another. Firstly, he's a brilliant player. He's aggressive but it is always contained and accurate. He reminds me of those great West Indian fast bowlers. They come loping along, nice and fluid, but, when they let the ball go, it's deadly serious. When Courtney hits people, they stay hit. He's one of our really respected guys. When he was young he was a bit of a lad at Northampton, but then he got married and had four kids. Courtney settled down and worked hard on his body. Rugby these days is suited to guys who look like short Exocet missiles, whereas Courtney was this tall, skinny guy, built like a basketballer. So he changed the shape of his body to adapt. But, most of all, I like the fact that when he talks, the players listen to him.

Mako Vunipola is the same. They're the quiet guys, but when they do talk then people look up to them. Courtney and Mako don't want to be at the head of the queue, but they want the team to win. And there is something almost spiritual about Mako. The players all look at him as if he's our chief.

In a different way, Tom Curry will become a standout player. When I look back over all the players I have worked with over 30 years, George Smith, the great Australian loose forward, is the one I come back to most often. I would say he is my favourite player, but if you asked me to identify someone who might fit the role in another 20 years, I would not be surprised if I chose Tom.

When I first saw him play, at a time when no one in England seemed to rate him, I knew within ten minutes he had something special about him. He had that innate competitiveness which reminded me immediately of Richie McCaw. I remember seeing Richie as a young player and even then he was the ultimate competitor. If you've got a player like that it brings the rest of the pack with him. Tom Curry is still young, but his development has been so rapid. The only risk for him, because of the way he plays, is that he could get too many injuries. But if he can have a consistent run, he'll be remembered as one of the greatest players in the world. He's well educated, very down to earth and comes from a good family. Just a lovely boy who is one of those people who mean so much when you have them around your squad.

George Kruis is now playing rugby in Japan, but he was another glue man for me. He has an unbelievable character which means he is just at it the whole time. George never flags and he lifts and unites everyone around him. These are the kind of people you want around you and your team. It has been fascinating to build a sense of togetherness with them and my fellow coaches.

So much comes down to identifying and choosing them in the first place. I think that's the test for every leader in terms of recruitment. I'm good friends now with the Goldman Sachs CEO in Japan and, talking about his own staff, he once said to me that 'I will never really know what they're made of until they're under pressure.' I believe that too because there's that great expression – the tea-bag test. You don't know if it will make you a great cup of tea until you put it under hot water.

You've got to discover who has the potential to be great under pressure. Great Test match players, just like great business people, are at their best when the pressure is on.

So when it comes to starting a new project, one of the most important skills you need as a leader is getting your recruitment right. From that point on you can follow three further key stages:

- Build togetherness

- Identify the quick wins and the big changes required

- Plan the transformation

In terms of quick wins and making the changes we needed after the 2019 World Cup, I had to wait until the following autumn and the Autumn Nations Cup tournament. The 2020 Six Nations came too soon. We won that competition, but we lost to France in the opening game because I under-prepared the team. I didn't think they were ready for a normal first-game preparation because they were still recovering from the World Cup. But my mistake will pay off for us in the longer term. Sometimes you have to lose a battle to win the war. Since that defeat in Paris, I've been re-energized and refocused on what we can do with this team. For this group of players, it's a once-in-a-lifetime opportunity to become one of the greatest teams in history and do something unforgettable in 2023.

So, in the Autumn Nations Cup, we looked for quick wins to build momentum because that tournament, in November 2020, started our rebuild. Our easy wins came through our defence and pressure game. With the limited preparation time, and the condition of the players, they were the easiest things to get right. And it helped that, to win the tournament, we had to go through extra time to beat a highly motivated young French team.

We were expected to win and it proved that we could survive and even thrive under pressure. During the Autumn Nations Cup we had worked on our ability to increase the pace of our game after half-time. This was one of our 'quick wins', because in 2019 this had not been a strong feature of our game. In the first 20 minutes against France, we averaged 103 metres per minute. Then, in the first 20 minutes of the second half, we averaged 130 metres per minute. The ability of our team to give that much energy was a good indication of their togetherness and clarity.

From that point we could plan our transformation. I knew there would be setbacks and disappointments in the short-term, but I believed in our vision. My confidence stemmed from the fact that I had paid close attention to this key factor:

BUILD TOGETHERNESS WITH THE RIGHT PEOPLE AROUND YOU

- Choose character over cover drive
- Identify the quick wins and the big changes required
- Plan the transformation
- All great teams have glue players

3

CLARITY IS THE NEW CLEVER

ASSESS EVERYTHING AND THEN PROVIDE THE CLARITY

Leadership is an exhilarating challenge but there are also bruising periods when it causes acute stress and worry. I was back in that dark and demanding place in the early hours of Wednesday 3 February 2021. The digits on my phone glowed in the dim light. *2.32 a.m.* I was already pacing the floor of my room so there was no point even thinking about going back to bed. My day had begun ten minutes before when, knowing that rest and sleep were both shot for another night, I got up in the hope I could find clarity amid the tangled uncertainty.

Insomnia had tracked me for five long nights. I was late joining the England camp, only arriving the previous Friday afternoon. Every early morning since then, a gut-deep concern had woken me from a restless sleep. We had been living with Covid in England for more than ten months and the strain couldn't be ignored. It was a suffocating and isolating reality which made the task of leading a high-performance programme so much more complex and difficult.

Every squad in the Six Nations, as well as every sport and business and family around the world, had been affected. It had been a crushing experience globally and it had eroded our individual lives with a sense of creeping dread and gathering disorientation. A global pandemic might be a communal experience but there are moments, especially in the dead of night, when you feel its baleful influence in an acutely personal way.

As a leader you have to address stress and anxiety. But, in our unsettling new era of Covid-19, you need to get on top of it so that you don't shift these negative emotions onto your staff or your squad. I dealt pretty well with it in the autumn of 2020. I stuck to my set routine where I did about 40 minutes of work soon after I woke up. That was usually around 5 a.m. I then went to the gym for an hour – and never missed a day. It gave me the clarity to move forward.

But, three months on, we were more fatigued by Covid. In the grip of a deadly winter, with infections and deaths rising at such a distressing rate, our own more minor problems were mounting. They contributed significantly to a sense that something was amiss in our camp. It began with my unexpected isolation from my fellow coaches and our players for ten long days.

I had been due to join everyone on the morning of Wednesday 27 January. We had thought carefully about our preparations and tried to show empathy for the players. These young men were in the prime of their lives but they were being locked up as if they were in a world war. It was not natural for them to be cooped up in bio-secure bubbles. We knew they were feeling it and we wanted to help them. Their club rugby commitments ended on Sunday 24 January. We could have met up with them the very next day but we wanted them to have time with their families. We asked them to come in on the Wednesday.

It was a good plan, but it was ruined by the fact that, when the players arrived at St George's Park in Staffordshire, 80 per cent of the coaching staff, including me as head coach, were not allowed to join them.

A few weeks earlier I had spent two days with our coaches at the Lensbury Hotel in Teddington. It felt important that we met face to face because we hadn't been able to see each other since the previous autumn. We observed social distancing protocols and it was a productive series of meetings which showed how much more effective it is to talk in person than over Zoom. But we hit trouble soon afterwards when Matt Proudfoot, our scrum coach, tested positive for coronavirus. We were worried for Matt because he became quite ill very quickly and he had to be taken to hospital by ambulance. He eventually made a full recovery but our camp was thrown into turmoil.

In a selection meeting both Simon Amor, our attack coach, and I had sat alongside Matt. We had maintained a sensible distance between each other and we tested negative. But we had been in Matt's company for more than 15 minutes and so Simon and I were compelled to isolate for ten days. This meant we could only join the squad on day three of a four-day preparation camp before the week of our first game against Scotland, at Twickenham, on 6 February 2021. It was frustrating being locked away in isolation while knowing John Mitchell was the only one of our five senior coaches able to work with the players for the first two and a half days.

Jason Ryles, our skills coach, was also missing. The lockdown regulations meant that he had to remain in Australia – as did Neil Craig, my closest ally, who could not leave Melbourne to join us. It made for a disastrous start to our Six Nations.

I knew it was important we turned these negatives into a positive, and so I called in Ed Robinson, a young coach who turned 28 in our first week together as a squad. Ed is the son of Andy Robinson, the former England and Scotland coach, and I had mentored him while working with young coaches in 2020. He impressed me because he is bright and courageous and I felt that, apart from helping him develop as a coach, Ed would be an asset to us as a short-term consultant. It did not matter to me that his coaching had, until then, been confined to working with Jersey. He has the right attributes to become an outstanding coach.

When I finally arrived at St George's on the Friday afternoon it felt like I had escaped prison. The relief did not last. We were scrambling from the moment I walked into camp.

In normal circumstances the first three days of a training camp are devoted to rekindling relationships between coaches and players. There is obviously a foundation to build on with most of the players because of our past experiences. But they have been at their clubs for months and exposed to different environments. There is also a vast gap in intensity and quality between club rugby and the Test arena. Readjustment is always necessary, but any chance of my catching up with all the individual players before intense training began was impossible.

We had scheduled our main training day for the Saturday. We trained in a blizzard that day. I've never felt so cold in my life. It was freezing and the wind was howling. Our players are really tough but, after 20 minutes, the backs couldn't feel their hands. It was a terrible session. The situation did not improve. We could not leave the site and, again because of Covid, we had to hold our meetings outside. I remember one meeting where we were sitting in as many layers as we could wear, in an attempt to keep out the cold, and the wind was blowing up a storm. It was really hard for the players and the staff to concentrate.

As coaches we had already mapped out a new system of attack. We had won both the Six Nations and the Autumn Nations Cup tournament in 2020. But our kicking game had taken a lot of criticism. We were accused of being frightened of the ball and ruining the game as a spectacle. I didn't care about the criticism. We were winning. But, knowing that elite sport is always evolving, we needed to develop a different way of playing before the 2023 World Cup. It was time to move our game on – not to placate the critics but to give us a better chance of winning.

The Lions tour of South Africa was still months away, but it would soon present us with yet more clear evidence that, when it comes to beating an ultra-physical side like the Springboks, you need to play a different style of rugby. You can't just try and outmuscle the Boks as this is their area of consuming excellence. It is important you can play another way to outwit them.

In 2020 we had been effective in playing a big ball game. We now wanted to introduce small ball skills to widen our repertoire.

These are basketball terms but they work well. Big ball rugby was based around our physicality, aggression and kicking game. Small ball rugby would be more nimble and versatile. It would see us move the ball and attack with pace and dexterity. Simon Amor was steeped in Sevens rugby and he was keen to develop our small ball game. It was the right vision, but our timing was awry. We were trying to introduce it to a team that had lost its cohesion.

One of reasons I paced the floor before three in the morning was because, rather than pushing the coaches harder, I gave them more scope. They were all new to the job and, as a leader, you want to give them time to make their mark. But we had lost our clarity.

We had also moved away from the highly disciplined training method of tactical periodization that had led to such success in 2019. Tactical periodization is a form of structured training which focuses on four fundamental areas: defensive organization, offensive organization, the transition from defence to attack, and the transition from attack to defence. Every aspect shapes key blocks of training so that your enhanced fitness and technical levels will carry through to game day. Essentially, you settle on your style of play and tailor your training to suit this philosophy.

I used it with England from day one in 2016. We also trained our World Cup coaching team to be advocates of tactical periodization. It means that the amount of time you have to work with the players, because we're doing everything through rugby, has to be monitored very closely. It puts pressure on coaches to coach in a fresh way – which is to explain the concept more dynamically. Raymond Verheijen – a Dutch football coach and expert in tactical periodization, who had worked with Guus Hiddink at three World Cups and three European Championships with the Netherlands, South Korea and Russia – put us through an intensive course. By the time we reached the 2019 World Cup we had fantastic discipline. We've since lost that rigour because we no longer have this same knowledge in a changed coaching team.

Tactical periodization is difficult to implement because it requires immense discipline and rigour. As a leader you also need to be a master of exclusion. Everyone wants to do everything at the same time. Most coaches hurtle headlong into a training session without excluding all but the three key ideas they need to impart that day.

Neil Craig has an amusing but accurate phrase which he uses when he watches training sessions done by a variety of teams: 'Half the time they're flat out doing fuck all.' They're dashing around trying to do everything but end up doing nothing with lasting discipline. One of your fundamental tasks as a head coach is to work out which three things are going to help you win on the weekend. And you need to insert that clarity and discipline into your training – and the best way to do this, for me, is through tactical periodization.

I paced the floor in the dark hours of the morning because I worried that our training had become cluttered. We were not being specific enough and that was bound to affect our performance. But I made the fatal error of allowing things to drift further.

Our situation was also difficult because the fallout from the Saracens debacle – after they had been relegated in 2020 as a consequence of flouting the salary cap – had hurt us massively. Six of our key players were not playing any rugby because the Championship was in lockdown and had yet to resume. We got away with it during the Autumn Nations Cup, but another three months of inactivity for our Saracens core damaged us in a new year.

The leadership group was dominated by Saracens players, which made sense because, in recent years, they had often been the best club side in England and Europe. There had been complications, inevitably, because of rivalries between players from different clubs. We had experienced these problems during the build-up to the 2019 World Cup but we had defused most of the conflict that summer. But I could sense the divisions and resentments rising to the surface again. Eventually the leadership group would crack as the influence of the Saracens contingent waned.

I couldn't admit any of this in public, but we had real problems. We had a squad of 28 players who, on average, had played 2.3 games in the previous nine weeks. And our leading Saracens players, who offered over 500 caps of experience, had played no rugby at all. Maro Itoje was recovering from coronavirus and he only joined the squad five days before we played Scotland. And club rugby had been decimated by the second wave of Covid and no one had played in the previous two weeks.

I picked the proven players even when they had not featured in any games. Would a more average club player who had four games under his belt in recent months have been better than the guys who had played in a World Cup final just over a year before? I knew I needed to place my trust in those with a proven track record of Test success. But we were unfit and in a mess.

In hindsight it could be argued that we should have left out all of them – Elliot Daly, Owen Farrell, Mako Vunipola, Jamie George, Maro Itoje and Billy Vunipola. But it's easy to say that now without any consequences to confront. What would have been the impact on the other players if that Saracens group had just been ripped out in one big chunk? It would have been traumatic. And what kind of message would it have sent to those six players who had been outstanding for us over the years? Did we not at least owe them a chance to prove they could overcome the disadvantage of not playing any rugby?

Maybe we believed they just needed to turn up against Scotland to pick up a routine win. At the same time, we were trying to move forward and generate fresh resolve and enthusiasm in a conflicted squad of players while playing Test rugby in an empty stadium.

So, on the weekend before the game against Scotland, we used the concept of a pre-mortem. We all know that you carry out a post-mortem after something has gone wrong. But we chose to do a pre-mortem where we did a mock-up of the kind of headlines we would see in the *Daily Mail* if the game went wrong. 'Rudder-less England embarrassed by Scotland' was an example of the media flak we could expect if we failed to win.

We had done a similar pre-mortem before we beat Ireland in 2019. Then, rather than using fictitious headlines, we did it with me verbalizing the kind of media abuse we would cop if it all went wrong against the Irish. It's not a new concept. But before the Scotland game, I wanted the players themselves to work on this project rather than just listening to me. I wanted them to go away in groups, think about it, and come up with the answers as to how best we could avoid the fate of our pre-mortem predic-tion. All the research shows that, if they think about it themselves, rather than being told, the chances of them then owning and solving the problem will be much higher.

It still felt like we were preparing a horse for a three-mile race when we had just one 600-metre warm-up. Are you going to back that horse? Not unless you like throwing your money away.

Sleep would not come, and rest proved impossible. I kept pacing, sensing the depth of our problems and mistakes.

Of course, the pre-mortem turned out to be the truth. The only difference was that the long headline to the *Daily Mail* column written by Sir Clive Woodward was far worse than we had pre-dicted: 'England's dismal defeat to Scotland was the worst I have EVER seen us play given what was at stake . . . Eddie Jones's men were bereft of ideas and it felt like a 30-point loss.' The *Mail* and Sir Clive are never slow to stir the pot, but this was a clear sign of the pundits' and the media's mood. They were out for blood.

After we lost 11–6 at home to Scotland, I took responsibility for my errors. I admitted that we played poorly and did not resemble a well-coached team. I had let them down. The endur-ing lesson is that if you want to win then you must prepare well. If your preparation's not up to the mark, then you're relying on luck and circumstances to get you through.

The pre-mortem did not cause the result and I will use it again in different circumstances. You always need to review every possible outcome because, even when you're flying, no project is ever complete. You are always moving – either out of conflict or back into conflict. At the time of the Scotland game we were trying to move out of a conflict zone. We're still doing the same late in 2021 and even when we reach seemingly clear waters, as we will, another source of conflict will be on its way.

There are consolations for me in these tough periods, which is why I actually enjoy them. It is here, between the discord and conflict, crisis and defeat, that you really find which players you can rely on in the future. Unlike in a smooth winning run, the true character of your squad emerges during these painful moments. It is an opportunity to learn and improve, and it helps that I like contrariness. Everyone thinks you're an idiot. Everyone thinks you don't have a clue what to do next. Everyone thinks that they know better than you. I really enjoy these situations.

Against Scotland the responsibility rested with me. I didn't coach well enough. We failed to give the players clear direction. When you make changes, particularly in attack, you struggle at the outset. I tried to explain this to the players on the Thursday before the game. I said when we changed the attack at the Brumbies we lost the first three games by 40 points but, two years later, we ended up being the best attacking team in the world. So we needed to be patient because attack is a complex process in rugby. It consumes so much thinking that it can look as if the players have got no energy. It looks like they don't know what they're doing. That's exactly what happened to us against Scotland.

Before the game I was confident it would work. Whenever you introduce something new, you never see the problems in the build-up because the players are excited by it. They want to add it to their games. But then the match starts and, under pressure, they can't follow the new methodology. We tried to coach it into them but we failed and so they became muddled in their thinking and we lost at home to Scotland for the first time in 38 years.

On reflection, I should have gone back to absolute basics. I should have simplified the game plan. I should not have underestimated the impact that Covid and the Saracens fiasco had had on the squad. Even before we were sent into isolation it was clear this would be a tournament like no other. We had to shut out the rumours that the Six Nations could be abandoned after the opening fixtures, while the politicians, in tandem with the scientists, scrambled to react to a changing and often depressing situation – as rates of infection, hospitalization and death reached frightening numbers. We were all aware that a far more important battle was being waged against a deadly virus, but we had to try and adapt to the shifting regulations which governed our already restricted lives within the England bubble. All six teams in the tournament faced the same challenge and so we cannot rely on excuses.

Early in our preparations I heard a phrase which seemed so striking during a global pandemic:

CLARITY IS THE NEW CLEVER

When there is so much uncertainty and confusion, the need for clarity is greater than ever. We didn't find such clarity in the Six Nations, but the importance of this concept will become more pertinent in the years it will take the world to recover from the physical, economic and psychological consequences of Covid.

There are not too many clever people around at the moment. Instead this is a time to adjust to the strange new normal. When you have so many changes swirling around, you need cohesion, stability and, above all, clarity. We learnt some hard and valuable lessons during the Six Nations. One of the most important is that the role of the leader has been reinforced. You need a strong voice and a clear direction – which is contingent on your ability and your knowledge of the situation.

It is not going to be easy, in sport or business, to plot our way out of the pandemic. The direction may be clear but it cannot be precise, because it is now harder than ever to predict future trends.

In the previous year's Autumn Nations Cup, you could see very clearly which sides had prepared for the Covid fallout. We won the tournament and were better equipped than we were in the Six Nations. I made sure that we approached the Autumn Nations Cup with an attitude that we should be grateful to have the opportunity to play rugby – even behind closed doors. I also stressed that we should adapt to whatever advice the government gave us. It was not easy, because there were times when the politicians did not know if they were coming or going. In the morning we would hear that it would be safe for kids to return to school and then, that evening, we would be told it was no longer considered a secure option.

It becomes difficult for people to be compliant if there is little clarity from leadership. It would be like me telling the players in the morning that they have to wear masks and then, that night, telling them they can ditch the masks. You need to give clear direction. We failed to do that in the Six Nations. We will learn from that.

In the meantime we had to take so much criticism. I sometimes think that the English media love to hate us. The more you win in England, it seems, the more they dislike you. I don't think there's anything nasty about it. They just know that putting the boot in generates great headlines. When I took over, and we won the Grand Slam and beat Australia 3–0 in a tough away series, the praise was excessive. We were then ridiculed as being hopeless when we lost five matches in a row in 2018. There were reasons for that little slump – and the source of it was that I purposely over-trained the squad before the Six Nations that year because I wanted to push them harder than ever. Of course I didn't tell the media that at the time. So I didn't expect them to understand.

Eighteen months later, we beat New Zealand to reach the World Cup final, and again the players and I were lauded. But a week later we lost to South Africa, and the media were like a hellhound on our trail. The Saracens story broke soon after we returned from Japan in late 2019, following which there seemed to be so much negative external noise around the team.

It's important to try and muffle that noise in elite sport. Top businesses are fortunate in rarely having to deal with this endless and often emotional scrutiny. Even the largest companies in the world might only have three big days a year when they launch a product or their share price soars or falls and they publish their year-end report. We have 12 or 15 big days a year. Every Test match is a big day, and a win or a loss affects our share price in terms of public perceptions.

This external noise explains why it is so bloody difficult to coach England. The media here are vociferous because individual outlets are competing so hard for attention. And a negative take on England, with a provocative headline, generates so much traffic. People are more likely to read a story of looming crisis than a more measured analysis addressing the very fine margins between perceived success and failure at the highest level of international sport. No one wants to hear about natural ebbs and flows. They want to talk about boom or bust. Extremes sell, and so I can understand why the media prefer black-and-white polarities.

The whole organization is affected by the external noise. I can block it out most of the time, and I can help the players try to do the same, but there are occasions when it seems draining. The board of directors above me at the RFU, and at any big organization, hate the noise. When any boards at big organizations have that noise, they react. Look at the fate of most football managers. As soon as the team gets put under pressure, the manager is dragged in and, to ease the pressure on the board, often sacked. Bringing in a new manager might not solve the long-term problems, but it takes the edge off the scrutiny in that moment. The board feel they have acted decisively and quelled the noise for a while.

I think that's a fascinating part of sport. Emotion often gets in the way of clarity. If the board was running a proper business, they probably wouldn't make such a speculative decision in haste. They would address the situation more calmly and allow the leader time to turn the situation around. But the emotion of sport makes it thrilling and addictive, and none of us who work at the sharp end can claim to be oblivious of how it functions. When you sign up for the job you understand the territory. And if you're willing to smile wryly when praised to the heavens, then you should be tough enough to take the insults.

It's not always easy and, despite winning two tournaments in 2020, it felt as if the media had had enough of me coaching England. There was fierce criticism of the way we had played – even though we were not the only team in the Autumn Nations Cup tournament to offer up stodgy rugby. France became the new darlings because they were a young and inexperienced team. They have not won anything yet, but their talented young players were venerated while my team, and specifically my coaching, was castigated. The noise kept building and we failed, this time, to block the clamour and the dissent.

The art of leadership is partly about finding the best way to get inside people's heads. Ultimately, we're trying to train the mind to get more out of the body. In every sphere of leadership, you shape the thinking of those who work with you or for you. You want them to believe that the seemingly impossible is possible. You want them to reach for greatness. So you've got to be really creative and innovative, and absolutely relentless in looking for an edge.

You always need to read the context of the situation and the ability of your group. You've got to know how much you lead and how much you guide. Sometimes the players will lead the charge. Sometimes it will be the coaches who drive the organization, and usually it will be you, as the leader. But you always need someone to lead, and for everyone to understand the vision and the end goal you have set for the group.

You will work out where the gaps and holes are in your organization. You will establish the kind of people you need around you and the strategies required to ensure that you travel forward along the carefully plotted line you have mapped to reach your end goal.

As you pursue the vision, you learn so much about your players. In the amateur age in the 1980s and 1990s, players were resilient as they lived tougher lives. They combined work, rugby and family. But young people today have to be resilient in other ways. Look at what they've had to endure with the pandemic. It's a terrible time for young people – but they will develop more resilience. And they're going to have to be resilient again to cope with its aftermath. I see that every time I examine our culture and environment in the England camp during this testing pandemic.

As we move into the Operation phase of the Vision stage of the cycle, it is vital that we:

ASSESS EVERYTHING

As a leader you can only discover how far people in your company can go if you are out there as often as possible, watching them at work and observing their attitudes and behaviour with scrupulous attention to detail. You need to react accordingly and know when to praise them and when to tell them they need to offer more.

Someone asked me, not so long ago, if this need to 'walk the factory floor' will ever change. I was definite in my answer: 'Never will, mate. Your eyes and your gut give you more information than anything else.'

I believe that intensely, because such information provides the ability to develop good conversations – whether they're robust or supportive or even 'nothing' conversations. Sometimes a nothing conversation can have a really positive effect on a player. It might be as simple as: 'How's your baby? How did he sleep last night?'

Those little moments can lift the person and encourage them to pursue our objectives even harder.

Wayne Bennett, the great Australian rugby league coach, often says that he has hundreds of meetings every day. It feels particularly true when I am in camp with the England squad. Some of those meetings will only last a minute as a player and I pass each other in the corridor. But they are still of value because our work is so dependent on communication and building relationships. Every time you see a player or a member of staff, there's a chance to have either a positive or negative effect on them. So I see this as an opportunity to coach the player – even to give them an idea to mull over or to reinforce a point we have discussed earlier.

I make sure there are also detailed group and one-to-one meetings where we really drill down into the core of a subject. Some players respond better to formal meetings where you have an agenda and you sit down together and look at some clips on video. But most of your meetings are informal, when you catch someone in passing and you get a chance to assess their mood and to say some appropriate and positive words. I might also pick up in our exchange that something is amiss and the player needs more attention paid to him. I won't be able to deduce this if I am not relentless in my observations and moving around the squad attentively. Those brief chats in passing are a valuable extension of walking the factory floor.

PROVIDE THE CLARITY

As a head coach in professional sport, it's obvious that you will be working with young people, mostly in their twenties, and you have to communicate in different ways with them. The view from outside might be that modern rugby players are one-dimensional and insular, that they spend so much time in the gym or on their game consoles that they have little imagination or wider general knowledge. But that is totally wrong. They have so much to watch on Netflix or Amazon, and so much information they can mine at the tap of a few keys on their phone, that they are well informed about a wide variety of subjects. The young player is also becoming smarter in using his mobile phone and is more aware of cognitive fitness. It is no longer a novelty, so I don't have to ban mobile phones in the England camp like I had to do when I coached Japan.

They're also keen to expand their horizons and are, generally, much better educated than we were in the 1980s. It is striking that they are so much more up-to-date with the news and more socially conscious and better informed about issues of race and gender. All of them can get on their phones and, within 20 seconds, tell you how many people are suffering from coronavirus in Nigeria today or what the political situation is in Myanmar this week. It's really positive.

It also means that there is often an insatiable desire for new ideas and new experiences among young players. Their attention span is noticeably shorter than it was for players when I turned out for Randwick and New South Wales back in Australia 35 years ago. They are also much more individualistic, and you have to find a way to connect with them personally.

The downside is that, sometimes, they have fewer life skills. They have also been slow on occasions to realize that it is part of their role to generate empathy with their teammates, and cohesion in the squad, and they have often focused more on their own games than the wider well-being of the squad. Will Carling has reminded them that it is not just down to the coaches to think about such issues. The players need to show the basic life skills to think of others. They are more used to being entertained and stimulated.

Nowadays, you have to put more thought into what you say to players than you did in the past. You need to be more nuanced and strategic in your thinking. It's interesting, but it's also challenging for a coach, because you've got to think of ways to keep the environment fresh. Your ideas need to be entertaining and meaningful to keep young players involved and right on the edge. You have to work very hard to keep them fully engaged.

For instance, in the Autumn Nations Cup tournament, we even had breathing lessons to help the players learn how to recover. People will say: 'You don't need that. We all know how to breathe.' But the truth is that you do need it, because young players thrive on learning more about something as seemingly simple as breathing. Singers have been doing it for decades and so why shouldn't elite rugby players? Young players are happy to work with specialists in recovery. They feel, rightly, that it will help them become even better players.

At the start of the professional era of rugby, players would enjoy a few beers at the end of training. Then the game embraced the idea of an ice bath or a sauna. We've now got different versions of both, but you continue to look for new ways in which you can improve their recovery. It just shows how much more complex it has become to run a high-performance team. It's the same with leading businesses now. They have to provide gymnasiums and mindfulness classes. You need experts to run them. And therefore the head coach, or the CEO of the business, needs to find the right people to do it, and then get them to work together. The risk is they become silos by themselves and they only worry about their unit. You've got to make sure that all these areas are connected.

It's also vital to ensure your presentations and team talks suit this younger generation. Our meetings with the players usually won't last longer than 15 minutes, and we'll generally have only three points that we need to get across. We break out into small groups for discussion and use a mixture of video, movement and infographics which make it more stimulating for them. We use news bulletins to distribute information before meetings and to help them feel they're part of something special.

For the players to learn, and to understand the vision you've set, you need to teach them in a way that elicits a positive response. I used to go to meeting presentations for businesses with 20 or 30 slides. I soon understood that by the time ten slides had been shown, no one was really learning anything more. This is especially true of young people. They want sharp and fast lessons. They want change. You need to provide this to be effective in elite sport, business or education.

When it comes to setting the vision or making changes in how we are going to train or play, there will be a process to follow. We will talk first to the players' leadership group and get feedback from them. We will modify the vision or our plans if necessary. Then we break the team up into smaller groups and run through these new ideas with them. We will again look closely at the feedback they give us. It's a little like when you run an advertising campaign. Before you launch it in public, you test it with focus groups. We do the same.

These small breakout groups also provide cohesive communication between the outside backs, the inside backs, the tight forwards and the loose forwards. They meet in their specific pods and discuss the new ideas and work out how best to utilize them within their role in the team.

But the essential nature of one-to-one communication has not changed. It's become popular psychology now to talk about the importance of relationships in sport or business. But it's never been that different. I can remember being on a bus as a 20-year-old, about to play my first game for Randwick against Brothers in the Australian club championship. The memory is still vivid more than 40 years later. Bob Dwyer, our head coach and a man we all revered, chose to sit next to me. He said: 'What do you think about today, mate? How do we approach this one?'

Bob was not looking for any nuggets of tactical acumen from a rookie like me. He was just opening up a relationship and making me feel as if I belonged – and that my opinion mattered. I couldn't tell you what I mumbled in reply, but I remember how good Bob made me feel. He drew me into the group with a simple gesture.

Those same dynamics apply today, but there is a caveat. You have to be much more subtle and nuanced in the way you communicate new information to young people now. I've got no doubt that this is even more important in business when you are dealing with a far wider age-range than in elite sport. Out in the real world, in big companies, your staff criss-crosses the generations from young people in their early twenties to more senior people in their sixties.

If I was running a business now, the first person I would employ would be a learning expert. The pressing question for me is always: 'How can I create the best learning environment?' The only reliable advantage we've got in life, in business or sport, is to learn faster than the opposition. To achieve this we need to make sure that any information that has to be disseminated is done in an appropriate way for all the different generations.

Let's look at our staff with England as an example. Apart from Neil Craig, I am the oldest bloke in camp. The coaching staff like to communicate through WhatsApp and that's not ideal for me. I can't read proper documents on WhatsApp. I need them sent to me by email so that I can print them off. I need to read the documents and write notes to absorb the information effectively because that's how I've been educated. So I think you've always got to be cognizant of the differences in how we communicate.

In the 2020 Six Nations we carried out a little experiment. We cut out all WhatsApp communication. The staff sent all documents by email. We found that the amount of traffic decreased by 50 per cent because it eradicated all the useless chatter that crops up on WhatsApp. Everything that was sent had the feel of a proper document, which gave each one a sense of gravitas, and the coaches put more thought into their presentation. I found it fascinating how it chopped out all these useless conversations we often had on our group chats. But once lockdown bit and we could not meet in person, we reverted to WhatsApp. You just need to be flexible and find the best way to communicate across the generations at the appropriate time.

These days you have to present ideas, especially critical ones, in a positive way. When I started out as a leader, you could go straight to being bluntly negative if something wasn't right. That has changed over the last 25 years. Now, even with the glue guys, you have to give them positivity to develop togetherness. It's neither right nor wrong. It's just the way it is.

But I still drive the players to be self-challenging. People who don't really know me might have heard a few stories from the 1990s when, in a totally different culture with the Brumbies, at the start of professional rugby, I could tear strips off a player if they were not putting in the work we needed. I never do that now because the modern player needs to be spoken to differently. I didn't use fear in the past either. It's always the wrong word to use but the media love it. They love hearing embellished stories about players quaking while a coach gives them the old hairdryer treatment. That's how we often communicated back then and I could be very direct. Now the approach is much more measured and subtle.

The aim is still the same – to convey to the player that there's always a bit more in them. The one thing players don't know, whether in the 1990s or the 2020s, is how good they can be. So the coach's job is to paint the full picture of the player's potential and get them to believe it. Sometimes you have to dig deep emotionally to get them to understand that. And sometimes it can be an encouraging conversation.

It's never about what they want. It's what they need to realize their potential. Every player wants to be loved but, to perform at your best, such an approach is not always necessarily going to be right.

You need to be honest and robust in deciding what the player needs to hear. You tailor the way you deliver that news to suit the character of the individual. You strive to be as honest as possible, depending on the player and the situation, but I think it's always important to give them hope too. It can't be false hope – it has to be based on sound knowledge.

Our job as leaders is to take them as close as we can to fulfilling their potential. In a company, a school or a team, no one knows how good they can be. And so the job of the leader is to keep pushing, keep insisting, keep demanding that they challenge themselves. When their focus dips, you need to challenge them to keep moving in the right direction.

Clarity has become more important than ever – as has developing leadership within your team or company. Firstly, you have to be able to identify people who you think can influence the organization in a positive way, and in line with your values and vision. Each person then needs their own plan to develop themselves as leaders. There's no one-size-fits-all when it comes to engendering leadership. Everyone needs different instructions and ways of being helped. So you have got to find the right people to help them.

I remember Ricky Ponting being made the Australian cricket captain. He was quite a rough and tough Tasmanian and pretty green. They recruited a guy from the National Bank of Australia to become Ponting's private leadership coach in 2004. He was a good man whom we also used with the Wallabies. His task was to add some sophistication to Ponting's captaincy. It was not to neuter the innate toughness and grit of Ponting – but to give him more confidence in dealing with the public scrutiny. It shows how personal leadership plans have been part of elite sport for years now.

When I became Australia's coach, I asked for help with the media. So they brought in an ABC newsreader and I had two lessons with him. I still remember him telling me always to talk as though I was addressing the back of a room. I still try to do that because it means that you're talking with confidence as you try to own the room. It's a little tip that is useful in leadership.

We've had leaders in our current team take acting classes. Not all of them – just a few select players to help them in terms of their confidence and delivery. It's finding what is right for each person to become a better leader. For some people it might be the way they talk to their teammates. For others it might be the way they behave in meetings or use their discretionary time to influence their teammates.

We arranged acting lessons for a senior England player who was one of our tactical leaders. Acting classes developed his presentation of information. That's important because we're all selling ideas – and the more effectively you can convey and sell your ideas, the more influential you will be as a leader. We organized his lessons when he was back at his club, with their approval, but other players have had acting tuition while in camp with England.

We have seen a huge improvement in levels of communication – especially with those players who don't usually command people's attention. Acting is a good way to learn because it brings out confidence and skill. If you look at the most successful coaches in rugby, many of them started out as schoolteachers. And when you are a schoolteacher, you learn how to talk in front of the class, how to position yourself and present your work. You learn how to command the room. This is important in terms of coaching and leadership.

As a leader, the best way I can assess people is face to face. You can have Zoom conversations, but you never get a real feeling for someone's mood unless you can see them in person. During the pandemic, it was important to be even better at reading people's body language because of the masks we all had to wear. People's faces were partially hidden, and so you had to find different ways of assessing how they were feeling.

The various coronavirus lockdowns taught me lessons that, I think, can be applied to any business or line of work. You should approach any meeting that you have, especially on a remote medium like Zoom, like an investment banker. You've got a certain amount of money you can invest. And you want to invest that money in the right area to get the best result. It's the same whenever you have a meeting. You've got a certain amount of attention time and focus at your disposal. The key to these Zoom meetings is investing in those areas that require very specific attention. Don't let those meetings become just talk-fests. You know how it is – most people want to talk, but they can waste a lot of time.

You need to work out what's important to your business, and go back to that old 80:20 rule. Invest 80 per cent of your time in the 20 per cent that's going to make the most difference. Keep it concise, keep it tight, summarize the key points, check their understanding, and don't let anyone go off track. If you want to have a social chitchat, then save that for a totally different time.

It comes back to clarity being the new clever. Understand where you most need to be clear and focus on that. Let go of the things you can't control. Don't let them become a discussion point.

There is no perfect blueprint out there – especially during a pandemic. But we have our vision and we know where we want to go. How we get there is much more uncertain. We know that there are going to be some ups and downs. We'll have to keep our seat belt on most of the ride. But, sometimes, we might even have to jump out of the car to get there.

Again, it all comes down to the vision you have set. You know where you want to finish because you have the end point in mind. You work back from it. At the moment, because we had a slump in the Six Nations, we know we need to be quicker to adjust. We have to be quicker on our feet and in our thinking. As a leader I need to clear my head. From this point on we can translate the vision we have set into achievable goals.

But this Operation phase, when creating your vision, is always driven by the same simple process:

ASSESS EVERYTHING AND THEN PROVIDE THE CLARITY

- Find the best way to get inside people's heads

- Provide the clarity – the code of operation, the expectations of delivery

- Translate the vision into achievable goals

- Block out the external noise

- Invest 80 per cent of your time in the 20 per cent that's going to make the most difference

4

THE GLUE OF KNOWLEDGE

KNOW YOURSELF, KNOW YOUR PLAYERS

Self-knowledge is always a cornerstone of leadership. The ability to confront your strengths and weaknesses, to know deep down what works for you and what you need to do to keep improving, and to understand the ways you influence your employees, is important every day you are in charge. A willingness to reflect on your leadership deepens your self-awareness. I believe that most leaders who have been successful for a sustained period of time have been very reflective. They've always been willing to sit down, after either success or failure, to work out what they have done well and where they have fallen short of their own highest standards. Once they have that knowledge, they attend to their findings to become even better leaders.

It helps to have a routine of reflective practice. Every day you should spend time reflecting on what you've done over the previous 24 hours. It should be a priority where you make notes. I try and do this when I am feeling mentally sharp rather than just ticking it off as a ritual chore at the end of a long day. It also helps if you have someone you trust with whom you can share these thoughts.

Self-knowledge is relatively easy to generate when you love your work. This is one of the many reasons why I am grateful to be involved in sport, because it is easy for me to love coaching. If you are in a different line of work, which might be a field you find harder to love, you need to find a strong reason to believe there is something special about your mission. If you don't have the spark for the job, it will be impossible to be a great leader, because there will be no motivation to put in that extra discretionary effort we all need.

If the job feels special to you, you'll do the hard yards and everyone will benefit. It's like when you have kids. There's nothing complicated about getting out of bed and looking after your kids. You simply want to be there for them. It's the same with leadership. You've got to find something special that makes you want to put in an enormous effort to lift other people. You might be doing something positive for society, or the environment, or you might be involved in a special project or building a business you believe in passionately. If people are exposed to your enthusiasm and engagement, and feel included, they will give you a little more. The combination of everyone putting in this additional effort becomes a mighty force – and it all starts with self-knowledge.

I know that, for me, international rugby is showtime. It's the biggest show of all. I could make much more money coaching full-time in Japan – but it's nowhere near as exciting or demanding. Here, with England, you're stretched all the time. We win and we get criticized for our style of play. We lose and we get hammered. England are by far the most difficult team I've ever coached. I am being tested and challenged all the time.

I feel I'm an immeasurably better coach now than when I was at the World Cup in 2019. From the outside it doesn't look that way; but my self-knowledge and exposure to various new problems have added fresh layers to my coaching. It's a damn difficult job, but that's what I want. I want to coach difficult teams on the international stage. I would get bored coaching at club level now – and I would only want to go to a club that kept winning. Coaching a club that loses consistently is not much fun. You can certainly improve players at club level, anywhere in the world, but those losing clubs generally don't have the economic resources to become champions. Professional sport is now dominated by money, so the challenge is more limited in club rugby.

I would be attracted, one day, by the prospect of taking over a lesser rugby nation, such as Germany, and attempting to turn them into a decent Test team. The dream could be US Rugby. The

United States could become a force in world rugby, and I would love to see if I could do something in American rugby, along the lines of what I achieved with Japan. Such different challenges are for the future, rather than now, and so to keep my coaching fresh with England, I mix it up when I can.

Someone asked me a pretty deep and meaningful question the other day when they encouraged me to describe my purpose in life. I could not give an immediate answer beyond saying that I think everyone has some sort of talent within them. I believe it's your task in life to maximize that gift. Maybe I've been given the talent to coach rugby. And so, if pushed, I would say that my purpose in life is to coach rugby as well as I can. I want to help young players to achieve their potential, and for my team to perform together like an orchestra; I want people to derive so much pleasure from watching us that they will never forget our rugby. I want to keep doing that for as long and as well as I can in the years ahead.

The clarity of this self-knowledge helps me to know everyone around me. This is the fundamental focus of part four, the Management phase, of the Vision section in our cycle:

UNDERSTAND THE GROUPS, UNDERSTAND THE INDIVIDUALS

There is a great story about Carlos Ghosn, the fallen business leader. In March 1999 he was approached by Louis Schweitzer, the CEO of Renault, and asked to lead a turnaround at Nissan, the struggling Japanese motor giant, in Tokyo. The two companies had agreed a major strategic alliance where Renault absorbed $5.4 billion of Nissan's debt in return for a 36.6 per cent equity stake. The new joint venture would be the world's fourth largest car-maker. But Nissan were in a mess, and it needed a dramatic transformation to get the staff firing again.

Ghosn, a Brazilian-born French businessman of Lebanese descent, wrote numerous fascinating articles about the way he operated on his arrival in Tokyo. He spent the first hundred days just walking the floors of the Nissan factories. He was resolute in finding out what was wrong and what needed to be changed. Ghosn had to know his staff before he set about making any plans. He seemed sincere in his desire to help people as well as rejuvenate the company.

Once he really understood the people working at Nissan, he formulated plans of how to set a new vision which he could use to transform, operate and manage the company. These plans were based on him walking into every area of the company and talking to people about their job. He practised leadership with the most fundamental units of his business. This is the opposite of the image of a CEO taking over a distressed company, staying in his office, poring over worrying balance sheets while devising new strategies. Ghosn had incredible success after that first burst of knowledge-hunting, and it's a tactic that has always stuck with me. Ghosn showed that if you can fix the fundamental units of any organization, the sophisticated units follow much more easily. Nissan were transformed into a powerhouse again.

The story then took a twist because, years later, in November 2018, Ghosn was arrested and charged with allegedly 'misusing company funds for personal benefit'. He was held under house arrest in Tokyo, for 132 days, while awaiting trial. Ghosn had already been fired by Nissan and, before the trial began, he made a daring escape from Japan.

Ghosn and his wife apparently hired a group of mercenaries who pretended to be musicians. They smuggled Ghosn, who is only five foot six, out of the country inside a six-foot-tall double-bass case. He managed to get to Lebanon, which has no extradition treaty with Japan, and held an emotional press conference. Ghosn claimed that 'I did not escape justice. I fled injustice.' He said that he had been 'brutally ripped from my work, my family and my friends' and insisted that he been pressured during solitary confinement into making false confessions. He also claimed to have been a victim of a coup to derail Renault's influence at Nissan.

I can only read this outlandish story from a distance and suspect that Ghosn became too narcissistic. He lost that searing focus which made such an impact at the outset, and he presumably became distracted by fame, money and power. When you're doing well, you have to keep those temptations at bay. When you're struggling, you're battling with criticism and lack of respect. As a leader I am less interested in the distractions than in Ghosn's initial determination to really know everyone at Nissan. He needed to understand them as a group and as individuals – and he was hugely successful until hubris brought him down.

You've always got to work on yourself and your core values and stay true to them. If you can be yourself, you will find it so much easier to understand your staff. We've recently had a coach at England who can't be himself. He's a bright man, but he always tries to play the part of a happy-go-lucky guy, and the players know it's just not him or his real character.

As a coach, or any kind of leader, you have to be a great actor on occasions so that you can find the right tone and demeanour for a vital moment. You might not be in that particular mood right there and then, but you've got to find it within yourself to convey the message that is needed. You can't be a good actor unless you know yourself. It goes back to one of our first points about self-awareness. Who am I as a coach? What do I do best? Where must I improve? That self-knowledge allows you to play the other roles you have to slip into from time to time.

I spoke to this specific coach about the need to be himself every day. But his trouble is that he wants to be popular with the players. However, it's important to find the right way to be popular. I remember reading Bill Walsh's *Finding the Winning Edge*, which is the encyclopaedia of coaching. The former National Football League coach said the first and most important thing you need to do is coach yourself. It's the same with leadership. If you can't lead yourself, you can't lead other people.

As a leader, while cultivating your self-knowledge, you need to understand that you don't know everything. You have always got so much more to learn even if, like me, you are in your sixties and approaching the end of your career. This acceptance should allow you to remain humble and respectful – and never to think you are the doyen of leadership.

But how do you keep building towards your planned destination as a leader? That's always a key factor, and it goes back to the beginning and knowing your direction. You're leading in the moment but, at the same time, you need to manage tomorrow as well. You have to keep pushing the group towards that end goal. So much of this comes down to the level of support or challenge you give to your employees. You can be too supportive and caring – and not challenging enough. Or you can be too challenging, in which case the environment becomes too abrasive. It's all about getting that balance right. Everything is handled more easily if you have the right mix of staff – people with hard analytical skills and others with softer and more subtle gifts.

Let's start with the group. A good leader will test the temperature of the room, and the group, every single day. What is the temperature and the health of the group at the moment? What do we need to do to get them even stronger and more focused? It's impossible to have a group filled with people of the same character and talent. When you're dealing with human beings, you get used to fluctuating levels of ability and commitment.

The chances are that 10 per cent of the people in your group are always going to be excellent. It doesn't matter where they are and what conditions they face. Your top three players are always going to work harder than the rest and be more valuable to the group. Yes, there will be days when their form dips a little, but it will never be down to attitude or ability. With England I know that the Farrells, Curries and Itojes are going to be right on it. You've then got your bottom three who you're trying to move on. Then you've got the middle group, around 24 of the 30 players. This is the group you're always trying to edge forward. Can you find another 3 per cent in those people? This is the real coaching task – to move this large middle group slightly forward. The people at the top end will drive that move forwards and the people at the bottom will be replaced or they will be pulled along by the sheer momentum of the group. Once this happens, you start to build a really strong team.

I've found this with every team I've coached. Sometimes you can get really lucky and have four or five standout players but, generally, this is just how most teams operate. They're normal distribution curves. You just need to understand quickly which players fit in a particular group and then work out strategies of how you move them forward. It's always about speed because often the only advantage we have is learning more quickly than the opposition.

You're always trying to build the team but, sometimes, your top guys need a bit more attention. The middle guys are fairly consistent, but you have got to be relentless with them. And you've always got to be ready for problems and to think that there could be a crisis coming unless you keep at it constantly. You need that urgency and diligence to keep doing it with a large group – and one of the problems in leadership is that it can become a grind.

Everyone wants to be comfortable. I understand that from a human perspective but, in elite sport or business, the enemy of excellence is concealed within layers of comfort. You need to find that relentlessness not to be comfortable – and to keep pushing the group to do more.

So while there will always be discrepancies in your group, you want the weakest to rise up rather than the best to slip down a level.

Humility is a big part of being successful. Those who are more capable than the others have to learn to be humble. Arrogance is just like complacency. It erodes everything that made you successful in the first place. The best people realize this and so, unlike Carlos Ghosn, they stay on track.

But as a leader you need to adapt to the people within your group to get the best out of them. The lazy view would suggest that you are at the apex of the leadership triangle. Some leaders might say: 'I am the boss so you dance to my tune. And when I stop, you stop dancing too.' I approach it from the opposite view. How can I get to know you better so that I can help you get the best out of yourself?

My underlying philosophy, and I know it doesn't come across like this in the media, is that I am always a servant to the players. How can I serve the players best? Now, sometimes, you have got to sit above them and be very clear and direct and tell them what they have to do. But, for the vast majority of the time, *you* are serving *them*. Sometimes the only thing that gets in your way is your own ego. But those are short-term failings that help no one, because we're trying to get the players to perform.

It's like a drama production. What is the director's role? Getting the actors to perform the best they can. So he's serving them. Occasionally he will berate or cajole them. But most of the time he is there to encourage them. In Japan, it's interesting that a film director is called the head coach. I think that's correct, because it is the role of a director or a head coach to be a servant of those people working with them.

The hardest aspect is that it takes a lot of time and sometimes you don't get it right. It's always a gamble. I spoke to a young coach the other day, and I told him that he has to be prepared to fail. I felt he was trying to be safe all the time and, because of that, he can never engage the players. He's not prepared to go somewhere difficult and more challenging – but, unless you do that, you can't get that little bit extra out of the group.

I also sometimes go harder on the younger players because I want to set them an early example and make them understand that they are entitled to nothing. One day, during the 2021 Six Nations, I pulled young Ollie Lawrence aside. He's still a kid, only 21, but the way that some of the media raves about him, you would think he's already assured of becoming one of the best players in the world. He might do that, one day, but his attitude was not hungry or disciplined enough. If you want to be the best player in your position, you simply have to work harder than anyone else. I had just got back from a coaching stint with Suntory and so the example of Beauden Barrett was fresh in my mind. To contrast his diligence and drive with what I was seeing among some of England's most entitled players was sobering.

'Mate,' I said to Ollie, 'I've just been working with Beauden Barrett for three weeks. He's one of the greatest players in the world right now and he is out playing club rugby in Japan. You know what I saw every day? Forty-five minutes before training even starts, there is one bloke out there. Beauden is working on his passing and kicking. He then does training, and afterwards who is still working? Beauden. So how about you? What do I see with you?'

Ollie admitted that he had not been working hard enough. It's simple for him to say it because we know it's the truth. So he understands. We will have to see if he sustains a change in behaviour. It is down to him and it is down to me to keep pushing him. We might need another 15 of those conversations. It all depends on how coachable a player is and that, in turn, depends on their background. So it's not straightforward.

But you can change a player's behaviour. I had the same kind of conversation with George Smith when he was 20. A year after exploding onto the scene, he was a key member of our title-winning Brumbies team, but I was on my way to coach Australia. I could tell George was enjoying life a little too much. He had started believing his press. He was exceptional, but his standards were slipping. He was in danger of not fulfilling his potential but, thinking he was entitled to have a great game every time he played, it also looked to me as if he could become very ordinary. So I had a serious conversation with him and that's all we needed. George changed and he worked very hard from then on.

It's difficult for players like Ollie to hear the truth because, at the same time, he reads articles by people who don't see him in training or around the camp, and they are saying that he should definitely be picked. It's going to be interesting but, sometimes, I am encouraged. We had a training session the other day and he was totally on it. You could see how much he wanted to work and to improve. But I want to see that every time. It's the same for every player we call up. They are not entitled to be here. They have to prove themselves every day.

In preparing the team for the 2019 World Cup, we needed to go to some difficult places with the squad as a way of clearing out some damaging disunity. I called in a specialist, Corinne Reid, to find any potential grenades in the group. We knew something was not quite right and we used this expression: we do not want to carry grenades in the back of the truck. So we had to find the grenades and detonate them safely. Corinne is an Australian academic; in 2018 she was the director of research and chair in Psychological Thera-pies at the University of Edinburgh. She had worked in elite sport before, and she could explain to the squad that exceptional sport-ing performances require an exceptional group environment.

Corinne helped us, as a group, to identify the grenades which had been lurking at the back of our truck since the 2015 World Cup. There had been a lot of negative press about the team after Sam Burgess spoke about some of the schisms and divides. It was also complicated because Owen Farrell's dad, Andy, had been one of the England coaches. Other players then chipped in and said their piece to the media, and so there were all kinds of cliques and divides within that group. When I took over as head coach in 2016, I deliberately sidestepped those issues. I didn't have enough time to deal with them and I just got on with coaching the team.

But it came to a head in the Six Nations in 2019 – six months before the World Cup. The frailties in the group were exposed in our final game of that tournament. We led Scotland 31–0 after half an hour but, at the death, we had to score a converted try to rescue a 38–38 draw. You could sense that the group lacked tight-ness and cohesion. Corinne, as a conflict psychologist, was able to help resolve some of those difficulties and divisions.

She confronted the group head on. It was full-frontal honesty and people felt exposed. This made it a difficult time. Even Neil Craig and I were caught up in the fallout. I remember the toughest day – a boiling hot afternoon at an England World Cup training camp in Treviso. After one of Corinne's grenade-exploding sessions, it felt as though there were bush fires raging across the whole camp. It was crazy. Neil and I went at each other as well. For the previous few days it had felt like anarchy, because so much ill-feeling and dissent had been unleashed. All the old wounds from 2015 had been opened up and players were still hurting. There was also a clear anti-Saracens feeling in sectors of the squad. It was emotional carnage.

I met Neil for a coffee and I really laid into him. I said: 'Neil, what is the leadership group doing about this mess? What are you fucking doing? You're not their mate. Mate.'

It was ferocious because I was worried. Neil came back at me just as hard. We were sitting outside a cafe that was in a thoroughfare leading to the players' bedrooms. They were walking past us as we ranted at each other, but I was beyond caring by that stage. We were caught up in a difficult conversation and the emotions of the players had got to us. I remember saying to him: 'Do you think you can do this job? Because I don't know whether you can get the leaders to do what they have to do.'

It was such a tough but helpful conversation that led to some practical solutions. We ended up cutting a couple of players adrift. The leadership group grew up, and Neil became a lot more focused on them. We all like to be liked, and Neil and I are guilty of that as well at times – even though we are two tough old Aussies. So we had to detonate those grenades, take the flak and not be afraid to face a difficult situation. We had to be reminded that adverse circumstances often lead to better solutions. You need to go through a bit of pain for a time, a sense that you're not in control. And in Treviso, in the summer of 2019, I didn't think we had control. We needed the players, the senior group in particular, to take some responsibility for the environment. The coaches are at the forefront, but then you need your leadership group to drive it, and that's what happened. Instead of allowing the old wounds to fester, they came together and began to heal.

Neil and I also had a real laugh after it was all over. It was flipping hot, 35 degrees day after day, and so we trained mostly in the mornings. In the afternoons we relaxed a little and the coaches played padel – which is a variation of tennis. It's like you're playing on half a tennis court with a back wall that resembles a squash wall. We had a coaches' tournament and, despite our feisty exchanges, Neil and I were doubles partners. He's older than me but a very skilful sportsman. So he was better than me and he was racing around as we won three of our four games. As the two eldest in the coaching group, by some way, we were pretty chuffed with ourselves. We had also totally overcome the harsh words we had spoken to each other during the previous days. But I felt a bit crook too. It was like I had heat stroke. So I suggested to Neil that we each have a little rest in our respective rooms and catch up late afternoon for a chat.

There was no sign of Neil later, and so I went in search of him. It was pretty hilarious, if painful for Neil. It turned out that, after his shower, he had fallen asleep naked on the bed – and then gone into a full body cramp. He couldn't move. We laughed about it later, once he got out of that painful and compromising position, and it proved again that if you have a tough conversation about professional performance in elite sport, it needn't affect your relationship going forward. We were still firm friends, and it was a healthy affirmation that these conversations are not about personalities. They're performance conversations where respect matters more than harmony.

Corinne taught everyone else in the group that they did not have to be best mates. They just needed to be honest with each other so that they could work together effectively. I think the skill is to create a space where robust conversations can happen so that these can improve the performance of the team. If you need to tell someone else what you think, then you should be able to do that without them feeling as if it's a personal attack. The coaching staff and the players did a lot of work in generating these tough exchanges, because it helped them understand each other and have a better relationship. The better the relationship, the more robust the conversation. As a result, we found greater cohesion as a team.

When Corinne returned to Australia to take up a new academic post, we were fortunate to be able to draft in Dr Andrea Furst – a psychologist who had worked with the GB women's hockey team which won gold at the 2016 Olympics. Corinne and Andrea had a real skill in helping our players open up to express their true emotions. It is not easy to do this in a male-dominated sport like rugby, where toughness is a core attribute. They were able to expose people's vulnerability, but to do so in a way where we could come up with solutions.

We've still got ongoing issues within our group in 2021. We will address these divides and power shifts later in the book, but in the Vision section it's vital just to understand the group. You also need to – generally – be more positive than ruthlessly honest with your group. Twenty years ago the message could be stark, and even negative, to force a change in attitude. But these days, unless you're in the state we were in Treviso, you need to soften your blunt candour with a positive tinge. You have to think of the well-being of your group and understand that they need a more subtle and upbeat approach.

I don't think it's a problem. I had an appreciably easier life than my father did. My dad worked down the gold mines at the age of 15. He worked two jobs his whole life. Life has never been that hard for me. And now my daughter has got an easier life than me. She was flying around the world with me at the age of 15. When I was 21, I had only made it as far as New Zealand. Her children will have an appreciably easier life than she did. It's all part of human development. Everyone wants things easier. So it's part of a natural progression that the players need a softer platform to absorb an honest message.

Twenty years ago, I could have used controlled anger to deliver a message without any problems. Now I use anger very sparingly. I pick the time and the place for it very carefully because, really, I don't think it has a beneficial effect any more. I can use it with individual players, occasionally, if this is what they need, but I would never show anger to the group as a whole. It would not be beneficial.

Within each group we have distinct individuals who all need to be treated differently. I remember when I was teaching, I could be fairly direct and even authoritarian. I was a Geography, Maths and PE teacher, and those subjects suit that approach. I then became the acting principal while still helping out as a teacher. One Year 12 class didn't have a teacher in a subject called General Studies. The course focused on essay-writing, and it needed to be driven by creativity. I had four girls at the top of the class, and they were so bright and effervescent. I remember trying to teach them using my normal direct style, and it was an absolute disaster.

I needed to change because I finally came to understand them –

both as a group and as individuals. I thought: 'I've just got to let go – and let them be themselves.' I did, and from then on classes became discussions. The four girls ended up in the top 10 per cent in the state. I was proud of them – but it was a good lesson for me as well. It translated to coaching. Some players need to be coached less. George Smith didn't need a lot of coaching. He just needed some guidance here and there. Tom Curry is the same. So you have to learn who you've got to coach hard and who you've got to coach less. Experience helps, but it's primarily about your observation skills, seeing what effect you have on people, and being courageous enough to be wrong.

I was wrong in my General Studies class with those individual girls, and I made a hash of it early on. But I had the courage to change. It would be a mistake to think that this was a gender issue and the girls were unhappy with a harder line of teaching. They were simply brighter than me. I realized that pretty quickly, and so I allowed them to bloom. Boys of similar intelligence would have been the same, but they might have been slower to show their emotions.

When it comes to assessing individual players, and the level of the team, their qualities should have nothing to do with the amount of effort and energy you put into your work. This is so important to me. I'm proud of my profession. I want to be the best coach that I can be every day, whether I am coaching Japanese club rugby or in the Test arena. I want to engage and inspire people, and make my players even better than they think they can be.

We're always trying to make the impossible possible for players. I remember Arsène Wenger saying in a conversation we had with coaches from across a variety of sports that he had one regret in his career – that he had not always pushed his players hard enough to be their best. I keep thinking about that. I feel that responsibility.

In all the decades I've been coaching, how many of my players have really reached their full potential? I was talking recently to a national hockey coach and he made me name five. I said George Smith, George Gregan, Stephen Larkham, Rod Kafer and Jonny

May. The first four were from the Brumbies. Alongside the brilliant Fourie du Preez of South Africa, they were the four brightest players I've ever coached. Jonny is different. I think I knew to give him the space to trust himself. If you pressed me there would probably be five more I could name, and so by the end of my career I expect to say I helped ten players maximize their abilities.

You might think ten players in 30 years is not a good percentage. But it's normal. We're dealing with human beings and so there is always conflict and complexity. Ric Charlesworth won two Olympic gold medals with the Australia teams he coached, and he also says his one lingering regret is not being able to unleash the full potential of more than a few players. I think every leading coach feels the same. It's really difficult to uncover the very best in a person. You've got to get everything right.

Earlier today I had quite a sharp conversation with a player about what he had done this week and how he had portrayed himself. I want him to be the very best version of himself and, at the moment, he's too preoccupied. I had to explain again that there is a delicate balance between being an individual and a team player. How much are you prepared to sacrifice to be part of the team?

All the great players know this sacrifice and they are willing to endure it. Look at the two greatest players of the last 20 years – Richie McCaw and Dan Carter. If you say just one thing about both of them, it should be that they were both great team players. If you don't teach a player to be a good team player, you're not giving him the opportunity to be the best.

We'll see whether this particular player takes on board what I told him about McCaw and Carter. You never know until you see evidence of change. Twenty years ago, I would have torn into him and told it to him straight. But this time I took a different approach. I said: 'Put yourself in my shoes. What would you do now?' So it was a conversation rather than me laying into him; I gave him the problem to solve. But the message was still blunt and honest.

When you are dealing with individuals, you need to be flexible in your communication. So it is vital to:

UNDERSTAND THE GAPS – IN CAPABILITY, VALUES AND BELIEF

The more creative players, as we have noted before, tend to be more neurotic. I don't mean neurotic to be demeaning. It's just that they have a much more mixed temperament. They are more up and down. When you're a tight forward it's different. You work much harder, doing the tough grind, and the personality traits of these individuals are fairly consistent. The tight forwards feel like they are going down a coal mine every day. They've got to dig, dig, dig and then come up for air. Take a breath and then they go back down again into that dark and often painful place where tight forwards operate. The backs are getting the jewellery, taking the gold and making it into something glittering. So they need to be more creative.

You need to talk differently to diverse parts of your team. It's the same in all organizations. The logistics department is different to the marketing department, which is different to the sales department which is different to the creative department. It's all about how you can create the same page – and end goal – for these various mini-teams. At the same time you need to look after the individuals in all groups in a distinct way so that you get the best out of them.

I sometimes get asked how important it is for your team or organization to have a maverick. My answer is always the same: 'Depends how good they are, mate. If they're really good, you want them all the time. But having one or two good performances is not good enough.'

This is one of the areas where the media gets it wrong all the time. I listen to those pundits on the television raving on about a guy who has one or two good games and how can he not be in the England squad? The reality is that you've got to have about 50 good games. It's the same in business. You want your employee performing at their best consistently.

I played with David Campese at Randwick. People loved to call him a maverick. He had wonderful individual skills, but he was a team player. He won you games with his magic. Over the course of ten games he might have one bad performance – which could be worse than the average player. But he won most of the other nine games he played, so the trade-off always made him a key player for Randwick, New South Wales and Australia. He was also the most professional rugby player I've ever seen. In those days, when we all had to work in a day job, he would still arrive at training 45 minutes before anyone else. He would practise his torpedo kicks diligently because he wanted to be the best possible player.

You find out the secret of the best players pretty fast. The reason they're the best is not because they're mavericks. It's because they work harder at their skills than anyone else. Beauden Barrett is another great example. He's first out there, practising his passing and his kicking before the rest of the team arrives. Owen Farrell is the same. Always practising his kicking before and after training begins. Who trained hardest in *The Last Dance* – that riveting series about the Chicago Bulls? The great Michael Jordan. He was the best player, by a mile, but he still worked harder than everyone else.

Working harder and smarter than anyone else gives you a great chance to be able to maximize your potential. No one knows what your best is, so there's always a bit more there than you expect.

I feel regret when I see individuals fail to utilize their own huge talent. Danny Cipriani is the obvious example for me. I remember seeing him as a 22-year-old. He was unbelievable. He was gifted, fast, inventive and endlessly creative. But he lost focus. When I worked later with him it was too late to get him back on track. In 2018 he had already turned 30. The pattern had been set and there was no changing him.

In some teams I've implanted the core values. On other occasions I've let them grow organically. With England, when I took over, we didn't talk about values or our belief system. We just focused on rugby. In a short period, after their disastrous 2015 World Cup, I said: 'Let's get our rugby right.' From there certain behaviours began to emerge. Then, in 2019, in our fourth year together, three values were embedded in the ethos of the team:

1. Bring it on – having the courage to take anything on

2. Togetherness – that sense of cohesion and unity is self-explanatory

3. Clear thinking – which underlined the importance of clarity

The players came up with those three values. It has been easy to reward behaviour that is consistent with these values – and to challenge behaviour that runs contrary to them. The values themselves aren't the most important thing. If you look at any religion in the world, it shares most of the same basic values as other religions. But this brings us back to the art of leadership. It all boils down to how you implement those values.

Finally, in this Management phase, you need to ensure that you:

ALIGN THE VISION YOU HAVE SET
TO INDIVIDUAL JOURNEYS

I think that corny old quote of 'There is no I in team' is essentially right. But, in today's environment, a lot of players are motivated by themselves. Twenty years ago, everyone wanted to play for England because they were motivated by the shirt. It struck me that this was changing, so three years ago I visited the football academy at Ajax Amsterdam to study how they produced so many outstanding young players. They've done this consistently through the generations, and in recent years they have been exceptional again. So I spent a couple of days there and I was so interested when they told me that, 30 years ago, they recruited players because they all wanted to play for Ajax – one of Europe's most iconic teams. That was motivation enough.

But, as Ajax have been unable to match the economic powerhouses of European football, a new motivation has been offered to the best young players. They are told that Ajax can be the first vehicle for them to be the best player they can be. Ajax can lead them to bigger and wealthier destinations, but they can help this club become great again. Even more than this, you need the team to make you great. This concept appeals to the gifted young individual.

They had this beautiful infographic showing the role of the coach. Initially the coach is like a teacher. He then becomes the mentor. Finally he becomes like a friend to the player. It made so much sense. So much of the psychology of the game, especially in regard to how we get the best out of players, is geared to individual desires within the team.

The overall message is still about the team. But it's about trying to work out how we can drive individual dreams so that they also benefit the team. So there is a nuanced but important change in how you frame your team meetings psychologically. You need to tap into these individual journeys.

James Haskell gave us an example of where we aligned the vision of the team successfully to the path of a specific player. We got a lot more out of him than any other England regime because I went out of my way to make him feel important. I said to him before the 2016 Six Nations that he was going to be in the team for every game. Some players need security, and some players need to be on the edge. He was the sort of bloke who craved security. As soon as he had security, he was able to be himself and give more to the team. He was brilliant for us but, even if he started the Six Nations badly, I would have kept to my word because I knew that he was an ebullient and hard-working bloke who was tough and had a good sense of humour. He was good value on and off the field.

Dylan Hartley was similar. He didn't really need the security but, by making him captain, we made him feel so valued; he had the best period of his England career with us for 18 months. Chris Robshaw was different. He obviously lost the captaincy, but we found a new role for him as the best number 6 in England and a mentor to the younger players. He did that superbly and became a really important leader – just without the (C) next to his name. I couldn't have asked for any more from Chris.

Those three players are good examples of guys who probably hadn't been at their best in the England shirt before. We were able to create a positive environment and a narrative for them because we understood how their individual ambitions and characters could drive the team. I think that's one of the things you're always trying to do in any sort of performance-based organization. You're trying to create the right narrative for the group to develop and the right narrative for specific individuals to come forward.

It matched our aim to know the group and to know the individuals. As always, this echoes the guiding principle of this phase of the first stage of our leadership cycle:

KNOW YOURSELF, KNOW YOUR PLAYERS

- Understand the groups, understand the individuals

- Understand the gaps – in capability, values and belief

- Test the temperature of the room, and the group, every single day

- Understand yourself – self-knowledge is a cornerstone of leadership

- Create a space for honest conversations to improve performance

- Find a way to drive individual dreams so they benefit the team

STAGE 2: BUILD

5. Growth Mondays
[STRATEGY]

- Provide the context – join the vision to the transformation
- Support change with clarity of direction
- Set the horizon – make the end game real

6: Disciplined Thinking and Emotional Journeys
[PEOPLE]

- Align the resources to the changes required
- Deliver the quick wins
- Deliver the fundamental changes – both upfront and over time

7: Conflict Is Healthy
[OPERATION]

- Plan and execute
- Highlight the goals – what will success look like?
- Apply the hard graft

8: Finding the Access Point
[MANAGEMENT]

- Build the individuals towards achieving their goals

5

GROWTH MONDAYS

BE CURIOUS AND OPEN TO NEW IDEAS

Lockdown came as a jolt to all of us, but it also presented a rare opportunity. We had more time to think and to explore different approaches to work and even life. There were also occasions when we stumbled across fascinating material which we would have otherwise missed during the typical rush of our pre-Covid existence. I had a slice of good luck when, during the second lockdown of 2020, I was drawn into the stimulating world of the Gonzaga Bulldogs – a small college basketball team. They offer up one of the most interesting stories in American sport.

An extended Six Nations had just ended, and England had won the tournament on the last day of October 2020, after the final series of games had been pushed back more than seven months because of the pandemic. We were about to start the Autumn Nations Cup but first, before those autumn internationals, we did our usual post-tournament review. A familiar problem stood out.

I have never felt that our Monday sessions are particularly effective, because it is a tricky day for training. If the players have taken part in a Test match on the Saturday, they are still getting over the impact of that brutal encounter. Even if we have just had a free weekend, we have never quite maximized our Monday work. I wanted to find a new way to start the week for our squad. Curiosity and an openness to new ideas helped change the old pattern.

I also benefited from a willingness, as a leader, to work with my rivals. I am old friends with another coach who is part of a different international group and, with both of us being eager to improve, we speak often about our work. This would never happen in a week when our teams face each other in a Test match but, outside direct competition, we share ideas regularly. These conversations remind me of the helpful exchanges I used to have with Jake White, when he was coaching South Africa and I was in charge of the Wallabies. Jake and I swapped notes on our rivals and discussed how we adapted to their strengths and weaknesses.

Bob Dwyer taught me this openness because he was never a coach who wanted to hide anything about his work. He was always open to sharing, and would allow all kinds of people to watch training when he was on his way to leading the Wallabies to winning the World Cup in 1991. Bob was keen to discuss ideas – and if someone seemed smarter than him he would just say: 'Well, that's a better way of doing it than our idea. I hope it might make me find something just as good.' That generous and positive response has always seemed the best way to operate.

In this spirit of openness, I told my coaching mate about the concerns I had with our Monday sessions. We had a really constructive conversation, and he mentioned the Gonzaga Bulldogs. The bare bones of their story hooked me, and I was intrigued when my mate told me that he'd had a Zoom meeting with Gonzaga's performance director. He said that they had had some novel ideas about Monday sessions with their college players, and he suggested we set up another Zoom call so we could talk to Travis Knight, Gonzaga's performance director. I said yes like a shot and, before we met Travis online, I spent time researching the Gonzaga programme. It's a pretty amazing journey.

Gonzaga is a small private university in Spokane, Washington. It is, historically, a Catholic college and, in keeping with its limited size and scope, Gonzaga is meant to be a sporting backwater. The huge and lavishly funded basketball teams that traditionally dominate the National Collegiate Athletic Association (NCAA) are UCLA, Duke, Kentucky and Kansas. Gonzaga were once puny no-hopers. However, for the last 22 years they have made the NCAA finals, which feature the leading 68 teams in college basketball as they play an elimination tournament known as March Madness – one of the most celebrated events on the American sporting calendar.

In 1999, when their long unbroken run started, they made it to the last eight. They were described as a sporting Cinderella who would soon return to obscurity. But since then, the Bulldogs have grown into a mighty force. The Cinderella riff grew so wearisome that people would yell, 'The slipper still fits!' each time they pulled off another victory. But something far more interesting and transformative had occurred.

Mark Few, their head coach, had taken charge in 1999 and, while even the juggernauts of the NCAA have had dips over the years, Gonzaga have been on a steady rise. They used to share their practice court with the women's basketball team, volleyball players and Physical Education classes. Before Few's arrival, the Bulldogs had never featured in pre-tournament previews or played on national TV. But the coach changed their culture and expectation.

Year after year the tiny Bulldogs made it to the NCAA finals. Their consistency shifted perceptions. Once they began to win the West Coast Conference in the regular season, a new task emerged. How far could the Bulldogs go in the tournament that really mattered – March Madness? It was not an easy transition to battle it out with the far richer and more established basketball colleges but, slowly, young players and sponsors began to flock to Gonzaga. The Bulldogs grew steadily and, once they built a larger new arena, they began to acquire the financial muscle they needed to close the gap on the traditional giants of the NCAA.

They became the second favourite team of many college basketball fans, who were won over by the smart and gritty Bulldogs. By 2013 they were the number one seed going into March

Madness – but they lost early to another university team, Wichita State, which had designs on becoming the new Gonzaga. Mark Few, Knight and the rest of the coaching staff refused to be deflated. Their determination grew, and they began to develop still further as they concentrated on improving the environment around the team. It helped that they could, at last, attract some of the best high-school talent in America. But they were still Gonzaga – a small Catholic university in Spokane.

Every year since 2015 they have made it to Sweet Sixteen – the round before the quarter-finals, when they are just four games away from becoming national champions. In 2017 they were in the lead in the NCAA final and about to become champions with just 30 seconds left on the clock. But they fell short at the death, just as they did in 2019 when they were tipped to win.

The year 2020 could have been the culmination of 21 seasons of incredible work as they chased down the elusive NCAA championship. Gonzaga were seeded number one as they prepared for March Madness, and Spokane was scheduled to be a tournament site – which would have meant playing games at home in front of their increasingly passionate supporters. The Bulldogs looked to be in the best possible position to finally win the national title. But, in early March 2020, the tournament was cancelled as Covid-19 took hold.

When we held a couple of Zoom meetings with Travis Knight in November 2020, a new season had begun. Gonzaga were already on their way to an extraordinary run. They soon became the first college team in history to beat four rivals ranked in the top 20 nationally in their first seven games. The procession continued without the Bulldogs missing a beat. Their record was 26–0 when the regular season ended. They then justified their number one seeding in March Madness as they cruised through to the NCAA final on 6 April 2021. Gonzaga were on course to become the first team to be crowned champions after a perfect season since the Indiana Hoosiers won the title with a 32–0 record. It would have been the Bulldogs' first national title.

But, as we all know, sport is unpredictable. The Bulldogs suffered their one-and-only off-day when the stakes were highest. Despite being the overwhelming favourites, they endured their first loss in 429 days and were defeated by Baylor in the final. Gonzaga will have to wait to make history.

We didn't know then, back in November 2020, how their memorable season would unfold, but I was swept away by the clarity and discipline of their programme. Travis and his assistant were generous with their time, but I don't think they had any idea who I was or what England rugby means. They thought I was this half-Japanese, half-Australian bloke from the outback. But that didn't matter. They were open to sharing their ideas.

They explained how they had improved their Monday sessions by giving the Bulldog players more responsibility. They made it a growth day for the players. It felt as if they owned Mondays. Travis explained how the players held small meetings as they explored new ideas with him. The rest of the coaching staff kept their distance as the players took control in response to Travis encouraging them to be more curious. It was clear to them that off-court growth leads to on-court leadership and victory.

Gonzaga make these Personal Growth Mondays a cornerstone of their programme. Travis stressed his belief that this special space helped the players become more connected, not only to each other but to an appreciation of their work on and off court in a surreal year. So much happened in 2020 – from a global pandemic and national recession to a deeper political activism in the wake of George Floyd's murder – and the world felt different. But Travis believed these Monday sessions helped keep his youthful players on track and reminded them how fortunate they were to play elite college basketball.

Travis explained that their Growth Mondays had also been prompted by an exercise he did with the players when they had to list the three issues in their life that were the biggest barrier to success. The players were asked to place the reasons in either a bucket for 'human' issues or a bucket for 'sports' issues. There were dozens of human issues. But the sports bucket remained empty. The players made it clear that they did not see a single sporting reason standing in their way of becoming national champions. This clarity underlined to Travis that they needed to ensure attention was paid constantly to improving the players' environment. Rather than just focusing on the cohesion of the group in pre-season, or during occasional bonding sessions, it was vital to attend to issues of communication and environment every day – with the foundation each week being reinforced by those Personal Growth Mondays.

Their Monday meetings were short and sharp. They would be around 15 minutes in length but the meaning and mood of them pulled the players out of the typical Monday low and set the tone for the rest of the week. Those meetings were then followed by drills or videos that could be drawn from all aspects of life, and even different sports, which encouraged the players to challenge themselves personally and work together more closely. The impact was evident as the Bulldogs unbeaten streak stretched from one week to the next.

So we began with that Gonzaga template; but we haven't done exactly what they did. We've followed an England way of changing our Monday schedule. But the thought pattern was established by our curiosity, and the generosity Gonzaga showed in their willingness to share.

The whole concept of a Growth Monday is to develop closer relationships with the players. When you're starting any sort of project, it's vital to grow the relationships between the coaches and their players. Team selection, specialist training drills, tactical coaching and planning, strength and conditioning and sports science all contribute to the overall success of a group – but I think developing those relationships is key to you getting the best out of your squad.

Neil Craig believes that, at the highest level of elite sport, selection and tactics and sheer talent perhaps count for 15 per cent when it comes to making the fundamental difference between winning and losing. This means that 85 per cent of the decisive balance is shaped by the communication of the group and the environment in which they operate. I think Neil is close to the mark, and so we need to start every week in camp by attending to the development and growth of the squad.

Mondays are difficult because the players are generally at their most fatigued. They're shattered and a little broken after playing a hard game on the Saturday, or they might be distracted after going home to see their families on the Sunday. Monday work is rarely very stimulating. It tends to be all organizational. So we've tried to give a sense of control back to the players, and encourage them to drive Mondays in the best direction for them so that they can keep growing. That's exciting for them – and for us as coaches.

As with any radical idea, I floated it first. I tested it on Owen Farrell, to gauge his reaction, and then chatted about it to a few other senior players. Their gut reaction allowed me to get a feel for the temperature of the water. The feedback was really positive. Young players today thrive on change, as we have noted before, unlike players from 30 years ago who liked consistency and routine. As long as you've got a strong enough rationale, you will find little resistance to change now. So I'm always looking to see how we can improve everything.

The players soon found a way that suited them. When the squad comes in on a Monday, they split up into four groups. Each has a leader. They also have an overall leader of the leaders. It doesn't have to be Owen. It's good to mix it up and have other players take charge. The players now organize their Monday mornings. They decide what kind of meeting each group needs and what work would benefit them the most. It's totally down to them if they do skill work, or organize something with the strength-and-conditioning coaches. They run the timetable. So they take ownership from the start of the week, by controlling their Monday mornings, as they get ready to prepare for the next game. After Monday lunch the coaches' schedule takes over. But we might think of extending it even further so that the whole of Monday is run exclusively by the players.

It varies of course, because of injury, but generally Anthony Watson is in charge of the outside backs. The inside backs were led by Willi Heinz, until he was injured, and the loose forwards are almost always taken by Tom Curry. When it comes to the tight forwards, it tends to be Jamie George or Mako Vunipola as the main man on Monday mornings. The leaders get together and they map out the timetable.

They understand the importance because I've pointed out that Monday is the key preparation day of the week. How they feel at the end of Monday is probably the strongest correlation we get to their performance on the Saturday. So we want them to feel energized at the end of Monday. It's the toughest day of the week, so allowing them to claim ownership of it is a welcome change.

It also enhances leadership. We think Anthony Watson has the potential to bring sustained excellence to the team. It doesn't even have anything to do with his personality. Rather, it relates more to the way he conducts himself. Anthony can be very influential and, clearly, he is starting to mature as a person. This is another lesson Bob Dwyer taught me. You always have to be looking for people who can, potentially, be world class. They don't have to be world-class leaders right now, but they need to have the capacity to develop in that way. Anthony's definitely got something about him.

Mondays also present the players with the opportunity, through their leaders, to come to me if they think the coaches or I have got it wrong the previous week. In a formal process they'll approach me. We've had occasional feedback sessions where we give them a week to go away, reflect on what we've been doing, discuss it in the team room, and then come back to tell me their thinking. We might want to make that a more regular exercise in the future. But, for now, we rely on the more informal process to understand the players' views.

Neil Craig is our high-performance leader. As I've said before, he is the one person I can trust to be totally truthful to me. He is

65 years old and has a real freedom about him. Neil doesn't do the job because he needs it. He does it because he likes it. Neil can walk away at any time, and that gives him the liberty to talk honestly to me.

If we are considering change and transformation in the Strategic window of the Build stage of the cycle I might, for example, float the idea of appointing a new England captain. I am constantly reviewing the leadership group but if I were to suggest changing captains now I know Neil will challenge me. His opinion would be limited in terms of rugby know-how, but his insights into character and context are valuable. He slips out of his normal amiable good cheer and assumes the role of an exacting devil's advocate.

He presses me hard – not because he wants to change my opinion, but simply because he wants me to consider the possibility from every angle. Neil asks deliberately provocative questions as we discuss a hypothetical situation. Neil is not trashing the idea that we need to review the role of England captain, but he does make me address the concept from every angle.

Neil doesn't just say: 'Yeah, good idea, mate.' That's not what England or I need.

Will Carling is also of great benefit here. He knows what it is like to captain England at 22. As Will said: 'There are some great things, and some really horrible things, about being England captain. It's also relentless.' Will said it put a terrible strain on his family and he felt battered by the job by the time he stepped away from it.

But Will is less cautious than Neil. He feels, like me, that we have to review the leadership group harder than ever. The internal debate is set to roll for months to come. It is a tough and complex decision because you always have an obligation to the current leader. But you need to divorce that sense of obligation from your judgement, which is based on the cold, hard evidence of the data. And when I say 'data' I mean both the actual information we derive from statistical and video reviews and the instinctive data you get from your gut. I am just glad I have Neil and Will to examine and probe my thinking at every turn.

It is of equal importance that, to the players and the other coaches, Neil and Will are seen as a benign presence. That is partly down to their characters – they are both warm and generous, but they are also non-threatening because neither of them is involved in selection. Neil even admits that he doesn't know much about the intricacies of rugby. This means the players are comfortable sharing their thoughts with him.

Neil plays such an important role because, while he is loyal to me, the players know they can speak to him in confidence. They trust him. And that trust comes from the only caveat Neil mentions when he first meets the players. He stresses to them that he will only relay to me what they tell him, in confidence, if he is sure that they have voiced something detrimental to the well-being and the future success of the squad. Anything else private remains strictly between him and the player. Word has got around since he arrived in 2017 that the players can bank on Neil. They can open up to him. I suspect that 95 per cent of the time the views they share with Neil are passed on to me because everyone accepts this is part of our informal process of feedback.

The same principles apply to Will and his interaction with the leadership group. It helps to have Neil and Will at my side because, with 30 players in a squad, you need more than just me, as head coach, to absorb all their views and insights. This information allows us to:

PROVIDE THE CONTEXT AND THEN JOIN THE VISION TO THE TRANSFORMATION

Our vision, to become the best team in the world, is bolstered by the transformation – which, in this instance, is the change instigated by Growth Mondays.

The context emerges through the constant and vital process of communication. Some players will come forward naturally and volunteer their observations. Other players will be more reserved or less confident. For some it is easier to talk in specific forums. We have a team communication session every week with the squad psychologists. This provides an opportunity to talk about the team. If there is an issue it will be addressed. Some players would prefer to talk to me or Neil in private – or to filter their views through a sub-team meeting when they just need to talk to a few of their teammates in a small group.

This is why we test-run ideas. They might suit the vision of the group, but the players have to buy into them as a positive way of transformation. The players are all-important because they go out there and perform. Coaches don't play the game. Our area of expertise is generating ideas and communicating them. But if the players say, 'No, this doesn't work for us', then we won't pursue it further. I am pleased to say that, most of the time, the buy-in is total. But it's important that they have the platform to disagree, because a healthy elite environment is dependent on clear honesty and robust conversations.

Occasionally they will say a tentative yes to a potentially transformative idea. But, if they fail to carry out the directive on the field, you know they're saying no. That's what I call 'the Japanese yes'. It is polite agreement on the surface, made out of deference, but it is meaningless without any togetherness. I don't mind that because it's just another way of saying that's not going to work. When you're a younger coach you want to keep pushing your idea because you think you're right. But you're not right every time. Sometimes you go down the wrong track and so it's vital that your team, and staff, can push back.

It is an ongoing process, because I would prefer them to come out with a clear no at the outset rather than a soft Japanese yes. This saves time and, as we know, time is the most valuable currency in elite sport and, I suspect, business circles. The biggest lament we make as coaches and leaders is that we don't have enough time. We want more time with our players, more time to develop our ideas and more time to prepare ourselves physically and mentally. But it always feels as if we are racing against time. So it is crucial that we:

SUPPORT CHANGE WITH CLARITY OF DIRECTION

I learnt this truth in Japan. There will often be many murmurs of 'yes' in a meeting but most people are saying a silent no. And then you end up spending so much time on more meetings as you try to address the problem. So it was in Japan, while pursuing a clarity of direction, that I began to use test runs as a way of establishing the validity of a new idea. I would make sure that I talked to all the influential people beforehand to get a feel for their thinking. Once I felt they were on board then I would deliver it in a formal meeting. If this works in Japan, a country built on consultation and group deliberation, then it's going to work with most organizations.

This clarity of direction is crucial because it will then help you to:

SET THE HORIZON – MAKE THE END GAME REAL

Our vision is to turn England into the best team in the world. We came close in 2019 when only South Africa were better than us in the World Cup. But the scale of our defeat in the final, and the disappointments we endured in the first three months of 2021, were sobering reminders of how far we still have to go to make our end game real.

There are powerful lessons we can glean from the past. For all great teams there will come a time when continued success might tempt them to divert their attention from the nitty-gritty work that made them brilliant in the first place. They are human, and so they can become complacent or arrogant. But, as a leader, you can stop this happening.

You don't need to change your vision but you do need to keep the ideas fresh. You have to keep stimulating the environment.

Secondly, you have got to keep changing personnel. Freshen up the staff around you. Reinvigorate your fellow coaches and the players with new people and different ideas. Always be brave enough to change a winning team if you sense a looming slump. It's tricky, but if you've been walking the shop floor, your eyes and your gut – combined with the arsenal of stats and data we have at our disposal these days – will tell you when to reboot your programme.

Thirdly, you need a psychology of certainty. That iron belief is often forged in adversity. Don't allow your staff or your team to become comfortable. It's no bad thing to keep people on edge so that they try to do more.

How do you instil this uncomfortable edge that means the intensity rarely drops?

Sometimes it comes through the selection process. Some players will become complacent, while some will never fall into that hole. You've got to move on the first group and find the players who hate and fear complacency – and are always restless, always relentless, always searching for the next stage of their development. If you have enough of those guys, you're going to have that certainty of will that all great teams possess.

Look at Michael Jordan in *The Last Dance*. Jordan, the greatest basketball player of them all, was never happy. He kept pushing himself. He was always bitching and moaning and making his teammates uncomfortable. Jordan left them on edge and, in so doing, he raised standards as the Bulls became an iconic team.

I find it fascinating that one player could have such a seismic impact on his team as well as an entire sport. But on a basketball court there are only five players at a time. You might have a group of 12 at courtside. In rugby you generally have a squad of at least 30. No one individual can have the same effect that Jordan had on game day. You need two or three monumental leaders in a great rugby squad. It is my job to find and develop those game-changers.

The aim is to make the opposition feel that we are almost

impossible to beat. New Zealand sometimes have that down to a fine dark art. Like Mike Tyson in his prime, the All Blacks have intimidated many of their rivals. But the real key to their greatness is that they never seem to be beaten. They are always coming at you. Even when you are 15 points ahead of them it still feels difficult. They usually never drop their intensity or utter certainty that they will prevail at the death. We beat them decisively in the World Cup, but the All Blacks retain the template when we consider rugby history. They are simply the hardest bastards to beat in rugby. That's the kind of side we aspire to become – a seemingly indestructible team.

Of course there will be blips and defeats along the way to creating such an aura. But we need the players to share this psychology of certainty, and you can only be sure you've got it when your team has been tested repeatedly, and prevailed, in the heat of battle. Until then you can only sense what might be brewing.

I remember, back in 2001, when I was coaching the Brumbies in Super 12 rugby, I came in one morning and the whole place was humming with conviction. The players were buzzing and working so hard in the gym and on the pitch. Our coaching was sharp and precise. The administrative staff were on top of everything off the field. We had won 11 out of 12 matches and were in the play-offs. You could feel and see the certainty, and I just knew we were on our way to winning the tournament. It was no surprise when we blitzed the Sharks 36–6 in the final.

You strive to reach that pitch of clinical, seemingly unbreakable belief. I regret that I didn't get to work for another few years with that brilliant team because I accepted the chance to coach Australia in 2001. It would have been an interesting challenge to have sustained that fleeting greatness. Few teams can maintain that excellence which, again, is why the All Blacks have been revered for so long. They have retained that psychology of certainty for years, only occasionally falling short of their own highest standards.

They failed to win the World Cup between 1987 and 2011,

even though they usually played the best rugby in the four years between tournaments. We can only assume it was down to mismanaging the pressure and the expectation. The longer they went on without winning the World Cup, the more they probably looked at those big games as a threat rather than an opportunity. But, finally, they controlled the pressure when it mattered most.

No other team has won a World Cup final after being reduced to their fourth choice number 10, as the All Blacks did in 2011 with Stephen Donald, who had been fishing when the tournament began in New Zealand. There were lots of injuries and mishaps, but the All Blacks were able to deal with everything that was thrown at them. They coped with the problems and the uncertainty, the expectation and the pressure, through a combination of talent, resolve, good coaching, and the right leadership in Graham Henry and Steve Hansen. They did it again four years later when they won the World Cup in England in 2015. Those are the markers of greatness we need to match.

The 2021 Six Nations was a sobering experience. We will delve into the reasons throughout this book but, as we consider our strategy in the Build section of the cycle, it seems timely to explain that England lost their way partly because of a creeping sense of entitlement which ate away at the core values and principles we had established in the Vision stage of the cycle.

Entitlement always becomes an issue when a team is successful. It often stems from external sources – from the media who hype up a player or the team, or from well-meaning fans who get carried away and can start to hero-worship individuals and turn them into 'stars' or, even worse, celebrities. Sponsors also muddy the waters because they offer seductive commercial deals and endorsements which can erode the focus of more impressionable players. They offer cars to drive, clothes to wear and money to burn.

When human beings start to have serial success, it is natural for them to drift in their thinking and work ethic. That is why coaches are so vital in cutting off this sense of entitlement before it settles and corrupts.

When we suffer this feeling of entitlement, and England clearly did at some points during the Six Nations, it gets in the way of the team when it matters most. In Test matches you often experience bad luck or poor decisions. This happened to us particularly in the game against Wales, who went on to become Six Nations champions. When decisions go against them, players can get dejected. They simply do not put in the extra effort they need to overcome misfortune. They lack that little bit of extra fight they had before. The tight games, which they had once always won, start to slip away.

There was a telling insight into this sense of entitlement when one of the security guards let slip to us during the Six Nations that a player felt pissed off during the tournament. He told the security guard: 'I'm not playing well and that means I'm not going to get into the Lions.'

Some of our management group were angry. I understood their reaction, because the implication was that this player felt as if playing for England was merely a stepping stone to the Lions. This was the kind of creeping entitlement that we needed to rip out once the Six Nations was out of the way.

Against Wales, in the third game of the tournament, we clawed our way back to parity at 24–24 after we had been hurt badly by two dubious refereeing decisions. But we then looked as if we thought we were entitled to win without maintaining that grit and hard work. The game slid away from us, and Wales won after they scored 16 unanswered points to give them a lopsided victory.

Entitlement also takes chunks out of a team during training and preparation. Players start taking short cuts and worrying about themselves individually. They no longer put in that extra discretionary effort that was second nature to them when they were hungry and desperate to improve. Complacency corrupts the soul of the team. When that happens, the core of the team cracks open and you have to start again. You've got to regenerate the team. It demands some personnel changes on and off the field and a drastic change in mindset. You almost need to start the cycle again.

I have said this before, but there are three types of people. The leading group are at it all the time. The group in the middle fluctuates according to the location of the tipping point. And then you've got the people in the last group who, basically, don't give a fuck. England don't really have any of those. But we've got too few in the top group and far too many in the middle group – and they are being affected by the disease of entitlement. Farrell, Itoje and Curry don't have enough lieutenants around them. In the Six Nations they missed Kruis, Launchbury and Underhill.

Most of all, we need as many leaders as possible because the effort we put in has to be unrelenting. And who really wants to be unrelenting? If you look at the normal curve of life, maybe 10 per cent of people want to work hard all the time, 80 per cent want to have a good life, and the bottom 10 per cent just can't be bothered or feel totally lost anyway.

It's natural that these longer cycles of success are harder to sustain. Even the All Blacks have gone from a 90 per cent winning ratio to 80 per cent. Whether they can recreate that period they had under Graham Henry, Steve Hansen and Richie McCaw has to be questioned. But that's part of their challenge now and I know they will want to take it on.

There's a lovely analogy which suggests that a sports team is like a piece of fruit. When it's perfectly ripe, it is at its best, and that's when you've got to win. But beyond that point, what starts happening? Decay. The next day the fruit is slightly overripe, not quite at its best. The job of the coach is to slow down that maturation as much as possible. Do you put it in the refrigerator or place it in water? In sport, you don't want to be facing decay the moment after you have reached peak performance. It's a constant challenge to keep the entitlement at bay and to put in the relentless work that will make you better than you were yesterday. And to do that you need the right lines of communication, the right culture and the right environment.

One of the best ways, as always, is to remember the words which started this stage of the cycle:

BE CURIOUS AND OPEN TO NEW IDEAS

■ Provide the context and then join the vision to the transformation

■ Support change with clarity of direction

■ Set the horizon – make the end game real

■ Keep stimulating the environment; change personnel, introduce new ideas

■ Be brave enough to change a winning team if you sense it is necessary

■ Develop a psychology of certainty

6

DISCIPLINED THINKING AND EMOTIONAL JOURNEYS

DON'T RELY ON CIRCUMSTANTIAL SUCCESS

My reading list is endless. Every week another two or three books get added, as there is always something new to learn about coaching, leadership and getting the best out of people. It helps that I am a voracious reader, because gaining knowledge this way always feels enjoyable rather than an effort. Reading deepens and expands my thinking in a way that works effectively alongside the Zoom calls and meetings that I have most weeks with fellow coaches from around the world. Hearing new ideas, and having the opportunity to share the pleasures and pressures of coaching, refreshes me. The third platform, in this constant search for improvement, is built on the additional coaching sessions I attend in places as far apart as Tokyo and Hull.

We will explore the obvious benefits of practising your coaching, and sharpening your leadership skills in diverse environments, throughout these pages. But first, as we consider how best to align our resources in this second stage of the Build cycle, here is a little sample of how these extracurricular activities can clear the head.

In mid-May 2021, I went up to East Yorkshire, to Hull FC, the rugby league team coached by Brett Hodgson. Brett was a fine full-back who won the Australian National Rugby League (NRL) Premiership with Wests Tigers, the great Sydney club, in

2005, before he moved to England. In 2009, while playing for Huddersfield, he was voted the Man of Steel, the award given to the Super League's Player of the Season. Brett is now a really interesting coach, and we have a reciprocal arrangement. He has visited the England camp and offered some astute insights while, in return, I did a two-day consultancy at Hull.

It tapped into a facet of coaching that has always fascinated me – how to best find access to both the brain and the heart of an individual player. A significant chunk of my reading relates to this theme, because rugby is a disciplined team game driven by distinct players who each have their own background and character which you need to understand to help them fulfil their potential. So much of this comes down to communication and working out how best to talk to specific players. While I was in Hull, I spoke to many of Brett's squad. I was keen to hear their stories while, at the same time, it helped me talk in different ways to a variety of young rugby players.

One of them made a simple but telling point. He is a good player, from Ireland, and I asked him an easy question: 'Who had the most influence on you as a coach?' He picked out a coach and when I asked him why he said: 'Because he asked me about my family all the time.' It was an illustration of this player's access point. To get to know him really well, and to earn his trust, you would need to pay attention to his family and the huge role they play in his story. So for each player there's an access point which you have to find to develop a relationship with them. As each person is different, you need courage to experiment before you find the right way into their character. Sometimes you get it wrong and they might think you're an idiot. But you've got to be prepared to be that idiot in order to find the key to their mentality.

While in Hull, I was in the midst of rereading *Moneyball*, which is one of my favourite books. Billy Beane is the key figure in Michael Lewis's book about the Oakland Athletics and how, despite their relatively modest budget, they built a successful major league baseball team by relying on data and statistics. This sabermetric approach, in which empirical evidence trumps big-money splurges, transformed Oakland and revolutionized baseball economics.

I have never met Billy Beane, but I would love to have a chance to talk to him in person. We participated in the same podcast once and I also heard him deliver a lecture in London. He was outstanding both times. His story in *Moneyball* is fantastic. No one really understood him as a player, but he came into his own as a general manager who not only implemented data analytics but retained an intuition and empathy for players. Most general managers hardly talk to a player after he signs his contract, but Billy was different. He kept talking to the players while revolutionizing the role of data analytics as he united the front office and the dugout. He did not rely on circumstantial success, where achievement seemed to happen either by chance or in a predictable way framed by advantageous circumstances. Billy, instead, used disciplined thinking while tapping into the emotional stories of his players.

But there is a scene in *Moneyball* that shows how even Billy and the Oakland coaches sometimes forget the scientific evidence and stick with the clichéd surface. As they sit around talking about players, they slip back into human nature, which is not the best way to identify and nurture elite sportsmen. They said: 'Oh, he's got a real good swing' or, 'He went to a good school.' They even start saying he has a good face and a good girlfriend. It's understandable to get swayed by the superficial and revert to such slim quantifiers of success. A good swing, a good school and a good face might have mattered once, but the really disciplined thinkers rely on reference thinking all the time. They go back and say: 'But what does the science tell you?' That is where the discipline of winning is based. Go back to that. Don't go back to circumstantial success, in which having a good background, a good swing and a good face made all the difference. You need to battle against this all the time – whether you're in elite sport or business. Billy Beane and the Oakland Athletics realized this basic truth.

I was reminded of it yet again soon after I got back from Hull and we went into a selection meeting to discuss the England squad for the 2021 summer Tests against the United States and Canada. We were in a difficult place, because the Six Nations had been disappointing and we had lost nearly an entire team of England players to the British and Irish Lions tour of South Africa.

We needed to align our limited resources to the changes required.

This was new territory as we considered a much wider pool of young players. I saw it as an opportunity to do something different and perhaps uncover two or three bolters who might make it all the way to the 2023 World Cup. We had achieved this unlikely feat in 2017 when – on a tour of Argentina while the Lions faced New Zealand – we had introduced Tom Curry and Sam Underhill to the Test team. They would be vital players for us in the World Cup two years later. We had another chance to do something similar.

The only problem was that some of the coaches at the meeting started discussing players who, clearly, they felt had the type of background and even the face to be successful. They liked the look of the player rather than basing their argument on tangible proof of his effectiveness. Of course I picked up on it and said: 'Mate, that's just not good enough.' I thought again of *Moneyball* when they soon reverted to the science.

All of this was on my mind because Kyle Sinckler had been in the news again. Kyle had become a lynchpin of my side and one of the best tighthead-props in the world. We saw how important he was to England when we lost him to injury early in the World Cup final and our scrum never gained parity with South Africa.

I had long been a believer in Sincks and he had also been picked for the Lions in 2017. But life rarely runs smoothly, especially not for a rugby player as distinctive as Kyle, and he was a shock omission from the Lions squad to tour South Africa.

Warren Gatland announced his 37-man squad early in May, and Sincks was devastated to hear that he had not been picked. I deliberately chose not to call or text him in the immediate aftermath because I know what happens. The excluded player is wounded and he spends the next 24 hours fielding messages from people saying either how sorry they are or how unlucky he has been. Everyone is well meaning, but those messages, from the anguished to the aggrieved, don't really help the poor bloke who has been axed. They just open the wound a little wider. I always wait a few days, even a week, before I make contact in such circumstances.

Sinckler did the right thing. He posted a dignified message on social media saying he was disappointed but that he wished the Lions well. And then in his very next game for Bristol, away to Bath on 8 May, he went out and produced a Man of the Match performance as he inspired his team to victory. Sincks then gave a powerful and emotive interview straight after the game, live on television, which revealed all the raw character I had admired for years.

Once the interviewer had praised another win on the road and Bristol's biggest-ever victory at the Rec, the 28-year-old made a painful noise which was meant to be a laugh. 'It's been an emotional week, especially for myself,' Sinckler said as his voice thickened and tears welled in his eyes. 'I want to thank my teammates, my family, my loved ones, Saviour World especially, for helping me. From a team perspective how good [was that]? First half wasn't great but in the second half we dug in and showed how much it meant to us and the fans.'

Commended by the interviewer for his performance and 'lovely tweet' earlier in the week, Sinckler nodded. He then paused, drawing breath and thinking time, before opening up. 'I'm not going to lie,' he said. 'I'm quite emotional right now. Yeah, it's been tough. It means so much to me.'

You could tell he was struggling not to cry but he found the strength to keep talking. 'I'm just lucky I had my mentor at Saviour World and we broke it down,' he continued. 'In a year or two's time I will look back on it and it will all make sense. But at the moment, right now, it doesn't make sense. But what I wanted to do was lead by example and show the kids how easy it would have been for me to play the victim and say: "How bad is it? Sorry me."'

I knew that Sinckler took great reassurance from Saviour World – an organization set up by the former rugby player Ollie Pryce-Tidd with the aim of helping men to cope with mental health issues. They mentor rugby players such as Sincks, Danny Cipriani and James O'Connor, who said they had helped him recover in time to play for Australia in the 2019 World Cup.

In an earlier interview discussing his involvement with Saviour World, Sincks said: 'My frustrations were nothing rugby-related. I was born in a single-parent home. I was always looking for that male father figure. Subconsciously, I put people in that position, put my trust in certain people who betrayed me. It was just about me taking control of my life and teaching myself how to be an actual man in control of his emotions. A man looks after his family, he does the right things. He doesn't let anything that frustrates him show, he just gets on with it. That's something I've really tried to work on because I know my behaviour in the past has cost the team and I didn't want to feel like that again. I had to look within and help [myself]. I feel like it's definitely working for me, but it's been tough.'

This was the big, tough prop I knew and cared about, and his personality shone out of him after he swallowed his disappointment with the Lions to drive Bristol to victory over Bath. As he was interviewed on the pitch at the Rec, not long after the final whistle, Sincks shook his head as he was asked about the Lions. 'It's been so tough. I've never experienced something like this in my whole life, let alone my career. I'm just lucky I've got a good support team around me. I wanted to show the kids and everyone at home how much it means to me and lead by example and don't throw my toys out of the pram. Do the tough stuff. Use that anger. I've got so much anger inside me right now but use it in a positive way and do what's best for the team. Do the unselfish stuff and I think I did that today. It's good the boys got the win.'

I was proud of Sincks – both for the way he played and the manner in which he spoke. There were times when it looked as if he could break down, but he kept the tears in check. He did not try to hide his emotion, or his vulnerability, but he used it to make a powerful statement. It was heartening to see because I had been a little worried about him. I could not be exactly sure how he would react because he was under immense personal pressure.

But I have always backed Sinckler from the moment I chose him and Ellis Genge for England's tour of Australia in 2016. The two wild young prop-forwards were unheralded then, and neither of them had 'the face' nor 'the look' of a successful rugby player. They come from the other side of the tracks and, as kids, were outside the English rugby system. Sincks is an interesting boy from, essentially, a non-rugby background. He was an emotional young black kid from Battersea in London who had struggled through a tough upbringing. Eventually he found some direction at Battersea Ironsides, a gritty old rugby club operating far from the often privileged heartlands of the English game. A smart scout for Harlequins spotted him.

He played the game with more emotion than most players. This makes him vulnerable but it's part of his allure. We thought he offered something different, even though he was always going to be a bit difficult to harness.

Genge, meanwhile, grew up on the Knowle West council estate in a poor area of Bristol, and his mullet told you that he would never be one of the pretty faces of English rugby. But he was like some of the other front-row forwards I liked in Joe Marler and Luke Cowan-Dickie. He was honest and forthright.

I picked Genge and Sinckler when England were on a high. We had just come through my first Six Nations when we won the Grand Slam. But I felt we needed to add an edge to the team as we headed to Australia. I wanted more aggression in the pack. Genge and Sinckler had that raw aggression from the wrong side of town. So they came on tour and were a handful at training. Both of them wanted to prove how rough and tough they were and they caused some grievance amongst the established players. Some of their physical impact was inappropriate for a training session. But it's all part of the learning process of international rugby. They adapted, and by the end of the tour these two wild young bulls had both grown and become part of the squad. They have gone on and represented their country with honour and distinction. But they are always going to have their problems.

There were some serious doubts about Sinckler within the England coaching fraternity. I listened to one voice in particular for I had great respect for his views; he was unsure of Sinckler. His initial perceptions of Kyle were of a self-centred, immature, volatile, emotional and angry young man. He acknowledged Kyle's obvious talent and liked him as a kid. But he argued forcefully that Kyle could blight the team with his ill-discipline. Could we really trust Sinckler in the heat of battle?

I listened because there was plenty of validity to the view. But my feel for the game, and for individual people, allied to concrete data around his performances, told me to persevere with Sinckler. We could have a special character if, somehow, we could control his emotion.

I believed in the values we had instilled in the England camp and I thought that being immersed in this environment would engender a positive change in Kyle. I am the keeper of the environment, but I have also developed much more patience and empathy as a mature coach. In my early years my own volatility and impatience would not have helped Kyle. I hope that my calm belief in him has been a boost. There are also plenty of people outside the programme who have helped him immensely – from coaches such as Adam Jones at Quins and Pat Lam at Bristol to his family and his mentor at Saviour World. They have all had a really positive influence on him. It's something of a team effort, but the most important person, of course, is Kyle. He has changed his behaviour in the most constructive way.

But I remember as recently as early 2019 when he had a real problem in a game for Quins up at Sale. He got sin-binned, raged at the referee and some of his teammates. He wasn't in a good place. I rang him up on the Sunday and said: 'Can we meet, mate?' He agreed and we met at the Petersham Hotel in Richmond. I got straight to the point but tried to use some delicacy as well. I said: 'We've got a problem, mate. I need your permission to discuss it with you so we can come up with a solution.' His response was immediate and positive. He wanted to talk about it. So we had a really transformative chat to see how we could come up with a solution to control his emotions.

Later that year he was a key performer when England reached the World Cup final. Eighteen months on he faced another big test when Gatland overlooked him for the Lions. He would be one of the crucial conversations I needed before I chose my England squad for the summer of 2021. It was important I made an assessment of what would be best for him – whether he'd need a spell in the paddock or be better off galloping right away again.

It's a bit like training a wild horse when you're dealing with young players like Sinckler and Genge. They just want to run free. But you have got to pull the reins in every now and then so that they add to the composition of the team. Remember how Alex Ferguson managed Eric Cantona? The Frenchman was brilliant, but a little dangerous, and they had difficulties with him. But he added something to the team that no one else could offer.

Sometimes these more difficult players need to be given more room to run fast and free but, at the same time, you've got to be strong enough to know when to hold them back. Hard analytical data won't help you here. It's important you really understand the emotion that drives the player. Experience counts because it's not easy to keep control of the team while allowing the individual enough space to really be themselves.

Even before I met Sinckler to discuss his readiness to play for England, instead of the Lions, I knew he had made the right choice. He could have gone away and sulked. But he was prepared to try hard again while showing his vulnerability. It was an admirable display of courage and honesty. So we only needed a short conversation to confirm his readiness to play for me – as, then, we obviously did not know that Kyle would be called up to the Lions squad after all as an injury replacement.

I went across to Bristol and we spoke about 2017 when he was still a young kid coming through and he got picked for the Lions. But great players and good people such as Chris Robshaw, Danny Care, Mike Brown, and Joe Launchbury had missed out on the Lions that year. He had heard how they created such a great environment for the next wave of young guys coming through for England on that tour of Argentina. I told him that it was his turn now, and his responsibility, to help create the right environment for the next group of young players. It's a transfer of responsibility that all the good people understand implicitly. If they're not good people, you can't have them in your organization.

Sincks is a good person, without a doubt, and so he got it. He also saw he had a real opportunity to grow as a player and as a leader in the squad – and in his community as well, which is just as important. It was not the time to cool his heels. He needed to get back out on the field and perform because we both believed he could still become one of the best players in the world.

It took a bit of courage to pick him in the first place because he did not have the face or the look of a safe bet. He was not rooted in the kind of rugby background which can produce circumstantial success. Sinckler had followed his own path and both the hard data tracking his work on the field, and empathy for him as a person, proved we were right to stick with him.

The coach who had doubted him has been totally won over. He spoke admiringly of Sinckler's Man of the Match performance against Bath, and his moving interview after the game. Sincks had done us all proud.

Someone suggested I have an affinity for outsiders, such as Sinckler, because I have felt like an outsider most of my life. Whether it was me being a funny little half-Japanese kid growing up in blue-collar Sydney or now, being the unpopular Aussie bloke coaching England, I have often been on the outside. I have never really fitted in, and I quite enjoy that position. Maybe my parents were like that because they shared a mixed marriage. It is always a theme for me. Early in 2021, after I had done another coaching consultancy stint with Suntory, I took flak from both sides. The English media was unhappy I was working with New Zealand's Beauden Barrett. Rather than doing the more acceptable thing and using my leisure time to play golf, I was working on my coaching skills and swapping ideas with one of the best players in world rugby. I knew it would help me, and England, much more than if I was trying to blast my way out of a bunker.

At the same time an article in Tokyo suggested the Japanese Rugby Union should bar me from being involved with Suntory. I know a lot of people in England were also saying the RFU should get rid of me. So it was pretty funny. But I have never cared much what people think of me, and I especially don't now. So I am not hung up on being an outsider. I am just going to work hard and try my heart out to become a better coach of the players I care about.

I never forget that I am a servant to the players. It's not the other way around. And so it is never a case of me trying to shoehorn outsiders into the establishment. I hope I pick players on a combination of clear data, disciplined thinking and an open mind to their attributes. So I am not interested in finding outsiders for the sake of it. I am consumed instead by developing diversity of thought and action. Such diversity can really help an organization.

Suntory in Japan is essentially a family business that has achieved massive success. But when the owner finally stepped down, they brought in a CEO from outside the family. At first it was really difficult for him because there was a lot of chat in the shadows. People said he didn't really understand the business because he was not part of the family. There were doubts about him because his face and his background didn't seem the right fit in his first year. Now, deep in his fifth year, they all speak glowingly of the influence he's had on the business. He has brought freshness and a new discipline of thinking as an outsider. This is more than circumstantial success. It is something deeper and more enduring.

All these thoughts framed my interaction with Sinckler and the first selection meeting we had as we began to pick a squad for the summer of 2021. As soon as some of the other coaches started talking about the school background, the look or even the face of a potential player, I pulled them up hard. We needed to go back to the science and really think about the character of the player in question. It seemed to me, yet again, that so much of the hype around English rugby is built on these fleeting measures of circumstantial success.

Some players get praised to the heavens because they have a dominant pack in club rugby, which is very different to the Test game, or because they have the look that people like and expect to be successful. I was always going to pick Marcus Smith for the summer squad, but I have long felt that all the talk around him has not been helpful – either to England or Marcus himself.

Why was Marcus Smith so popular when he first came on the scene with Harlequins? He was a good-looking boy who had been to a big public school where rugby success was part of the culture. He had a Filipino background, so he also offered something a little bit different. There was a lot to like about him. I actually saw him play as a schoolboy. At the 2015 World Cup, when I was coaching Japan in England, I went to watch him play in a game at Brighton College because everyone said he was going to be the next best thing. I went out of curiosity, as a coach, and not because I had any involvement with England then. I was impressed as he definitely had a great skill set. But, somewhere down the line, he had lost that.

I don't have to tear down the story of him being the next great England rugby star. Some people in the English media would like him to occupy this role, but my task is to make sure Marcus doesn't believe in this story, because it's being written by other people. I want him to believe in his own story. I want him to write his own story. When the first lockdown hit in 2020, I called him so we could have a proper conversation. I've had my eye on him for a while because I think he's got real potential. But I was not sure whether Marcus had the desire to be the best he can be. I wondered if he might be happy being a nice Harlequins player, talked about for England in glowing terms, without really testing the limits of his ability or character.

I had thought this for over a year when I rang him up in April 2020. We had a reasonably blunt conversation about the state of his game. I suggested that he needed to come up with his own identity. I wanted him to outline that identity as a player on a piece of paper for me. He did that and sent it over to me. We've been continuing that conversation ever since.

He had identified the strengths he had first shown as a schoolboy. How could he utilize those strengths again at elite level? What is his role in the team? What did he need to do, especially as a number 10, to develop? Those were the three areas we tried to explore. I asked him to fill in those answers and I gave him a little feedback. He still has to fulfil that identity, but he only turned 22 in February 2021. Marcus is probably only going to be at his best in his late twenties. So we need to help him along this emotional journey and remind him about the journeys taken by some other great number 10s. When was Dan Carter at his best? At his last World Cup in 2015. Not before that. Is Beauden Barrett a fully mature 10? The answer is no. He is a great player, but the best is still to come for him.

Number 10s are like quarterbacks. You've got to allow them to fail. You've got to give them time to mature. The good ones come through. They repay you. They might have two or three years at their very best. But it is a demanding position. George Ford was the best 18-year-old number 10 I have ever seen. I love George and he has been such an important player for me and for England so often. But I am not sure he has even been as brilliant as he was at 18. Marcus Smith will take a different route. He was also an outstanding teenager, but he fell away and he needs time to develop away from the expectations of an overheated media.

I have seen it happen again and again in the six years I have been head coach of England. Young players who are often outstanding in club rugby get showered with unsettling praise. They often forget that success with your club does not automatically turn you into a proven international. Test rugby is very different and far more demanding than the club game.

Jack Willis was very good for Wasps in the 2019–20 season and he won three individual awards – as the Players' Player of the Year, the Premiership's Player of the Season as well as the Discovery of the Season. But I knew he faced some problems breaking into the Test side. All the data and the evidence of my own eyes suggested that he lacked the speed of the great international loose forwards. I had to be clear with Jack and explain that I needed him to find more gas to get past the likes of Tom Curry and Sam Underhill and into my starting XV. It was hard for him to hear as there is no easy solution to become faster around the field. But he listened and he heard that I would give him the opportunity to adapt. We're always looking for adaptability and so he still has a chance to really make it as a Test player. It was so unfortunate that, not long afterwards, in March 2021, he suffered a bad knee ligament injury, tearing his medial collateral ligament off the bone while playing against Italy, and needed surgery that would keep him out of the game for a year. But Jack will do all he can to get back into the England side.

Other players, such as Sam Simmonds, are also subjected to heavy media attention. Sam is excellent for Exeter Chiefs and, apart from all his hard work in the pack, he is a try-scoring machine in club rugby. He was picked for the Lions to tour South Africa and I know he can play well for England. But at Test level players come up against opponents who have that elusive X factor. I watched Grégory Alldritt, the French international back-row player, in the European Champions Cup final for La Rochelle against Toulouse in May 2021. Alldritt must be around 115 kg but he has an exceptional work rate. He's an unbelievable player and our back-row boys have to work hard to match a beast like Alldritt. Sam weighs around 105 kg but he is a smart player and so the door is still open for him.

The nice part of the job is announcing the names of players who are in the team. The unpleasant part is when you're giving other players bad news that they are out. I felt this with Dylan Hartley. I've got a lot of affection for him but, in the end, his body gave out on him, and we couldn't pick him any more. I said: 'You're fucked, mate.' I was being truthful, and he knew it, so I felt emotional telling him. But I had to be driven by loyalty to the team rather than the person. Dylan understood.

It doesn't take a toll on me. If it did I would never be able to do the job. But I can only think of two players who I know carry a grudge against me because I left them out of my squad. Owen Finegan is one of them. He was very upset when I didn't pick him for Australia's 2003 World Cup squad. I think he might carry that to his grave.

In terms of England, our well-being as a team is tied to our winning. We have to keep winning. It's always a balance of using your best players and, at the same time, trying to find players who are even better. You also need to establish the right time to get them in. It's a melding exercise so, usually, you're looking at about 20–30 per cent change every year.

In 2018 we had Hartley, Robshaw, Brown and Care. They were still good players but I didn't think they could be at their best at the World Cup. So I made the decision to phase them out quietly. We regenerated the squad but the timing was tight. Now, two years out from the next World Cup, I would say 70 per cent of my squad, if they keep their desire, will be close to their best. The other 30 per cent is debatable. There is a serious timeline for me to find new talent and give them enough experience to be at their best for the World Cup. We've brought in guys like Ollie Lawrence, Harry Randall, Will Stuart and Jonny Hill. We're giving them time to mature, but at some stage I've got to expose them to red-hot situations. This is probably the most difficult, and the most exciting, part of the job.

It's always a balance between stability and disruption. I think that's very true for business as well. You need a certain amount of stability, but disruption gives you bigger jumps. So when we had to get rid of Robshaw and Haskell, and we brought in Curry and Underhill, we were unstable for a period. We had lost 150 caps and were introducing two young guys who had no influence on the team apart from their performance in the game. So that was a difficult period, but we managed it well because we had stability in other areas.

These are the kind of decisions you need to make – especially as you align your resources to the changes you need. I often have to change my staff too. Of course it's important that you give people a reasonable chance. If you've given them the opportunity to work for you, then you've got to allow them time to adapt to the environment. But if it's not working then, for the benefit of the organization and the person, you're better off moving them on in the most respectful way you can.

From there you aim to deliver the quick wins that allow you to deliver fundamental changes, both immediately and over a longer period of time. In terms of quick wins an obvious example occurred when we were in transformation after the 2019 World Cup. We set our new vision and we also worked hard on the team taking more responsibility for themselves. We drove that with more internal leadership. In a military situation, all decisions are made by small teams out in the field. They are not made by a higher level of command. Similarly, on a rugby field, we wanted good decisions to be made when the players are in the heat of battle. We were quite aggressive in trying to drive the team here but, as our difficult 2021 showed, we're not anywhere near the finished product.

The third quick win is understanding the metrics of the game. We probably stole a march in data analytics but, over the last year, that gap has closed because every team now seems to understand what wins games of rugby. That disciplined, data-driven knowledge is now a big part of rugby. When we lost five games in a row in 2018, we kicked less than the opposition in every one. Yet, in the previous 18 games, all of which we won, we kicked more than the opposition. But the team wanted to play more attractive rugby. This was not just the desire of the players. The coaches wanted to embrace that more expansive style as well. It's like the batsman who averages 50. He wants to come in and play his shots straightaway. He no longer gives himself time to settle at the crease so that 50 average dips down to 40. That's what happened when we had that run of five losses. We have graphs that predict all these outcomes but it was hard, in this period, to convince the players to go back to what works. When they did, we came close to winning the World Cup.

As discussed in Chapter 5, in 2020 we began to make some fundamental changes, breaking the squad up into four groups – the tight five, back row, inside backs and outside backs – and assigning a coach to lead each one. Most of our meetings are done in those four groups. Each group devises their own game plan and they help with training. We've spoken about our Growth Mondays. So the team is developing and growing because we've evolved and they are running it. At the same time, we operate under a stricter framework. But within that new order they're allowed to mix and match and pass on what they have learnt to each other. We're still in the infancy of this and we have more stages and cycles to pass through. But the outline is clear as we try to merge disciplined thinking with emotional empathy and:

- Align the resources to the changes required

- Deliver the quick wins and then deliver the fundamental changes

All the time we remember a key point as we look to learn, develop and improve as individuals and as a squad:

DON'T RELY ON CIRCUMSTANTIAL SUCCESS

- Understand the importance of disciplined thinking and emotional journeys

- Align the resources to the changes required

- Deliver the quick wins

- Deliver the fundamental changes – both upfront and over time

- Understand the emotion that drives the player

7

CONFLICT IS HEALTHY

FEEL UNCOMFORTABLE WHEN EVERYTHING ELSE SEEMS COMFORTABLE

Imagine sitting in as a guest at a boardroom or departmental meeting of an organization you are visiting. Your aim is clear and unbiased. You want to learn from them as to how they function and succeed so you might apply those lessons to your own work and communication. There are two scenarios for you to consider. In the first setting the meeting is smooth and harmonious and the chair presides over the business of the day briskly and efficiently. Everyone nods approvingly and makes supportive noises. We are wrapped up in a little over half an hour and there has been no rancour or discord.

The second meeting is very different. Conflict ripples through the room. People are challenged and questioned. There are difficult and even fractious conversations and some long and awkward silences as people mull over what has just been said. It is uncomfortable to witness from the outside and, for an insider, it is even harder.

Which would you say is likely to be the high-functioning boardroom or department? For me it's obvious. If you had shares in the first company, I would suggest you sell them pretty fast. They sound far too comfortable and dictatorial for my liking. If every meeting replicates that tendency to push everything through, without any rigour or thought as how to improve, they're being lazy at best and dysfunctional at worst. The second organization is much more interesting. Of course it's important to stress that respect for each other is paramount, as is a willingness to listen to opposing views, but if the arguing and debating is focused and fair, then we're looking at a highly functional organization that values healthy conflict.

In high-performance sport, the first way of doing things simply cannot lead to success. If you want to be the best in the world, or the best you can possibly be in your situation, then you have to be asking questions constantly. What could we do better? Why are we not doing it already? Whose responsibility is it to make those specific changes? How can we help him or her bring about a successful transformation in this specific area? Where do we expect the next problem to emerge? How do we stop it becoming a crisis? These are all pretty basic questions, but they are essential in any elite sports body or ambitious business or organization.

If you attended some of our England coaching meetings you would probably walk out and think to yourself: 'Boy, there is a hell of a lot wrong with this programme.' But, in this robust environment, we have a feeling of safety that enables everyone to voice their opinion. The buzz phrase is 'psychological safety'. This is the ideal state you need in your staff communication so that people can voice their thoughts freely and openly. They should be challenged and questioned but they deserve the right, as valued members of the organization, to be heard. It is imperative that they feel able to speak up in a different way without any fear that they will be belittled, dismissed or shouted down.

I might not agree with everything they say, but I want my coaches to push and question me. I want them to tell me how they think we might do our work better because there will be times when they are smarter and more astute than anyone else in the room. Once people know that they have a platform, and a net of psychological safety, they won't be afraid to speak out and suggest ways of changing and improving our environment. Healthy conflict flourishes then.

It's essential to hear different opinions and new ideas. There is no secret about the fact that, following the 2021 Six Nations, England have problems. We need to shake the players out of their sense of entitlement and fill the power vacuum that has resulted from the break-up of the Saracens group and the old contingent of players. We need to improve as coaches and find ways of fixing the problems while bringing in the right kind of players to rejuvenate the squad.

There is always something to fix. Problems sprout all the time, even in the midst of a long run of success. You would be very wrong to think everything is OK then. Everything is never, ever OK. There are always schisms and doubts, headaches and complexities. They might not be clearly visible when you are winning game after game, or having one bumper sales quarter after another, but they are just beneath the surface or around the corner. You will crash into them much sooner than you think if you don't go looking for them. The best way is to confront these looming challenges before they bring you down.

Neil Craig has been invaluable in helping me to find the right tone when I am leading a meeting where I sometimes engender conflict. He shares my belief that a robust environment is essential in elite sport, but Neil lets me know when I get it wrong. I remember one particular meeting when, afterwards, he asked me how I thought I had led the coaching group.

'I might have gone in a little too hard,' I said after a long pause.

'No shit, mate,' Neil said in his blunt but friendly way. 'It was counter-productive. You made everyone else clam up. Hardly anyone else said a word.'

Neil was right. I would have worked it out for myself after a while but, straight after the meeting, he pulled me up on it quickly. This form of conflict – with me tearing everyone down for not doing their jobs well enough – achieved nothing. I made the other coaches retreat into their shells and we shared nothing but my brief flurry of anger. I had wasted the meeting.

'OK, mate,' I said to Neil. 'I hear you.'

Neil said I surprised him by opening our next meeting with an apology to the other coaches for my attitude. But he liked it because it immediately changed the atmosphere. The coaches had thought about the views I had expressed too harshly and, overnight, they had formulated some answers. They were free to express them now and, having cleared the decks, I also felt at liberty to engage with them directly but in a much more considered way. I had learnt a good lesson – even at the age of 61.

Conflict can only be healthy if it is constructive and searching. Being deliberately argumentative or always prickly is obviously not going to help anyone. You need a sense of clarity and even calm when healthy conflict bubbles up. Neil told me a story of how an outsider made him understand this with real force when he was one of the leading coaches in Aussie Rules. He had invited a retired policeman, who had specialized in crisis and emergency situations, to observe his coaching team during a big game. The policeman joined them in the coaching box and Neil forgot about him during a tense and bruising match. Afterwards, Neil asked the policeman for his observations.

The policeman nodded tersely and then launched into a cutting assessment. Words like 'disgraceful' and 'embarrassing' were said and Neil was taken aback. But he was soon struck by the good sense of the policeman's argument when Neil was asked to imagine that he and his fellow coaches were in the cockpit of a plane. The players resembled the passengers on the plane. What would the passengers make of Neil and the coaches in the box if they had watched them shouting and cursing and gesticulating all through the game. If they were in a plane and they hit a crisis, would the passengers have confidence in Neil and his colleagues to get them down safely on the ground amid all that unnecessary emotion? You don't want your pilot whipped up and furious when the plane goes into a spin. Your life depends on him being calm under pressure and liaising closely with his colleagues as they work out how to get the plane back on course.

When the pressure is really on, we need composure more than conflict. But, away from the heat of battle, and when strategies are being planned and systems organized, a healthy dose of conflict can make everyone much sharper and more focused in their thinking.

Neil knows me well and he always says I am at my most uncomfortable when everything around me seems comfortable. If it looks as if the team is running perfectly then I am at my twitchiest. I instinctively understand that we are operating under a delusion. There is no such thing as a perfect run. So I start looking for the flaw and the kink in the system that could rise up soon and knock us off kilter. I know it's there and I need to root it out before it becomes a real issue.

I've become much more tolerant of other people over the years. I accept that we are all different and not everyone is going to work at the same remorseless pace as me or see everything exactly the way I do. Twenty years ago, I didn't like to see much dissent regarding my way of doing things as a coach. Now, I welcome it. I want to be challenged and made to think in a new way if it will improve the team. But my attention to detail and the high standards I endorse have not changed at all. I just feel more aware that everything is so fluid and changeable because problems are always looming even when you seem to have cracked the game.

It could be something as simple as player dissatisfaction when you are racking up win after win. The players who get on the field regularly are happy and fulfilled. But the other members of the team are disappointed or even angry. I watched an interview that Pep Guardiola did with Rio Ferdinand, the former England international, shortly before Manchester City played Chelsea in the Champions League final in late May 2021. City were just about to complete a phenomenal year. They had won two trophies, including the Premier League, with their bitter local rivals, Manchester United, 12 points adrift in second place. They had reached the semi-finals of the FA Cup and had made their first Champions League final.

Rather than delighting in their brilliant football and sustained success, Guardiola spoke of his certainty that, in the summer break, he would need to 'shake' the side to shed some of the problems which had begun to emerge behind closed doors. Most of these, at least the ones he was willing to discuss with Ferdinand, centred on dissatisfied players who had been shunted to the fringes of the squad and robbed of regular playing time.

'The players, like teams, are not a stable situation,' Guardiola said when he discussed the young forward Ferran Torres's burst of goals at the end of the season. 'There is up and down with all players. Ferran was in an incredible mood when he arrived, then upset with the world for many situations and he didn't play good. When he smiled again, he started playing good. It depends on the confidence of the players. We can help them, but it's up to them. Football rewards you when you are positive. When you complain all the time, people go over you and they play. Football doesn't wait. If you're not in the right moment, another guy will take your position. When you are positive, they always play good.'

Guardiola smiled, wryly, when he said: 'That's why they hate me, the players. When you have these alternatives [in City's squad], it's so difficult to let all the players play.'

He suggested that in the off-season they would shed numerous great players, selling them or allowing them to leave, and bring in fresh alternatives to rid the squad of both lingering bitterness and sudden complacency. He then asked Ferdinand a question: 'How many Premier Leagues did you win?' The answer was six at Manchester United under Sir Alex Ferguson, the master manager.

'Did you have the same squad for the first Premier League as the sixth one?' Guardiola asked next. It was a rhetorical question. We all knew how Ferguson had rebuilt his squad at United again and again, so Guardiola pressed on to distil this key point of coaching and management. 'You have to shake, you have to move.

With the same guys, it's almost impossible. We change, after a defeat. We change after a win. We change – me included.'

When I spent time with both Sir Alex Ferguson and Pep Guardiola, as we discussed coaching and management, I realized how much I could learn from both of them. That same desire to learn and improve burns just as deeply inside me now as it did then. It's why I will always feel uncomfortable, even when it seems as if everything is comfortable. I know how much more I need to absorb about coaching and leadership from so many people in sport, business and education. Each little snippet of knowledge will help me deal more effectively, I hope, with the problems and difficulties woven into the fabric of our work.

I met Pep when I spent time with him at Bayern Munich – where he had moved following all his success at Barcelona. He dominated and influenced the Bundesliga in much the same way that he has since done with the Premier League. It was a privilege to see him working in close-up and then to be given so many hours to talk to him. The day began at nine o'clock on a freezing morning in Munich. Pep was happy for me to watch their training session and their tactical work. It was fascinating to witness the intensity of his coaching and the sheer attention to detail in everything that he did.

He had a busy afternoon and so we agreed I would see him at seven that evening. I spent part of the afternoon going to a photo shoot with Thomas Müller, who is such an intelligent player for both Bayern and Germany, and that was interesting in itself. But nothing quite prepared me for the three hours I spent with Pep in his office that evening. His love of coaching, and of trying to find different ways to be the best attacking football team in the world, shone out of him. He told me how he had even studied rugby and handball to learn different approaches, and he asked me about Japan and the way we wanted to play rugby. I could explain how our vision of the game was built on some of the concepts of space and movement for our physically small players which he had refined into such an art form at Barcelona. The insights into his work there, combined with his plans to develop new strategies at Bayern, were outstanding.

I came away from that illuminating encounter feeling like an amateur who had just learnt so much from a master. But I thought of Pep in a different way when I spent time with Sean Dyche at Burnley. We all know that Pep is a great coach, but he is the first to stress that he has always worked with incredible players. It would be fascinating to see how he would coach if he stepped into the manager's role at Burnley. Could we be sure he would do a better job than the magnificent Sean Dyche?

The RFU are a juggernaut and the England rugby team have huge advantages over most of our rivals in terms of financial muscle and the depth of its professional playing pool. Of course these attributes are often tangled up in the endless acrimony and confusion that blights the structure of the game over here. Sometimes the chaotic problems totally overshadow the positives and make the England job so difficult. But I find it energizing and inspiring to visit a much more nimble and smaller organization at Turf Moor – where Burnley are based.

I believe that the smaller and more disadvantaged you are, the more initiative and creativity you show. These are the places where you often learn most. I've been around a fair number of football clubs – and most of them are giants of the game – but Burnley are the club I've probably enjoyed visiting the most. They're a relatively small team, with a small budget, and they've got a coach who's been there longer than any other Premier League manager. Sean took charge of Burnley in October 2012 and in his first full season he helped them gain promotion from the Championship. While they were relegated after one campaign, it did not take Sean long to get them back into the Premier League after the 2015–16 season. They have stayed up ever since, with a highest end-of-season position of seventh in 2018 which was enough to earn them a place in European football.

They've had to be inventive to get the best from their players and Sean is outstanding. The way he conducts himself is a lesson to us all. He keeps his composure in difficult situations and remains very considered in the way he talks to people. Sean chooses the right language and the right tone and he makes sure that Burnley are very clear about who they are and how they want to play. They don't get interference from owners or a governing body, and Sean turns the simplicity of their modest backdrop into a huge advantage.

Burnley have consistent and excellent theming around the club. Everyone can have snappy slogans and beautiful pictures on the wall. But they are meaningless unless you really drive home and live the meaning of those messages. Burnley have a very clear identity as a team and they understand the non-negotiables. They will always have to work harder than the opposition. You see it in the way they train, the way they talk to players, the way their training ground is set up. Other teams will have 35 different messages dotted around the place. They might have a slogan from Muhammad Ali, a quote from Martin Luther King or Steve Jobs, a soundbite from Elon Musk or Stormzy. All are fine on their own but when they are just flung together the messaging is muddled.

It is done in a much more coherent and lovely way at Burnley. Quotes from the players, reinforcing the vision of the club, are displayed all around the club. These quotes change every three months, and they are as powerful as they are personal. I had never seen that before and I thought it was fantastic as a reflection of what they're trying to achieve at Burnley.

This explains why I'm always looking out for the smaller teams that do well – whether it's the Gonzaga Bulldogs in American college basketball or Burnley in the Premier League. I am hungry to work out what they're doing because they're such intelligent and disciplined thinkers. Small clubs and leaders who have just retired, and have the time to tell you their secrets, are my touchstones.

They are all different and it's fascinating to compare managers like Ferguson and Dyche. At a powerhouse in Manchester United, Ferguson had the resources to build a large and stable squad. Many of his best players stayed at the club for years. So, in order to maintain the freshness and sense of change that is so essential to success in elite sport, he ensured a constant regeneration in his coaching set-up. Think of all the different number twos Fergie had over the years. The senior players benefit from the new input of ideas, and Ferguson could allow the latest assistant coach to run these revitalized training sessions while he watched from a more detached and clear-eyed managerial perspective.

Dyche operates differently. As soon as Burnley produce a really good player, what happens? He gets sold. So he is constantly on the lookout for lesser-known players to come in as replacements and, as a consequence, he needs real consistency in his backroom staff. He does not change the coaches around him in the same way that Ferguson did because they need that bedrock of solidity and a guaranteed knowledge of the Burnley way.

We all know that Pep Guardiola is a brilliant coach – and probably the best in the world right now. He is fizzing with ideas and totally dedicated to every job he does – just like Sir Alex Ferguson and Sean Dyche. When it comes to the Operation phase of the Build section of the leadership cycle, these are the examples of leadership I always remember.

As we lay out our plans, and execute them, I rely again on Neil Craig to tell me the truth about my work and the squad. When you sit in the chair as head coach – and this is probably similar to CEOs in the corporate world – it is often very difficult to get honest feedback. I try to change this pattern by walking the floor, and talking to everyone as often as I can, but the nature of my role obviously creates a barrier. All leaders face this dilemma. How do they sidestep the intimidating authority of the chair they occupy? If there are problems, it is sometimes human nature to try to hide them from the boss. So how do you ensure that there is a free flow of information from the equivalent of the shop floor to my office?

It's not good enough to say that you have an open-door policy. The reality is that most people are not going to stroll through that doorway to voice their difficulties. For me this is where Neil again does work of such value. He is a conduit between the coaches, the players and me. We are always striving to build cohesion, which is particularly difficult at international level because of a lack of time. Our players leave club-land and we have them for nine weeks in the Six Nations and then they disappear again. We might be lucky and work with them in the summer, but some years we won't see them again as a group until the autumn series in November.

In a club environment, when you've got access to your squad pretty much the whole year, it is easier to keep patient with them. In the Test arena it can sometimes become frustrating, because your plans and their execution of them do not move at the speed you would like. But the players have little time to adjust. When they arrive in camp we're pretty much straight into competition conditions. This is testing when you are trying to build and operate at the same time. It is much easier in a World Cup year when you have access to them for two or even three months before the tournament starts. It's amazing how you see the acceleration of your plans when you've got the players with you on a full-time basis for a longer period of time.

I always back myself in a World Cup because I have that crucial currency of time. Three World Cup finals with Australia, South Africa and England, and a ground-breaking tournament for Japan, offer the proof that our methods work when it matters most. But whatever the period in a four-year cycle, you need to be really clear about where you're going to spend that currency. When time is limited and you try to cover everything in the Operation phase of the Build stage, you can dilute your principles and vision.

I have found that an 80/20 philosophy gives me the biggest bang for my buck.

In my planning, I identify the most significant factors in our operation and we spend 80 per cent of our time making sure that these are running smoothly. It stems from being a student of the game, and understanding team dynamics and human behaviour, to know where you're going to spend most of your time in your programme. The technical and tactical side of the game might account for 20 per cent of your success. But so much else depends on your culture and cohesion as a squad. We can all rattle off the importance of communication, good planning, quality training, accountability of standards, having a world-class coaching team and a similar level of on-field leadership. Just go on the Internet and type in the phrase 'key characteristics of high-performance sporting environment'. You will be able to expand the list of obvious attributes and think you've got the secret sauce. But the defining feature is how you apply this information and make the most of the nuances.

I turn to Neil sometimes and suggest that we are not making the most of our time. The coaches are not talking enough or the players aren't listening closely. Neil will look at me and say: 'There is a reason why no one is talking or listening.' It is his way of reminding me about tone. How can we have healthy conflict and debate if the tone is wrong? I reset the scene and get the balance right because, as always, I am in the business of trying to change behaviour.

Neil compares the role of head coach, or any kind of leader, to a behavioural scientist or psychologist. He makes this analogy because you're trying to modify and improve behaviour. It's a complex, tricky task because we're dealing with human beings who are always riven with complexity. This is why I so value the opinions and insights of others in the organization. I am not interested in being the kingpin. I am interested in doing things better – and differently if necessary. There is never a day when I have all the answers myself. I need to create an environment where I can extract that information. If I get complacent and shut people down, or don't allow them enough space to be heard, Neil says: 'That's not good enough, mate.' He recently pointed out that, for all the problems we still face with England, that's happening less and less. But I can still learn and improve because I certainly don't always get it right. None of us does, and thank God for that. It would be a very boring world if we were all flawless.

The inner workings of the high-performance environment are highly complex and complicated. There's always so much going on because you're dealing with human emotions and human behaviour. Not everyone is set for a great day every time they get up. This leads to tension between staff members, between coaches, and in the playing group. Who is gelling? Who is disrupting cohesion? How do you rectify the blips and smooth away the bumps? These are all human behaviours, and you need to know so much to bind together 30 highly competitive professional athletes.

We draw a comparison with big commercial planes today. They use the best technology, so they are complicated. No matter the quality and experience of your lead pilot, he can't fly the plane on his own any longer. It's the same with serious high-performance sport. If you try and fly everything yourself, and you don't trust anyone else to have an opinion or add some vital knowledge or information, you miss too much. You will end up crashing and burning.

Of course there is still the great fallacy which encourages people on the outside to say: 'You're the head coach. You should know how to do it all because that's why they appointed you.' But all the best coaches who have been in the job for a big chunk of time understand that there are only some things they can do on their own. They can set the vision and always remain the keeper of the vision. But they require help and additional expertise in every other sphere because the job is too big for one person to do at world-class level on their own.

But, as in setting and maintaining the vision, the leader should always have the courage and the insight to:

- Highlight the goals – what will success look like?

- Apply the hard graft

When we made the unlikely aim of reaching a World Cup quarter-final with Japan in 2015, one of my hardest tasks was to engender a sense of healthy conflict in a squad of players whose entire lives had, up until then, been mostly built around them being quiet and compliant. Japanese culture was shaped by hierarchical order and traditional subservience. But, once I highlighted the goal, I needed the players to stop being comfortable. We introduced conflict into their previously calm and ordered routine.

I would tell them the time for an important meeting in our team room that evening. They were expected to be punctual and ready a few minutes before I and the other coaches arrived. They were obedient and duly gathered together to wait at least five minutes before the scheduled start. They found their places in the room, sitting down in their usual seats, and settled down to wait. I watched all this unfold in predictable fashion in a different part of the camp. The other coaches and I had set up secret cameras in the team room a few hours before so we could film them while we observed their interactions as a group. At first all was muted and peaceful. Ten minutes after the expected start there were a few glances at their watches to check the time. I had already barred them for using their phones in camp because, back then, players were less savvy about when and how to use their mobiles at work. So without the distracting comfort of their phones, and feeling constricted in a formal meeting, they waited and fidgeted.

Fifteen minutes passed. We could see the emerging signs of conflict as one or two players began to voice their dissatisfaction. Twenty minutes passed and the dissenting voices bubbled up, only to be hushed again. Half an hour passed and most of the players looked fed up and even angry. I watched and waited for some leadership to emerge out of this small situation of muted conflict. Finally, some of the older players took charge. We were obviously not turning up and so, slowly, they rose from their chairs and began to talk amongst each other. There were only a few sparks, but it was heartening to hear them turn the focus of the squad to the next training session and what they needed to do that day. It was a start in identifying the real leaders.

The next few days passed without any disruption. I made sure that everything ran on time with clockwork precision. Everyone settled back into a comfortable routine. They knew where they stood and what they were expected to do. We arranged a training game at a different venue and I told the players that they would be picked up by the team bus at 1 p.m. They were all on time at the appointed hour as they waited for the bus to arrive. Of course I had told the driver to keep the bus locked away in the garage. We were going nowhere, and so I and the other coaches again watched from a distance as the players milled around, their quiet expectation soon turning to impatience and then exasperation. A few irate voices were raised, which was no bad thing, and they decided to send someone to find me to check whether the game was still on.

They didn't like being messed around, but they came together as a squad much more quickly this time. The lesson had been absorbed. They agreed it was a small reminder from me that they should prepare for the unexpected on and off the field. We began to speak more openly.

I also needed to push them to a state of ragged exhaustion and acute discomfort. We could then force through change. Dissent and questions about my methods would emerge, when they were most uncomfortable, and in an area of new conflict we could debate the reasons as to why I was pushing them so hard.

We agreed that we played a tough and intensely physical game in international rugby and so our training equipped them to

handle the physical intensity. Through hard work we were giving
them the tools to put themselves in a position to win against the
best in the world. I was training them physically and mentally to
handle that intensity of opportunity. We hadn't won a World Cup
game for 24 years but, against South Africa, we had the cohesion,
the commitment and the courage to go for a try at the death when
a simple penalty would have earnt us a famous 32–32 draw. But
my boys went for the win because they were equipped to handle
it. My captain Michael Leitch came off the field, after we had won
the game, and he said to me: 'Mate, that was easier than training.'

I was proud in that moment because it's my job to apply the
hard graft and prepare them for the most difficult moments. My
players had been comfortable in the white-heat fever of the last
minute of a relentless game of rugby. The adversity and discomfort of training had steeled them for such moments. It's the
same if you go to a difficult business meeting. If you're not
equipped to handle that pressure, then your preparation has been
inadequate.

So we grafted in the long build-up to that camp. I worked them
hard but, also, I worked them smartly. We trained at 5 a.m.,
10 a.m. and 3 p.m. At the start, the players hated it. They couldn't
sleep at night because they were nervous about not waking up at
4.15 in time to drink their protein shake at 4.30. There was conflict and stress, and when I took them to a high-altitude camp for
two weeks we trained five times a day. By the time we returned
to our three-stints-a-day, training almost seemed easy. At the end
of our preparation, their ability to withstand adversity and discomfort was considered a sign of our strength.

Now nearly every team in Japan trains at 5 a.m. They've got no
idea why they are doing it, but they think it's the right thing. If I
was back in charge of Japan I would break that new tradition and
look for something different. You want the player, and the organization, to feel they're part of something special and doing
something different to everyone else.

To achieve that you need a sense of healthy conflict and, as a leader, an acceptance that you should:

FEEL UNCOMFORTABLE WHEN EVERYTHING ELSE SEEMS COMFORTABLE

- Plan and execute

- Highlight the goals – what will success look like?

- Apply the hard graft

- Create a platform for healthy (searching and constructive) conflict

- Ensure a sense of clarity and calm when healthy conflict bubbles up

8

FINDING THE ACCESS POINT

**EMOTIONAL CONNECTIONS HELP INDIVIDUALS
ACHIEVE THEIR GOALS**

In June 2015 I cranked up the pressure on my Japan World Cup squad. We trained hard on 28 days out of the 30 in a mad month. We were in the midst of typhoon weather, so it was hot and it rained constantly. We were training in mud. Every Saturday that month we had an open session so that hundreds of local fans could come and watch us play a practice match. To make it even more difficult we played a 12 versus 12 game. We also extended the width of the pitch from 60 metres to 80 metres. It proved a real test of the players' resolve. How much did they want to go to the World Cup? How much discomfort and pain could they tolerate? Were they ready to go deep into that muddy torture chamber to show me their character?

On the third Saturday of the month, after training so hard, the players were exhausted. They were right on the edge. But I told them we would go again in another brutal 12 versus 12 battle on a huge mud heap. These were the toughest conditions they had ever faced and Ayumu Goromaru, our full-back, could not cope. Everyone else was close to dropping away but they kept trying. Goromaru, however, gave up in the game. He got beaten for pace and he didn't even try. He walked back slowly, head down, in an act of complete surrender.

I didn't say anything to him in that lonely moment. I ignored

him and the game continued. But, at the end of it, I got the interpreter to tell Goromaru I would be talking to him. So he knew I
had rumbled him and I was not just going to let it fade away. Players always know when they have performed badly or with less
courage than usual, so he waited for me to approach him in the
dressing room. But I said nothing. As we usually did on a Saturday
night, after such a tough practice game at the end of an unforgiving week, we went out for a few beers as a squad. It was important
to relax and have a good time. I mixed freely with the rest of the
players, chatting away to them, but I avoided Goromaru.

On Sunday, he started ringing the interpreter. 'When are we
meeting?' he asked. The interpreter said he did not know. I had
not been in touch. A few hours later he called again. 'When are we
meeting?' He got the same answer. I had Goromaru exactly where
I wanted him. But I also knew there was value in letting his story
cook a little longer. On the Monday, the interpreter's phone was
clogged with more messages. 'When are we meeting?'

I finally responded: 'Tonight. Six thirty, in the restaurant.'

It was a beautiful little sushi restaurant in the hotel, which we
normally wouldn't use because it was so swanky and high class.
Goromaru was surprised to be meeting there because he had
expected he would be torn to shreds in an empty team room. But
I knew I had to find a different access point into Goromaru's
complex character. When I had first taken charge of Japan, he had
been the most openly defiant of all the players.

Goromaru had been burnt by his exclusion from the 2011
World Cup when John Kirwan, my predecessor, had not picked
him for a tournament held in New Zealand. Kirwan, a great former All Black, believed Japan needed to be bolstered by the
inclusion of foreign players. Numerous New Zealanders and
Pacific Islanders playing rugby in Japan were co-opted into the
national side. Goromaru is intensely patriotic and so he took
offence at Kirwan's selection strategy – not only did it cost him
his place in the squad, but it also appeared to insult all Japanese
players.

When I took over from Kirwan in April 2012, I adopted a different approach. I wanted to return to a Japanese core, and so I deliberately favoured local players over foreign imports. Goromaru was in the first crop I picked because, after years of coaching in Japanese club rugby, I knew he was an excellent full-back and a good goal-kicker. I would have picked him on merit anyway, but it fitted neatly with my plan to bring back patriotic Japanese players into the squad.

There was a problem, however, because Goromaru did not seem happy to be back. He made it clear that his problem centred on me. I was another bloody foreigner and so he was very cold and distant in all our interaction. Whenever we had a meeting, he would sit at the back of the room and never willingly engage in any team discussion. Sometimes, at a distance, I would see him talking to his teammates, but as soon as I came near them he would withdraw again. I knew he had the potential to be one of our very best players and so it was vital I broke down the wall and forged some kind of connection with him.

I knew patriotism was one of the key access points to Goromaru. So I turned to some of the friendlier Japanese players and encouraged them to talk to Goromaru on my behalf. I asked them to explain our vision to him in their own words. We wanted to pick a predominantly Japanese team to play a very clear Japanese style of rugby, a running and passing game, which suited our players. It took time but, slowly, Goromaru was convinced by the sincerity of our message. I knew he was on board when he began to sit in the front row of team meetings and to participate in our discussions.

Three years later, after his surrender on the mud heap, I looked for another access point to reach him. We were alone in the restaurant and I used a very different approach. For almost an hour and a half we just ate and spoke about his family. This was unusual because discussions of family were not often shared in a professional context. The Japanese players, as in polite society, tend not to talk about their private life. But I sensed this could be an emotional key to Goromaru. We had a really good conversation about his family. It was open and interesting.

Neither of us, obviously, had forgotten the purpose of the meeting, and I kept my laptop and notebook on display next to me. It offered a little bit of theatre. And so, after we finished our meal, I said: 'So, what do you think, mate?'

Goromaru spoke passionately and clearly. He started by saying he had let the team down and he had let himself down. Then, he identified the three key changes he needed to make. It was beautiful. In the three days I had let him stew he had addressed and then owned his problem rather than needing me to tell him what to do. I knew that our emotional connection had also deepened significantly because I had met him and we had spoken so personally. He could tell that I cared about him. This made him feel more secure and settled, and the fact that he had solved the problem, without needing me to do it, produced a remarkable change of behaviour in him. He went to the World Cup and had an unbelievable series of games which meant he was selected in the composite team of the tournament.

It showed, again, that there is more than one way to transform a player. Fifteen years earlier, if I had seen someone give up in training I would have exploded and berated him. But I made a far more lasting impression on Goromaru by finding the right access point to reach him.

When I worked in Japan, my first captain was Toshiaki Hirose. He was a small, slow winger but he had a great story. He was a really smart boy, who went to Keio University, which is one of the most prestigious in Japan. Hirose could have walked into a job with any company he wanted because, from Goldman Sachs to Ernst & Young, they were interested in him. He chose to go to Toshiba to work in nuclear engineering. But that plan was knocked off course as, after the tsunami, the nuclear industry fell apart. His future was suddenly clouded, but he saw how rugby was developing in Japan and so, while realizing that he had limitations as a player, he set about making an impact on the game by using his intelligence.

I brought Hirose in as my first captain because I knew he would help me lead a team that was outward looking. While I wanted the core of the squad to be Japanese, I didn't want them to be parochial like some previous national squads. Hirose's intelligence meant he was open and curious and he set the right tone. He was my captain for two years, but he had to bear the brunt of my anger in the early days.

A month into my tenure, we played abysmally against the French Barbarians and, afterwards, we went out as coach and captain to face the media. The performance had been totally unacceptable and I criticized the team in a blistering attack. As Japanese people often do when they are nervous, Hirose laughed anxiously midway through my tirade. 'It's not funny,' I said, before repeating myself even more icily. 'It's not funny. That's the problem with Japanese rugby. They're not serious about winning. If we want to win we've got to go out and physically smash people. Some players are never going to play for Japan again – unless they change, unless they grow up. What are we going to do with Japanese rugby? Do you want to carry on like this, or do you want to go down the path of choosing a side half-full of New Zealanders?'

There was genuine anger in my reaction, but I was also making a calculated attempt to find the access point to the players' deepest emotions. I wanted to open up bright young men like Hirose and Goromaru and tap into the trigger points which would change them as players. In this case it worked, and Japan began to play with much more cohesion, determination and fire after that.

Hirose was a unifying figure for us, and I always appealed to his intelligence to get the best out of him. But as our team improved, he couldn't retain his position as a first-choice winger on merit. I made Michael Leitch our captain. He was a New Zealander by birth but he had lived in Japan for many years. He

spoke Japanese perfectly and he understood the culture even
better than I did. But I decided to keep Hirose in the squad –
basically as a non-playing captain. He made 28 appearances for
Japan, but he was the only player in our 31-man World Cup
squad in 2015 who didn't play a minute in the tournament itself.
But off the field he was brilliant and he shared total responsibility
with Leitch. He was our equivalent of Mike Brearley – who had
been such an inspirational cricket captain for England, despite
not being selected on merit as a batsman.

It proved that, in elite sport, it's all about making connections
and forging strong relationships. When you're in the heat of the
moment, whether in sport or business, the people you trust are
the people who have given you something off the field to make
you feel good in terms of an emotional connection.

All these years later, I still speak to a sports psychologist who
works with swimmers. He is an old mate of mine and an invaluable sounding board when I discuss ways to strengthen my
players mentally and to help them find the right psychological
equilibrium. One of the fundamental points he makes to me is
that you always need to have an access point with the player. You
have to find a way to help him feel an emotional connection in
your relationship as player and coach. If you can understand
what matters most to him, and identify the drivers in his motivation to play rugby, you will be able to find the words to forge that
connection.

In recent years I have felt the truth of these words because,
with young players today, you've got to be able to find something
within that engages them emotionally. If you think back to your
school days, the only conversations you'll remember with your
teachers are the ones that emotionally touched you. They either
made you think about yourself in a new way or about what you
should be doing to improve yourself and make a difference. We're
also finding in elite sport that different behaviours are now coming through. Young players are quite happy to share their feelings

in a way that the older guys would resist. There is much more openness about emotion, and feeling vulnerable, but you still always need to find a way to access the hopes and fears that shape them.

Some players are hard to reach at first because there are no obvious access points to their inner lives. Will Stuart, the young prop-forward, was difficult to read, but we finally found the right access point with him. He really wants to make his mother happy, and we found a way to get him to understand how he can do that while playing rugby.

Each player is different because we are dealing with individuals in a team setting. But if they know that you care about them then you can share a good relationship. It becomes easy to work out how to tap into their character and to understand their story. You then work out how they respond best to your coaching. I often say that it's a bit like training horses. Some of them need the whip and some of them need lots of pats on the back. Some of them need to be kept on a tight rein and some of them should be allowed to run free. It's all about getting the horse to run faster – which you do by making the player feel valued and appreciated.

When I was coaching Australia, I used the same tactics on Wendell Sailor as I had done with Goromaru. Sailor was a larger-than-life character who had been a huge star in rugby league which, in Australia, is a much bigger sport than union. On reflection he reminds me of James Haskell. Those kind of big characters are very secure when they're on top and so they give full vent to their showmanship and sense of fun. But when you scratch away at the surface, and life becomes less straightforward, they can be very insecure.

I used to play little games with Sailor. He would have a bad performance and he'd be waiting for me to read him the riot act. But I'd pretend not to talk to him for a couple of days. This would be my way of keeping him on edge. Then, just when he was wondering what was happening, we'd have a conversation. I would build him up and tell him he was a great star of the game and to just go out there and show everyone why we loved him. He would be brilliant in the next game. He needed to feel really valued, but he could succumb to complacency, so you just needed to use the right psychological approach to get the best out of him.

I usually don't need to play any psychological games with English players because, generally, they are stable characters. They're used to playing long seasons, where they have to retain emotional control, so it's more a case of having to find an edge. Most of the English boys are pretty uncomplicated. Haskell was probably the most complex of them all so he would be one that I teased a little in the way I did with Goromaru and Sailor. It was a lot of fun but, also, to keep him on his toes. I knew it was import-ant that he felt loved by me and the squad, but I also had to remind him that he needed to be at his best to make a differ-ence.

We actually forged a friendly relationship even before I be-came England coach. In 2011 and 2012, Hask played for Ricoh Black Rams in Japanese club rugby. We spent a bit of time with each other in a pub in Tokyo called Trader Vic's. He used to go there with some ex-pats and we ended up having lunch and a few laughs. I liked him because he was a bit of a character and brought humour to everything he did. He liked me, especially when I picked him for England. Players like you when you pick them. They're not so keen, as we've said, when you don't.

Haskell was always going to be in my England team when I took over in 2016 and, as mentioned previously, I assured him that he would stay in the side for the whole of the Six Nations. That made him feel loved and secure, but I still knew I could have a joke with Haskell in front of the team. It was a way of keeping the mood light but, also, a reminder to Hask that he had to keep performing. So I walked into the team room on the second floor one day. Haskell was in the corner of the room close to the window and I said: 'Hask, have you been working on your finger muscles?'

He looked very worried and very serious when he asked: 'Why?'

'Because you're just hanging on,' I replied. 'You've got to keep working on them, mate.'

He laughed, along with everyone else – Hask likes being the centre of attention. But I also knew he was thinking, while looking at me: 'Yeah, I know he likes me. But then why does he say this?' He wasn't quite sure where he stood and that's where you want a bloke like him. Cocky but always on his toes. Then you find a moment to pull him aside for a private word. I said: 'Mate, don't worry about that. It was just shit to amuse the boys. You're doing great for us. We love you, mate, and we love how much you give to the team.'

Hask would light up like he was a million dollars again, and he would be on fire in the next training session. It was a way of finding the access point to play the right notes with him.

When the time came, in late 2017, to shake up the team and make some changes, I tried to let Hask go in a gentle and dignified way because I had great respect for him. He had done so much for the team but his time had come. I actually went to his place to talk to him face to face. He knew I was coming and so he had prepared some green tea. I offered him an opportunity to ease himself out of the team but, to his credit, he didn't want to do that. He wanted to keep fighting, which I accepted, but I made it clear that his Test career looked to have run its course. It was an example of the way you need to handle things a lot more sensitively these days. In the old days a coach would just axe the player. But, considering our emotional connection, it was right that I discussed what I planned to do openly with Hask.

Our relationship remained strong and he was over in Japan during the 2019 World Cup doing some commercial and media work. We were in the knockout stages and I brought him into the camp to lighten the atmosphere. He came in and, of course, he was brilliant, regaling the young players with stories that everyone had heard four or five times. Everyone loved it. I asked him to sit in on a team meeting and the first video we showed was Hask's huge hit on David Pocock in that second Test of our 3–0 series sweep of the Wallabies in Australia in 2016.

Hask piped up: 'Look boys, you only need to make one tackle to have a good career.'

That summed up our light-hearted interaction, which was always intended to help him get even better. But, these days, with players far younger than Haskell, you can't play as many games with them. They're sharper and they just want the truth quicker. They're used to having everything at their fingertips on their iPhone, so they don't like anything drawn out. It tends to be much more straightforward with most young players. Give them a problem to solve and no messing. Whereas the older generation, from the early years of professionalism all the way to Haskell, you could kid around with them a bit more.

But there is always place for a little humour, and I think we found the right touch, and the correct access point, with Beno Obano, the young Bath prop who made his England debut against Scotland in the 2021 Six Nations. Neil Craig and I met him in the bar area at Pennyhill Park, where England are based during some training camps. I asked Craigie to join me because I was going to go a bit hard on Beno. He was overweight and seemed to resist every suggestion that he needed to be in better shape for Test rugby. Craigie always reminds me that we should try to reach the players in different ways, so we saw Beno together.

Beno walked in and after some chitchat Craigie asked him about his physical condition. Did he feel in good shape?

Beno lifted his shirt up and, even for a prop-forward who doesn't need to be body beautiful, it didn't look too good.

We sat down and we began a general discussion about what he needed to do to have any chance of playing at Test level. It was a friendly chat but we weren't getting too far. Craigie pointed out that Beno didn't drink, so what was he eating that was not doing him any good?

There was a long pause and then Beno put his hand on Craigie's knee while he turned to look at me: 'I love my burgers.'

He did it in such an endearing way that we had to work hard not to laugh. There was also a warmth and confidentiality in the way he put his hand on Neil's knee while telling me the truth. It might sound silly, but we made a real connection in that small admission from Beno. He was implying that he would find it really difficult to give up the burgers.

I encouraged him: 'It's not that hard, mate. You can do it.'

I looked at Neil at that point and our eye contact allowed us to share a silent message. We could tell that he understood the point we were making but, also, that he's a good guy. There was no need for us to go hard on him.

We then became more serious. Was he prepared to give up hamburgers to find his best self?

'Yes,' Beno said simply. He has been true to his word, and since then he has come a long way. He has earnt his first England cap and he has become so much better on and off the field. He has also not eaten any burgers in that time, and he is in really good shape now. I reckon Beno will remember that conversation for the rest of his life – as Neil and I will too.

It was light-hearted on the surface, but also pertinent and full of good intentions. We were not trying to embarrass Beno or make him feel bad, but we needed to find a way to gain access to his brain. It also really showed the value of Neil to me. If I had done it on my own I would probably have gone in much harder and not been as effective. But Beno is a lovely young guy with a real sense of humour. The way he said 'I love my burgers', with just the right tone and timing, forged such a connection with us.

It also meant we had got it right because, with a different player, it would have been offensive to have discussed his body shape.

But Beno was just coming into the Test arena and, in that new environment, he was not fully aware of the high standards we expect. He had probably never been challenged about his commitment and we didn't want to crush him. We wanted him to absorb the message but also to understand that we cared about him and his future. It worked because we did it in an organic way without any planning. Neil and I just went in together and reacted naturally to the mood and to Beno's body language.

High-performance sport, as we have said, often feels deadly serious. But it's still important to remember that it is, after all, a game. Yes, it is big business, and it can make or break players and coaches. The pressure is intense and the scrutiny unforgiving. But if we forget the joy and the sheer pleasure we felt when we played as kids then we are getting it drastically wrong. There is still a place for joy and humour in elite sport.

The ability to have a laugh at yourself, your teammates and the staff members, without belittling anyone, is really important in our performance environment. It's a great tool to have because there's nothing better than having a laugh. It makes you feel good. Even in tough times, if you can have a laugh with someone and a bit of a joke, you are halfway to a much better place.

It's all about context and knowing when is the right time to have a laugh. With Beno it was the first serious conversation about discipline in Test rugby. Humour helped us as we shared the information that would educate him about the expectations he now faced. Other coaches would have said we needed to go in hard right away to set the standard for Beno.

But I have learnt over the years that you need to be very careful and thoughtful when using the spoken word. Once it leaves your lips you can't get it back. You can do some inspirational work and lift up people with the right set of words. But, if you get them wrong, you can also do unbelievable damage. Communication is everything, so pause before you speak. It will help you find the right access point to develop a lasting emotional connection with those you lead.

Sometimes the bond we forge with our players and fellow coaches is intensely personal and profound. There was an occasion that the father of one of them had lost his job. The dad was in his sixties, and so his chance of getting another job was minimal. So a member of our camp ended up paying the monthly mortgage on his parents' house. It had become part of his story and one of his goals – to look after his parents when they needed him most. He was OK but it was tough. Yet sharing it with me and the leadership group helped us understand his situation and make allowances for those difficult circumstances.

The aim is always to help the individual achieve his personal goals. If we can help them do that, then it is inevitable that the team will benefit significantly. But you need to assess each player in isolation and see how best you support them on their personal journey.

Maro Itoje is an interesting example. When he burst onto the scene you could have come from Mars and still been able to tell that he was going to be a special player. You didn't need any deep rugby knowledge or foresight to predict an outstanding career for him if he stayed on track.

But these are also the standout players that you have to manage carefully at the outset. He has developed really well since I gave him his debut as a substitute against Italy in 2016. Maro has a good head on his shoulders, and he doesn't get too far ahead of himself. I think the way we dealt with him early on in his international career helped a little in establishing those good habits. The media usually get it right when they pick out the exceptional talents but my job is to protect this kind of player. I am not interested in him being a new sensation. I want to look at him long term so that he eventually becomes a 50-cap or, hopefully in Maro's case, a 100-cap player one day. So we try to manage the media for him and we go out of our way to ensure that he does not start thinking he is better than anyone else. As in any job, if you start thinking that way, it will end in disaster. We try and get him to concentrate instead and to understand very clearly what he needs to do to keep improving his game. If he's got the right character, then he will keep getting better at a sustainable pace. You don't want a shooting star because, while it goes up very quickly, it also plummets back to earth soon afterwards. So we want these extraordinary players to rise slowly so they end up playing a huge amount of Test matches.

After Maro's first game for England I said: 'Not bad for Vauxhall Viva . . .'

That was me talking directly to the media rather than to Maro. He came up to me afterwards and said: 'I don't even know what a Vauxhall Viva is.'

I replied: 'Don't worry about it, mate. Just play even better next time.'

But I was telling the media to slow down the hype machine. Maro was still just a kid. He was nowhere near his full potential. We all needed to show much more patience.

Maro himself needed, more than anyone else, to understand the value of patience. He needed to trust us. I think we helped him do that because he quickly came to understand that we care for him. He's an important player for us but he's also got a responsibility to his family and himself. It is vital that he feels he can fulfil all his personal goals while realizing that the best way to do this is by applying himself to the cause of the team.

If the team are flying, so will Maro Itoje.

As with all the players, we do this in both a group setting and with one-to-one meetings. You're always looking to have conversations that the players will remember and to find an emotional hold that unites us. You need something that makes them feel really good or something that sparks an uncomfortable feeling. They will be inspired or they will see the need to take a hard look at themselves to see how they can improve. Again, it's searching for that access point to find an emotional connection which will get more out of the player.

For me, Jonny May has been one of the best England players in recent years. He's gone from being a hard-working fast winger to a sublime performer who lifts his teammates. I remember watching him in the 2015 World Cup, and at one stage he seemed to be doing little more than running at 45 degrees every time he got the ball. I was thinking: 'Who is this guy? Is he using his brain at all?' And now, on his day, I would say that he's close to being the best winger in the world. I haven't had a great deal to do with Jonny. He's one of those players you can allow to get on with things and work it out for himself. He is quite an unusual bloke, with quirky interests, but he is one of my best glue players. He binds everyone closer together.

Jonny also offers a reminder that, sometimes, it's not about the conversations you have. It's more the conversations you don't have. You build a certain picture for the player as to how he can get better. And then you leave it to the players. You don't encroach too much on their space because some people need room to grow. Jonny is one of those guys who needs his own space. So to have a lot of one-to-one meetings with Jonny would be a disadvantage for him. As a leader, you have to work out who needs close attention and who needs room to develop in his own way.

You are always trying to open the players' eyes to the opportunities that are ahead of them. But you also need to accept that many of them learn this from a young age – from their parents who will always have the deepest influence on them. When I think about building individuals towards achieving their goals, one of my best stories is Will Genia. When I took over the Reds in Queensland in Super Rugby in 2007, I remember going to watch one of our academy games.

A fat little half back caught my eye. I said to the academy coach: 'Who's that?'

'Will Genia,' the coach said. 'But he's no good. He's lazy, he's overweight and he doesn't work hard enough.'

I replied. 'But shit, mate, he can pass the ball beautifully.'

The academy coach wasn't having it. He said Genia was too soft and he blamed it on the fact that his father was a parliamentarian in Papua New Guinea. The coach said that this was why Genia didn't work hard. He was pampered.

My job was to look after the first-team squad and we were in for a rough season. I had my hands full, but I was still really interested in the chubby kid. I got Will in and had a good chat with him. I told him that he had real talent but he needed to apply himself. It was simple stuff.

A day or so later his father came down to the training ground to see me. He was a big guy wearing a really expensive suit. It looked to me as if he had probably got a small chunk of the GDP of Papua New Guinea invested in that suit. We talked about his son, with Will sitting alongside us, and I said to the dad: 'Mate, your boy has got incredible potential. But he needs to start working.'

The father looked at his son and he said: 'You hear that? You've got a real opportunity now, haven't you?'

That's all he said, at least in front of me, and the change in Will Genia was remarkable from then on. It all came from the father and, obviously, Will himself.

Whenever there was a day off for the players, I would find Will at the training ground, getting himself fitter and fitter and kicking balls on his own, hour after hour. He was soon playing for the first team and he eventually turned himself, for a while, into the world's best half back, winning 110 caps for Australia before his Test career finally ended in 2019.

The intervention of his father, and the application of Will himself, made all the difference as he went from being a dismissed player to achieving his great individual goals.

All these different examples have communication at their heart. Communication is the key to cohesion and improvement in your squad or your organization. This is especially true in any high-performance environment when you're asking people to do extraordinary things on a consistent basis. Communication here is obviously vital as you search for the right access points to their inner hopes and fears. Most of all you want to help them fulfil those hopes and overcome their fears. So always remember that:

EMOTIONAL CONNECTIONS HELP INDIVIDUALS ACHIEVE THEIR GOALS

- Find the access point to an individual's motivation

- Forge a connection to inspire change and development

- Build the individual towards achieving their goals

STAGE 3: EXPERIMENT

9. Review Constantly
[STRATEGY]

- Review the vision versus progress
- Take the key course-correcting decisions
- Make the revisions
- Re-engage with the evolved strategy

10. The 3 Per Cent Reminder
[PEOPLE]

- Assess transformation delivery versus goals in value terms
- Embed the changes made

11. Other Voices
[OPERATION]

- Review and improve
- Re-plan, re-execute
- Move at pace

12. A Close Examination
[MANAGEMENT]

- Study the working parts – the individuals, the processes, the organization

9

REVIEW CONSTANTLY

DON'T GIVE IN TO EMOTION . . . MAINTAIN
DISCIPLINE WITH YOUR PLAN

The most difficult challenge in sport is to keep believing in your plan when you are swamped by external criticism and doubt. I call it noise. When outsiders bring the noise, and threaten to derail you, it is vital you maintain discipline and stick to the essential components of your strategy. Block out the noise and adhere to your principles and your plan. You have to remember that sport, because it is so intensely emotional, always has the capacity to subvert and even ruin logic. It can drown you in a sea of froth, unless you keep vigilant and remember your aims and ambitions when you set the vision. As we move into the Experiment stage of the leadership cycle, it is important to review the plan and chart the progress you have made up to this point.

Of course there are always going to be blips and dips, and leaders need to brace themselves for the inevitable emotive reaction. To passionate fans, a defeat for their team can seem disastrous. Two losses feel like a crisis, while defeat in a third game in close succession seals a catastrophe. This was the unhappy outcome for my England team in the 2021 Six Nations.

We lost to Scotland, Wales and Ireland, and it was discussed heatedly in some quarters as proof that my work with England was over. It was the end of our world, as team and head coach, and everything we had worked on for five and a half years had to be obliterated. There were calls for my sacking and searing analyses of my shortcomings. The fact we still had a winning record of 77 per cent, and had reached the World Cup final 18 months earlier, counted for little.

We live in an emotionally volatile world where vitriolic opinions are to be expected. The media and England supporters have every right to question our performances and demand my removal. Why should we be protected from fierce scrutiny and scathing criticism? Every other leading coach and team is subjected to similar treatment. This is the nature of modern sport.

I really didn't care about all the negative press. But there is no point claiming I was oblivious to it, because people kept telling me what was being written or said and so there was no escape. But I avoided reading it, or listening to it, because I can't control the outside noise. I have lost enough jobs in rugby to understand the pattern to these campaigns. I was not surprised when a leak to the media confirmed that there was a break clause in my contract. This echoed what happened when I was fired as Australia's head coach in 2005. You could see it as a testing of the waters to gauge how high the media temperature against me had risen.

If the RFU's internal review of our Six Nations tournament concluded it was the right decision, they could dismiss me. It added to the debate and the hoo-hah, but all you can do is concentrate on your work and let others make the decision about your future.

I had set the vision in late 2019 for England to become the best team in the world, the ultimate aim being to play the best rugby anyone has ever seen. We won the 2020 Six Nations championship, but finished fifth in the 2021 competition. That outcome does not mean the vision is wrong or that we are following a poor plan as we build towards the next World Cup. The job for me after temporary disappointment, and the job of any leader, is to be disciplined in maintaining our plan.

At the same time, you have to keep reflecting on and evaluating your strategy. You cannot be blind to its shortcomings and how best to rectify them. But you have to be rigorous when putting a plan in place, and sticking to it. There will be ups and downs, and bad outcomes along the way, but that's why sport is endlessly fascinating.

After 25 years of coaching in professional sport I know that, in these inevitable tough periods, it's essential to stay calm and remain committed to your strategy. But in the short-term you also need to show leadership by pointing the way in a direction which can take you from the low you're in to where you want to be as quickly as you can. You have to find the right people to help you do this because others will fall away amid the adversity. They aren't robust enough or they find it too uncomfortable. So they need to be eased out. As a leader, your ability to identify effective replacements quickly is a clear way to change a downward trend.

We've got a plan for the 2023 World Cup and we're working methodically towards that tournament. But, within that strategy, our short-term goal is to win games. You have to keep winning in high-performance sport, but we're also always looking at the bigger picture. Bob Dwyer had a great saying: 'If your long-term strategies are right, the short-term benefits will follow.'

The key to current and future success is to review constantly. I occasionally get asked how companies can use their annual or quarterly reviews to maximum effect and I always offer a simple answer: 'Stop doing them.'

It is totally wrong to carry out sporadic performance reviews. You need to review your work, your staff and yourself constantly. This relentless review process is draining and difficult but it is the best way to improve and succeed.

My daily reviews during the Six Nations, and the more exhaustive overview we carried out once the tournament was over, confirmed a simple truth. I really struggled as a coach in lockdown. I missed exposure to the players and my fellow coaches. I missed the healthy conflict of my daily briefings over coffee with Neil. I spent long periods of time by myself in a room. It was not healthy or positive because coaching is a people-based job. If you're not dealing with people, you're not practising the skills you need to be razor-sharp as a coach.

There is no doubt that the isolation impacted negatively on me both personally and professionally. I felt it acutely before the opening game against Scotland. I didn't feel prepared because I had spent so much time in isolation. You're not people-sharp. An integral part of our strategy are the conversations where we believe we can elevate a player from a seven-out-of-ten to an eight-out-of-ten performance. If you're able to continually develop those conversations, using the right words at the right time, you can lift the individual player and your team. But if you're not seeing the players and your staff in the build-up, then it's very difficult.

I am sure it must be the same in other forms of work – even if I am surprised by the number of people in business who say Zoom is fantastic and the future of their communication because it cuts back on travel and saves so much time and so much hassle. Maybe in some businesses remote conversations might work. But in a people-based activity like high-performance sport, I can't see how that could ever succeed at the sustained level you need.

Consider this contrast. In late May 2021, I left Bristol at 5.30 in the morning so that I could travel over two hours to meet Jack Nowell just after 8 a.m. in Exeter. It was just a quick catch-up, face to face, and not much more than a ten-minute conversation because he was playing later that day for the Chiefs. But those ten minutes in person were worth ten long Zoom conversations to me. Jack had been out injured and I got to see his state of mind and physical readiness for rugby with my own eyes. He looked great and we rekindled our bond very quickly and it made the four-hour round trip totally worthwhile. Those one-to-one meetings, especially when I go out of my way to make them happen, show the player how much I care about them.

I could not do anything of that nature before we met up for the Scotland game. It was one of the reasons why I stressed publicly after the game that I did not coach the team well. I didn't give the players the best opportunity to perform at an optimum level.

It's important to admit your mistakes and poor coaching because it builds trust. I have always seen trust as a bank where you make deposits and withdrawals. You have got to avoid making too many withdrawals and instead concentrate on building your deposits of trust so that the players know you're there for them. You start doing that by making the time and the effort to see them personally. You're doing it for them rather than yourself. It is the same for any leader of an organization.

I remember being the acting principal of the International Grammar School in Sydney in the 1990s. One of the first things I did in that role was to meet every single member of my large teaching staff on a one-to-one basis. It was a boiling hot summer's day, with the temperature rising way past 30 degrees, and I was in an office in Surry Hills which, unlike today, was not a salubrious suburb of Sydney. Back then it was a gritty neighbourhood which matched my surroundings. My cramped office had no air conditioning and it was a very basic room where I interviewed all 77 teachers, one after the other, on that one day. Sweat poured down my face and my back and it took almost 12 hours to see everyone for five or ten minutes each. But meeting people face to face on an individual basis was so much more meaningful than me just holding another mass staff meeting. It showed each teacher that I cared about them and I wanted to take responsibility for my own new role.

In accepting responsibility for my errors after we lost to Scotland, I had to admit that clear mistakes had been made in the selection process. I could have chosen a much younger side, but you can't pick a player if he's not ready for international rugby. You've got to find the right time to bring the player in, and that's usually after they have had some experience of being around the squad on match days, and training with them in the week of a

Test. George Martin is the best example. We had him in for five weeks of training before we gave him 20 minutes against Ireland at the end of the tournament. He acquitted himself well and he is now ready for more time in Test rugby. But if I had thrown him in too early, against Scotland or France in the Six Nations, and they had driven him back, we might not have seen George again for a long time. We could have lost a player with the potential to win at least 50 caps for England.

I like the fact that George has some real dog in him. Those kind of players are rare. Let's be honest here. Rugby was a potentially violent game until 20 years ago. When teams wanted to stop certain players, they often resorted to violent tactics. But it's a much cleaner game now. You still need to stop opposition players, but when you hit someone hard you have to do it cleanly. Sam Underhill and Tom Curry like to hit hard, but fairly, and they're special players. George Martin has that same dog inside him and I'm always trying to find players who have got things I can't coach. Bob Dwyer taught me this valuable lesson. You've got to search for players that have an uncoachable magic, that fierce attitude or innate feel for the game. George has both but he's still developing. It would be wrong to rush him.

Fans and pundits want to see him in as soon as possible, but they're not worried about his long-term career. They just want to see him when choosing him is the flavour of the month. But we're trying to make educated decisions about building a squad and, sometimes, you have to go more slowly than you want. It didn't work out for us as a team, but it was the right decision for George – who was still only 19 years old at the time.

The review process never goes well on a Sunday after you've just lost a game. The players were really down after the Scotland defeat. I knew there was no point going into the detail immediately in any depth. So we highlighted a problem for them to look at on video and asked them to come back the next day with a solution. We do this much more these days. Rather than telling the players where they went wrong, we ask them to find solutions to the problem. Then, in a series of meetings, we point them towards the right answer out of the few they offer. Their suggested solutions are always pretty simple. It usually focuses on a problem in attitude or a tactical issue and, generally, they're right. From there we develop a shared plan on how we move forward.

On the Monday the review process really cranked into gear. I met each player individually and reviewed their performance in a five-minute meeting. I would point out what they did well and, also, where they let themselves and the team down. It was not excessively detailed but it gave them the essence, with pointers on what they needed to do before the next game against Italy the following weekend. I strive for honesty, clarity and engagement with the player. Rather than me just dominating the exchange, I get the player to comment on his performance. If it was unsatisfactory, where is the gap between the plan and its execution? How do we bridge that gap? Do they need help to bridge that gap? Or can they do it by themselves?

I put a lot of work into the coaching and leadership group on the Monday to ensure that we were back on track. They were part of the loss and needed to take responsibility. They also needed to coach the players better in the week ahead – with the onus on me to lead from the front.

After a defeat the temptation is to tear into the next game and make amends without paying the necessary attention to the basics of your performance. But that turnaround rarely happens in the first minutes of a game, so it is important to stay calm and measured and not to get disappointed again. This is one of the increasingly interesting conversations we have with young players today and I think it pertains to people in general. Everyone wants to get excited. Everyone wants to feel good. But the game generally doesn't make you feel good.

Rugby is tough and attritional. It's not a free-flowing game where you can be instantly exciting. But the perception of sport, more and more, is that it should be seen as entertainment. People want to be entertained. But coaching and playing Test rugby is not like making a movie. Most of the time you have to dig in and do the dirty work. It's always about trying to find the balance for the player between their dream of what they would like to be and the reality of the game.

Test cricket sets a great example. The best batsmen find the right time to be exciting and the right time to be dour. Test rugby is the same, so you're always trying to get that difficult but balanced picture in the players' heads. We also want them to understand that the achievements of the team dictate their individual success. It's fascinating but demanding.

The challenges were amplified during Covid. We had studied research done in the Austrian Bundesliga where they compared the emotion of players in regular games to their reactions when playing behind closed doors in bio-secure bubbles. The researchers were clear in saying that players had become less aggressive and that this was especially evident in home games, where the absence of crowds was having a detrimental effect on them. Were our players pacified by the sterile environment at Twickenham? Was it easier for Scotland to be more aggressive away from home in an empty stadium? We really don't know.

All that mattered was that, after a slow start, the players picked up the intensity and pace at training on the Wednesday. It took 50 minutes to get there but then they trained superbly. We beat Italy 41–18 on the Saturday and then prepared really well for the vital game away to Wales two weeks later. After the isolation-ravaged problems of the Scotland game, all the old excitement of coaching and leadership returned. I wanted to keep pushing, keep insisting, keep demanding that the players challenge themselves. There were still many difficulties and areas of conflict, but we were in better shape as we headed for Cardiff.

In the end we lost a contentious match to Wales and, on the Sunday morning of 28 February 2021, I came down to the team room. I heard the hubbub and chatter die away. Silence descended. I felt all eyes turn to me but, as soon as I returned anyone's gaze, they

Will Genia of the Wallabies runs around Sitiveni Sivivatu of the All Blacks during the 2009 Bledisloe Cup match. I sat down with Genia and his father when he was playing for Queensland Reds Academy and told him that only he could decide whether he wanted to be a great player. He went on to win 110 caps for the Wallabies.

Ayumu Goromaru signs autographs for fans prior to the opening of the Kamaishi Recovery Memorial Stadium on 19 August 2018 in Kamaishi, Iwate, Japan. My relationship with Goromaru was key to the way Japan was able to change both their mindset and the way they played. He was a modern-day samurai warrior.

James Haskell breaks with the ball during the first Test match between the Wallabies and England at Suncorp Stadium on 11 June 2016 in Brisbane, Australia. Haskell was a key part of my early years with England, particularly in the 2016 whitewash of Australia down under. He was a good team man with a real sense of humour. We enjoyed some good banter together.

We arrived in Australia in the summer of 2016 on the back of a Six Nations Grand Slam, and, in winning all three Test matches, did what no other England team had done before. The tour was hugely instructive in bringing together a mix of players, like Haskell, who had been part of the previous England regime, but also introducing Ellis Genge and Kyle Sinckler to the England set-up as we looked to build a squad that could compete for the 2019 World Cup.

England training session at Pennyhill Park in November 2016. We were unbeaten throughout 2016, which I was delighted with, but part of my philosophy is that you need to avoid getting comfortable at all costs and I am always looking for ways to test the players and develop healthy conflict on and off the pitch.

Jonny May breaks past Conrad Smith on the way to scoring the opening try during the QBE Test match between England and New Zealand in November 2014. Jonny is one of those players who doesn't need a great deal of coaching, only encouragement, and he is one of the most gifted natural athletes England has ever produced.

Scotland's lock Jonny Gray *(left)* and England's lock Maro Itoje compete in the lineout during the Six Nations match at Twickenham in 2021. Due to enforced Covid isolation at the beginning of the 2021 Six Nations, I barely had any time to coach the England team, and I took full responsibility for our loss to Scotland.

Billy Vunipola is tackled by Alun Wyn Jones *(left)* and Cory Hill during the Six Nations match between Wales and England in 2021. It was a tough game in a tough season for one of our most valuable and experienced players, but Billy's honesty and ability to show others how to react to adversity is a huge inspiration to everyone in the England set-up.

Josh Adams of Wales scores their side's first try as George Ford tackles during that 2021 Six Nations match. We were on the wrong side of two refereeing decisions and clawed our way back into the game, which I was immensely proud of, but ultimately it wasn't enough.

England players celebrate victory after the Six Nations match between England and France in 2021. We had beaten France in an extra-time nail-biter during the Autumn Nations Cup, but this was a different kind of win and we put together the best team performance since we had beaten the All Blacks in the 2019 World Cup semi-finals eighteen months previously.

Bristol Bears' Kyle Sinckler during the Gallagher Premiership Rugby match between Bath and Bristol in May 2021. Sincks put in a Man of the Match performance after the disappointment of hearing that, initially, he wouldn't be going on the Lions Tour to South Africa in 2021. His emotional post-match interview showed me how much he had grown as a man since he had toured with us to Australia in 2016. I was delighted for him that he was called up for Lions duty a few weeks later when Andrew Porter unfortunately had to withdraw through injury.

Golden State Warriors' head coach Steve Kerr *(centre)* and his assistant coach Ron Adams *(holding paper)* watch the game against the Milwaukee Bucks. Every coach has a truth-teller, someone who is unafraid to tell them how things really are. Steve Kerr, formerly a teammate of Michael Jordan, has Ron Adams, and I am lucky enough to have Neil Craig by my side to fulfil a similar role.

Arsenal's former manager Arsène Wenger looks on during the English Premier League football match between Huddersfield Town and Arsenal. Wenger is the ultimate thinker in the game. We have invited him to speak to the England squad in the past, and he is as eloquent in dissection of the game as he is profound.

Pep Guardiola talks to his Bayern Munich squad at their Säbener Strasse training ground on 29 January 2016. I went to visit Pep while he coached at Bayern and was put to shame by his attention to detail.

Neil Craig, the RFU head of elite performance, during the England training session at the Sapporo Dome on 20 September 2019 in Sapporo, Japan. I brought Neil in to join the England set-up in 2017 to help with the team's leadership, communication and teamwork. He is also invaluable to me as a truth-teller and we've had some healthy disagreements over the years.

Burnley's head coach Sean Dyche leads a training session. I have huge respect for Sean and what he has achieved at Burnley. Every coach can learn from Sean about how to make the most of limited resources.

General manager Billy Beane of the Oakland Athletics talks to pitching coach Curt Young and bench coach Mike Aldrete in the clubhouse. I have never met Billy Beane, but *Moneyball* is a book I have revisited numerous times.

The class of 2021: Jacob Umaga, Marcus Smith, Ben Curry, Freddie Steward, Harry Randall, Lewis Ludlow, Josh McNally, Joe Heyes, Curtis Langdon, Jamie Blamire, Callum Chick and Trevor Davison pose for a photograph wearing England caps after their debuts in the Summer International between England and the USA at Twickenham in July 2021. With twelve England regulars on tour with the Lions, the summer of 2021 was a chance to uncover two or three more players who could put their hands up for the 2023 World Cup squad.

looked away. It was a strange feeling. It made me feel as though I had murdered someone and I was still in the same blood-stained clothes I'd worn when carrying out the grim act the day before. This is how elite sport can make you feel when you're in charge and you've lost a game that you should have won. It is lonely and uncomfortable, but you learn so much about yourself and your players.

Everyone was feeling their own personal guilt over the loss, and it was important that I found a way to lift my staff because their demeanour could affect the players. Curious glances were still directed towards me and that was completely natural. Everyone was looking towards me, as the leader, to set the mood after a bizarre defeat. That's the job of a leader – to empower your people to do their job well. You back them to do it, and when the outcome is disappointing you learn from it.

But we need to resist the idea that failure is terrible, that it brings only doom and gloom. In the short-term, obviously, failure feels horrible. I hate losing; but the opportunity to learn from defeat is enormous. So it is vital, as a leader, not to look at failure as terminal. I find that it is a very English trait to fall into this trap of allowing defeat to distract you from your overall goal.

I got so many texts after the game saying, 'I'm still behind you', as though I was suddenly doubting their support or it was the beginning of the end for me. These same doubts probably led to many of the looks that were directed my way the following morning. I am sure some of the players were thinking: 'Maybe he's going to get the sack now? Maybe he's not the right man for the job?' That is often the mentality in England after temporary failure. To be honest it makes me laugh.

Despite the seemingly murderous implications of the loss, I was much happier with the team than I had been after the Scotland game. After so much ill-discipline, controversy, misfortune and problematic officiating against Wales, we had been impressive in the way we came back to level the score at 24–24 with 15 minutes left. I found that encouraging, even though I had been angered by the officiating and disappointed in our mistakes. Maro Itoje conceded five of the 14 penalties we conceded. The individual and the team count was unacceptable, but I knew that Maro and the other players would learn from their persistent offending. I had less hope that the officials would be as reflective as my players.

Pascal Gaüzère, the referee, had an indifferent game in allowing two tries from Josh Adams and Liam Williams which should never have been awarded. The first came after a blatant knock-on by Louis Rees-Zammit was overturned by Gaüzère and another Frenchman, Alex Ruiz, the TMO, but the resulting try by Adams should have been overruled. A look of utter incredulity spread across the face of young Rees-Zammit when he realized that he had not been penalized.

The second try occurred in even more bizarre circumstances, when Gaüzère called over Owen Farrell to tell him that he needed to talk to our players and tell them to get a grip on the ill-discipline that was causing so much trouble. Owen listened and agreed with Gaüzère that he would relay the instruction immediately. He ran over to talk to the team but, inexplicably, Gaüzère allowed Dan Biggar to take a quick tap penalty and run the ball even though we were preparing a team huddle to absorb the referee's message. Williams scored another unjust try.

But even after those two illegal scores, Wales were only 17–14 ahead at half-time. Kieran Hardy scored a legitimate try in the second half and Ben Youngs responded with an absolute beauty. With the scores level as we entered the final 15 minutes, the game should have been won by England. But we conceded another three penalties, and a try which Cory Hill scored. Callum Sheedy, on as a replacement, kicked the conversion and all the penalties as Wales won 40–24. The press picked up on the fact that it was the highest score Wales had made against England, but we knew that 14 of those points, from the first two tries, should not have been allowed. We also gave up another 12 points by gifting Wales four penalties they kicked through the sticks. A combination of poor officiating and our own lack of discipline ruined an otherwise good performance.

We received an apology from World Rugby the following day, but it hardly made up for the scarcely credible decisions. I have never known a team get so burnt by two wrongly awarded tries in the first 20 minutes of a Test.

At the end of it I could have made a long video of complaint like Rassie Erasmus did after South Africa lost the first Test against the Lions in late July 2021. In terms of leadership all international coaches could emulate Rassie's stunt, but would that benefit the game? We would put more pressure on the officials and, as we saw, the refereeing got worse as the Lions series went on, to the benefit of South Africa. Rassie might feel his tactics were justified but you need to take a wider view for the sake of rugby.

One of the problems affecting the game at the moment is that we're trying to make it into a science. But it's absolutely not a science. We're dealing with a very messy game. When we've got a contest for the ball there will invariably be a mistake and a penalty. This happens all the time because, unlike in football or basketball, you're trying to play the game in a constricted space which is made even more restrictive by the brutal physicality of rugby. So we are handing the game over to technology. Rather than relying on common sense, we're turning to the TMO and video technology incessantly. We should limit the use of the TMO to crucial decisions – which are tries. Let the referee decide on everything else.

But there is indifferent leadership in world rugby officiating at the moment. It means that our game is becoming like American Football. We had 80-minute games of rugby in the Lions series stretching across almost two hours. It's ridiculous. We need to give more power back to the referee and we need to help him.

For this reason we held back in our criticism of the officials after the Wales game. It was bloody embarrassing for them and I decided to keep quiet. If I had gone down the Rassie Erasmus route we would have got so much more leeway from referees in the next couple of games because they would have felt under extreme pressure. But that's not how I want the game to be run.

So we swallowed the 14 points that were taken from us early in the match, even though one try was highly dubious and the other was simply outrageous. I focused instead on the fact that we battled really well most of the game. We put in a lot of effort but, in the end, we looked mentally fatigued.

But here is the key point: a really great team would have still fought through those mistakes and won the Test. We were in a position to do exactly that with 20 minutes left on the clock. But we succumbed when it mattered most. We lacked discipline and we gave the game away.

It was difficult to take because whenever you get beaten by Wales you feel, as England coach, that you've let the country down. In the Six Nations the rivalry is intense. The Celtic countries love beating England, and England hate getting beaten by them. It's natural. But when you lose those sort of games you've got to front up. Accept that it's not good enough and look at ourselves as to how best we can improve. Don't blame the officials. Just make sure that, next time, you play so much better that the win is never in doubt.

The hardest thing for the players was dealing with the noise in the aftermath. They were bombarded with people telling them they're no good, that the team are no good. That's simply not true. They'd had two bad performances, but they are still good players and we're still a good team. So I had an important task to give them the positivity to think clearly despite the commotion. When you're under pressure, the neutrality of your conversation becomes even more exposed. Everything you talk about can be spun either positively or negatively.

But the margins between success and failure in international rugby are small. They're never as big as they're portrayed to be amid the outside noise. In the game against Wales the narrow difference would have disappeared had Maro not conceded five penalties.

After breakfast that Sunday morning we had a short meeting with the squad. Of course the mood was flat because, as Bobby Robson always said, after a game there is one happy dressing room and one sad dressing room. We ended up in the sad room. But I spoke about the tiny differences which had decided the game. I tried to explain that, in spite of the refereeing decisions, we should have still won. I also reminded them that, sometimes, you can play good rugby and still lose. Sometimes, you can play lousy rugby and win. But to win we had to stem the flow of penalties we were conceding. The penalty count was 14–9 and there were at least five avoidable penalties. So if the penalty count is 9–9 who wins the game? The team that plays the better rugby. The simplicity of the message is important.

We ended the meeting by showing them the brilliant Youngs try which had epitomized the quality of rugby we were striving to produce. We had been deep in our half but we won the ball back, through Jonny May, and then attacked fluently and scored the try. It was full of beautifully crisp movement and true to the vision of how we wanted to play the game when the opportunities emerge. We used the try to reinforce how good they are, and what a good team we remain, despite the external noise.

'Remember how good you really are,' I said. 'And that there's so much more to come.'

It was a positive note to end on and I hoped we had left the sad dressing room with renewed resolve. Nothing had been solved, but we felt better about ourselves in this transitional phase of the cycle.

Some valuable lessons had been handed down and it was a reminder that we had a unique challenge with England. It was different for Wales. When Wayne Pivac succeeded Warren Gatland as national coach after the 2019 World Cup, he set out to introduce a new vision and encourage Wales to play a much more expansive style of rugby. But Wales were exposed and Wayne suffered in his first year. Wales lost four out of their five games in the Six Nations and finished second bottom. They won only three Tests out of the ten they played in 2020. Wales is a rugby country and so there were calls for Wayne to be sacked.

Wayne knew he needed to win games to keep his job and, as a leader, he was under pressure to resort to a much more pragmatic brand of rugby. He was also reliant on a hardcore of older players; the only young Welsh guy coming through was Rees-Zammit. So Wales went back to the tried-and-tested methods. The thinking was clear, because if he lost too many more matches early on in 2021, he was in danger of being on a plane back to his native New Zealand.

The average age of their team that weekend was 29. Our average age was 26. A World Cup-winning side usually has an average age of around 29. So, by 2023, Wales may have to renew. They will be older, and potentially past their peak. We aim to peak at the World Cup.

Luck returned to the Welsh in the 2021 Six Nations. They came from behind both times to narrowly beat Ireland and Scotland, who had also each been reduced to 14 men. The officiating against England was hugely beneficial in another tight Test and, suddenly, after three matches which could have all ended in defeat, Wales were chasing the Grand Slam. It was a graphic illustration, yet again, of those desperately tight margins in international rugby. In their final game of the tournament, in Paris, they came so close to winning the Grand Slam – only for France to score a last-minute try that meant Wales lost 32–30.

Wales still ended as Six Nations champions – with our positions from the 2020 tournament having been reversed.

Can you imagine the reaction if England had played like Wales mostly did in 2021? We would have been criticized for the style of rugby, because it's not just enough for England to win – we need to win with style. I understand because people love the romance and entertainment of sport. They want their team to win but they also want to be swept away by the magic and spectacle, rather than just watch analytically correct rugby. In this era I accept the demand for entertainment alongside winning rugby. The Premier League and the NBA see their games as a product that has to be exciting. That's how they make so much money. Rugby is still a purer sport but, as the pressure increases to stay financially healthy, it's moving more towards entertainment.

We're searching for the right balance. We didn't find it in the Six Nations, but we will play some lovely rugby in the next year or so. But I know that by the time the World Cup begins in 2023, we will revert to more pragmatic rugby.

I accept our responsibility to play good rugby. But I also understand that if you want to win every game now, or maximize your chances of winning, you have to pay attention to your kicking game. All the cold hard analytical data tells us that, in 2021, kicking metrics were more significant than running metrics. But it's also our responsibility to do something different. It is vital to stay true to our vision of trying to build a team that can play some of the best rugby that has ever been seen.

We were under the cosh, having lost two out of our first three games of the tournament, and with France, the new darlings of rugby, heading our way next. But I felt calm. I felt optimistic.

As our relentless review continued, I knew we would do the following:

- Prioritize the key decisions

- Make the revisions

- Re-engage with the evolved strategy

The waves of noise rolled over me and I stuck to the core vision. This is the best way:

DON'T GIVE IN TO EMOTION . . .
MAINTAIN DISCIPLINE WITH YOUR PLAN

- Review the vision versus progress

- Take the key course-correcting decisions

- Make the revisions

- Re-engage with the evolved strategy

10

THE 3 PER CENT REMINDER

REMEMBER, IT'S NEVER AS GOOD OR AS BAD AS THEY SAY IT IS

The best advice I ever received in elite sport was given to me by a rugby league coach who had worked in the game for a very long time. 'Just remember this,' he said. 'When you win, it's never as good as they say it is. And when you lose, it's never as bad as they say it is.' I thought of those words often in the two weeks that separated our games against Wales in late February and France on 13 March 2021. I knew that the difference between being seen as 'a good team' and 'a terrible team' is usually around 3 per cent.

Even though we weren't great against Wales, we would have won if we had been just 3 per cent better. So the task was to change the team by 3 per cent. But if we made the wrong decision, and picked the wrong variable, we would be 6 per cent away. It would then start to get really difficult. While the margins between success and failure are small and agonizing, you need to think carefully before you make the changes that will close or widen the narrow gap that defines Test rugby.

The French had hammered Italy in Rome and then travelled to Dublin where they beat Ireland 15–13. It seemed as if everyone loved Fabien Galthié's promising young team, even though they had yet to be really tested in a sustained way. They were described as being 'thrilling' and 'exhilarating', but I still thought we would beat them if we played disciplined rugby.

I was intrigued to see how France did at home against Scotland, but that third-round fixture had to be postponed after Galthié, three of his staff and 12 of the playing squad contracted Covid. It was reported that the virus came into the French camp after Galthié left the bubble so that he could watch his son play rugby. Can you imagine the reaction in England if I had broken curfew, caught coronavirus, infected 14 other people and caused the cancellation of a Six Nations game at Twickenham against Scotland? It would not have been pretty.

The break between rounds three and four of the tournament gave the French time to recover and regroup. It offered us the same opportunity, and I relished the chance to face the adversity which had gripped our squad. I welcomed the challenge, rather than feared it, because you cannot become the best in the world unless you go through adversity. As a leader, whether in the military or business or sport or any other form of high-pressure activity, you almost need to seek out adversity because, one day, it will come gunning for you in a big way. If you can sharpen your adversity skills in times of low-level skirmishes, you will be hardened and strengthened. One day you will have to confront acute adversity and you need to be able to handle that situation.

I did not want to lose games in the Six Nations but, midway through two World Cup cycles, I knew that defeat to Scotland and Wales would at least offer me and my players the opportunity to deal with adversity and prepare for more difficult future periods of conflict. When adversity finds you, your eyes need to light up as you say: 'Right, here we go. Here is an opportunity to test myself as a leader.' That should be your response whether you're a coach, a captain or a player. It should be the same whether you're a chief executive or a middle manager, a head of department or a teacher.

Here's the question you want to answer: 'How good can I be now that things are going against us?' It's the ultimate challenge as you go out to prove yourself, and show your best attributes, just when everything seems hard and testing. How do you lift yourself and those who follow you when the odds seem against you? It's a defining test, and that's why I love these difficult moments as a head coach. Nothing is easy or handed to you. It's down to you and your skills, your character and your desire, to show how good you can be under intense pressure. I feel alive and ready to thrive in these situations.

If your response to adversity is different then you're in trouble. If you don't like the pressure or the scrutiny then you will be spat out of the system. You will be happier away from the stress, and able to enjoy a quieter and less draining life. It is no slight on you as a person because we can't all be expected to gain such perverse enjoyment from adversity. I accept it is a more logical reaction to want to step away from the heat and strife and live an easier life. But some of us have been born with this contrary trait, or lived complicated lives which have forged the fight inside us, and so we love the toughest tests.

There are generally three types of people in a larger group. You see this most clearly under extreme pressure. The first type tend to stay calm and focused. They say: 'Stay strong. We need to make a few changes but we're on the right track. The good results will come and we will get out of trouble.'

Most people are in the second sub-group and, under pressure, they feel uncertain. They are not sure why it's going wrong and whether or not it will come right again. They don't really know what to do or what will happen. They're looking to be led.

We then come to a third type. These are people who are looking to blame someone else. It's the fault of the head coach or the captain. It's the fault of his lazy teammates or the barracking fans or the hysterical media. This kind of person is always looking for an excuse or a way out.

I give this same speech in three slightly different ways. The staff come first, followed by the assistant coaches and then the players. I always ended up asking them one short question: 'So which group are you in?' You can almost hear their brains whirring and see their expressions changing, as no one wants to be in the third group of moaners. One of the coaches asked me afterwards: 'Where did you get that from?' I had read it before but, really, I learnt it from experience. I know how people operate under pressure. And it's the same when you win – the same three groups remain but you've just got more in the first set and fewer in the third.

Owen Farrell said to me the next day: 'I really understand what you're saying about those three groups. I can see them here.'

There was much more argy-bargy in the build-up to the France game than there had been prior to Scotland and Wales. Everyone was fighting for a spot in the team. They were also fed up after losing two games and determined to show the world that we were still a special team. There was a healthy sense of conflict. They all knew that the leadership group would soon break up. The Saracens players would no longer be as dominant as a unit and a power vacuum would emerge. Everyone could sense that and, as people strove to get out of the bottom group, there were some really good internal discussions, which I felt the squad had not had since the World Cup 18 months earlier.

Our lives consist of both success and failure. No person, and no team or organization, has constant success. We all fail. This is especially true in high-performance competition, where sometimes you come up against people and teams that will be a little bit better than you on a specific day. The skill, and the attitude you need, is to accept that defeat and failure will inevitably happen. You need to look at ways you can minimize being in this period of coming second but, sometimes, there will be external issues or circumstances that don't allow you to get out of a dip quickly. It's then that you really want the right characters around you. You want people with a good attitude while those with the opposite mindset need to be eased out.

It's the old teabag theory again. You don't know what your players and staff are really like until you put them under hot water. So that's why you actually welcome adversity and stress because that's when you learn most about people. When you move to the next challenge, it's going to be even hotter. The bigger the challenge, the hotter the water. You need people who can withstand the scalding temperatures.

Amid the heat and the glare of adversity, people's traits tend to be more obvious. So it actually helps you in terms of where you need to go. One of the worst things for us would have been if we had continued the same trend from the previous two years. We'd had a reasonably successful World Cup and a reasonably successful Six Nations in 2020. But we had not developed as quickly as we hoped and suffered from a lack of growth in the team.

We've also learnt a lot about the players – while having some of our already clear impressions reinforced. The most obvious example is Owen. He really stepped forward, as expected, in the face of adversity. Owen was in a difficult state at the start of the tournament. He lacked game time and he'd also caught Covid. He had a poor game against Scotland and so many problems with the referee in Cardiff. But he really applied himself and worked hard to get back to his best. He looks ready to take a massive step forward in an already stellar career. Tom Curry had been outstanding and driven again. Kyle Sinckler too. Remember how Sincks imploded against Wales a few years ago? He had matured and grown so much since then. The maturation of players like Sincks is key to the growth of the team.

On our return from Wales, Maro Itoje had more reason than anyone in the squad to feel dejected. Five penalties is a huge amount for one player to concede and, in the aftermath, Maro could have sulked or tried to hide. But he was so impressive in the way he reflected on his mistakes and in working out how he needed to rectify the errors in his game. He responded really well, and in training he was a beast. I knew that if he played as well as he trained, he would be hard for the French to handle.

We also helped him dig for the root cause of his problems against Wales. Ill-discipline almost always obscures other issues, and it's important to identify them. Maro was in only his second year as our lineout leader. The lineout is probably the most cognitively taxing part of the game, and George Kruis used to run it for us until the end of the World Cup. In 2020, with George playing rugby in Japan, Maro ran the lineout with Joe Launchbury assisting him. Launchbury's a good lieutenant, and he took a lot of pressure off Maro. But in 2021 he was out injured, and so Maro had to take this leadership role on by himself. He found it taxing. Most of all he missed the cognitive assistance that Launchbury always gave him. So, as the lineout struggled, he went to other parts of the game to try and make an impression. He chased a bit too hard and conceded penalties.

Maro has always played close to the edge because that's how good players operate. Richie McCaw always played at the edge. So did George Smith. Their ability to manage that themselves, while understanding the situation and the referee and their own emotions, is the great challenge. Some players learn it quickly and others take time to find the balance.

It is particularly hard for those kind of players in a leadership role. Owen is at his best when he's playing aggressive and belligerent rugby. But those characteristics certainly don't help you as a captain when you're trying to forge a positive relationship with a tricky referee.

At the end of the season, which culminated in him being chosen to lead the Lions in South Africa, Alun Wyn Jones had won 160 Test caps – 148 of them for Wales. No other player in the history of international rugby has won more caps than Jones. He is a master at separating the raw physicality of being a lock forward with the calm presence of a captain who encourages his players and talks cannily to the ref. Owen is still learning how leadership is all about acting appropriately in different situations.

It takes time to mature as a leader and understand the art of captaincy. If either Curry or Itoje were to become Test captains in the future, they would face a similar challenge to Farrell because, unlike Jones, they also play close to the edge.

In an effort to help Farrell, Itoje and the entire England squad, we asked Wayne Barnes, the referee, to join us in camp before we played France. He told us about the thinking of referees and it was a revelation. On the surface, referees are meant to be like policemen. We all know what happens if a policeman sees you go through a red light or overtake on a solid white line. You get pulled over and fined. A rugby referee is also there to ensure that the laws of the game are enforced.

But we learnt how officiating is changing in the modern game. Barnes explained that referees have their own game plan now. Just as we will study the opposition before a game, refs today will analyse our previous matches on tape and work out what they will need to manage once they blow the whistle. So they are not really approaching each game with a clean slate and on its own merits. They would mark Itoje's card even before they blow the first whistle. So they're looking for him to make the same illegality. It's been a self-fulfilling prophecy, and we didn't realize how far they'd gone down that track.

It made me understand that our players just have to accept that the referee is going to come to the game with some preconceptions. So there is no point getting agitated because it eats up so much emotional energy. We have to learn not to be distracted by the referee and to keep playing the game – legally, of course. The best way of managing the referee is to manage ourselves.

I am not blaming the officials because the game has become so much quicker and more contestable. They might have to officiate 180 rucks a game, with three or four players colliding at the same time with speed and aggression. They've got to make the right decisions and try to control the teams. It's a hell of a lot for them to cover, and everyone finds a way of surviving the jungle of Test rugby. So their way of surviving is to study past indiscretions.

The players absorbed this message in a short, sharp meeting. The best meetings are always the shortest meetings. This is when you're able to identify the problems quickly, and then come up with solutions. When the issues are more complicated and need detailed attention then, as staff, we break up into smaller groups and we go away and discuss them. Once we pool our ideas and decide on the best way forward, we make sure we can transmit this to the players in a 15-minute meeting. Most players, and most people, are at their most receptive and open to learning for a quarter of an hour. Our meetings before we played France were precise.

The modern player is much more involved in the planning before a big game. When I played, and in the early years of pro rugby, coaches tended to be very dictatorial. But today we avoid giving them lectures. We provide them with a framework in which to operate, but they have become far better than their predecessors at working it out for themselves.

In terms of planning for France, the players were 100 per cent involved in the detail of it. I would move from one group to another to ensure that they and the assistant coaches were on the right track. Without exception, the tight five, the back row, the inside backs and the outside backs were totally on it. Each unit was humming.

We got it right against France. There had been constructive and positive discussion and complete ownership of the game plan which we had set out in clear detail. Unlike the match against Scotland, I felt we sent the team out to battle with real dynamism. We were motivated, determined and uncluttered by the past.

It is the same in business. Nokia once produced the best phones, and dominated the market, but they sat back and enjoyed their success too much. Who owns a Nokia phone these days? Blackberry then seemed to have crushed their opposition. But they also sat back and, in their inertia, they ended up being decimated. Who owns a Blackberry now? They got complacent and failed to make the changes they needed to stay ahead of everyone else. Their fall was as complete as it was sudden.

You must keep growing in thought while reinforcing your core values.

I like to think we would have made the necessary changes even if the 2021 Six Nations had ended up with our retaining the title. But the adversity we endured encouraged real clarity. We could not ignore the need for transition any longer. I brought in 24-year-old Max Malins at full back in place of Elliot Daly. Luke Cowan-Dickie replaced Jamie George at hooker and Charlie Ewels came in for Jonny Hill at lock alongside Itoje. Timing is always crucial and it just felt like the right time for this trio of players. Introducing three new players in the starting XV meant we had changed 20 per cent of the team. It felt significant, even if Cowan-Dickie had been an integral member of the squad since I took over and had made a rare start against Italy the previous month. We might well change another three in the autumn and then, suddenly, 40 per cent of the team is new and it has a fresher look to it. Three changes here and three changes six months later might not look really radical, but we had begun a considerable shake-up as we took the team to the next level.

But we also maintained our disciplined belief in the overall plan, because we were only 3 per cent away from being seen as a very good side after being dismissed as a terrible team following those defeats to Scotland and Wales. So much comes down to perception when we consider views from outside the camp.

In the week before the French game, I had a chat on Zoom with other leaders in elite sport including David Moyes and Dave Brailsford. There were familiar themes when Brailsford spoke about public perceptions of his team in the Tour de France and other major events on the road. Brailsford said that, as Team Sky, they won nearly everything but no one liked them. They were seen as a voracious machine – hard-nosed, clinical, on the edge, relentless. Then, in March 2019, Sky pulled out and Brailsford's team was bought by Jim Ratcliffe, a Monaco-based British billionaire who had made his money in petrochemicals and established an industry giant called Ineos.

Ratcliffe had started to invest heavily in sport and, before he became so interested in Team Sky, he had poured over £100 million into Ben Ainslie's dream of winning the America's Cup. He has since become involved in football and Formula One – he bought the French Ligue 1 club Nice, and Ineos became a principal partner with Mercedes's F1 team and now own a third of their shareholding. They are involved with the All Blacks and Ratcliffe's sponsorship also helped Eliud Kipchoge become the first man to run the marathon in under two hours at the Ineos 1:59 Challenge event in October 2019.

Fracking is highly contentious, and Ratcliffe wanted to change the image of Ineos from a company loosely associated with that practice. His love of sport merged with a desire to become more popular, and so Ineos's sponsorship of Brailsford's team came with a clear instruction. Off their bikes, Team Ineos needed to become much more approachable and friendlier than Team Sky. A driven outfit, interested in little else apart from winning, suddenly had to smile more, dress better, appear friendly and try to engage the public. They needed to win while also becoming more likeable to help the Ineos brand.

England's rugby team have never been popular. I felt it in 2020 when we won both the Six Nations and the Autumn Nations Cup and the criticism seemed endless. The source of the condemnation stemmed from the perception we were boring and kicked everything in pursuit of victory. As explained earlier, all the data had told us before anyone else that a kicking game is a winning game in this era of rugby. Beyond public perception, I was more concerned that if you concentrate on one style of game, your rivals catch up fast. France have done this and now kick more than us. The perception on the outside is that they play wonderful rugby. But the cold, hard analytical data tells us that France kicked the ball more than England in 2021.

We need to add to our game and go to the next level because

the power of that kicking style is slowly evaporating. The laws are also changing again. So we are actively trying to create a more hybrid style of rugby. This will be good for us as a team, making us more adaptable, and it will also chime with the desire for us to be more entertaining and exciting. These aims should not be dismissed against the uncertain backdrop of a global pandemic. But it's bloody difficult because, at the moment, we're struggling to play this more dynamic, hybrid style of rugby. We will master it and we will become very good but it will take time to develop. It might not seem that way in terms of our performance in the first part of 2021, but we're on the right path with this transformative style of play.

We had no fear of the French as we approached another key game against them at home. They're full of promise, and their young players will get even better, but I have always believed that we can beat them. In the Autumn Nations Cup final in the autumn of 2020, we let France impose themselves on the game. They had a very young team at Twickenham that day and we were just off the pace in the first half. But we spoke to the players at half-time and then came out after the break with a clearer focus. We needed to win the territorial battle and, slowly, we did. It was tough but we came out on top.

In March 2021 it was on again. There was something in the air that week – and it was the distinctive scent of the English boys firing themselves up for battle. When the heat is on the England team, we see the best of our players. We have a little tendency to drift when the stakes are less high. Backed up against a wall, we'll give you a bit more. When we're playing France, and we've been embarrassed by Scotland and Wales, you know we are going to reach deep within ourselves. My aim, as head coach, is to find that every week, but we are dealing with young men who are not robots. They're human, after all, and so consistency still eludes them. Our goal is to be more consistent in our mindset.

We made a big leap forward, however, against France this time. The previous autumn, in the corresponding fixture against

France, our average running speed was 102 metres per minute. In the 2021 Six Nations it rose to 120 metres per minute against France. That 20 per cent increase was a clear sign of our raised intensity and commitment – and the changing nature of rugby.

We played our best rugby since beating New Zealand in the World Cup, and we did it with the hybrid game we've been trying to build for a while. It was not circumstantial. Instead it was planned and precise; this is the way we can beat France, as they play the same style of rugby. They play it with real panache and, after just 80 seconds, we conceded a try that was full of French swagger. Virimi Vakatawa and Gaël Fickou punched a hole in the middle of our defence, and Teddy Thomas's chip with the outside of his right boot was snaffled and bundled over the line by their brilliant young scrum-half, Antoine Dupont.

But all the great work we had done in the week, in terms of strengthening our confidence and intent, meant that we refused to shrink. We came back hard at France and put them under real pressure immediately. We mixed up our game, kicking to contest the ball and then spinning it from one player after another. Henry Slade, Jonny May and Anthony Watson all looked sharp, and Tom Curry and Mark Wilson came close to scoring, only to be held up just short of the line. Malins had a real opportunity to send Watson over in the corner but, on his starting debut, his pass was wayward and it flew straight into touch.

Slade found a gap, bursting through while resisting the clutches of the defenders in blue. After the forwards drove for the line, George Ford spotted the overlap and sent a long, looping pass safely into the arms of Watson, who scored a lovely try on his 50th Test appearance. The score was 7–7 after ten minutes and a special Test was underway.

We maintained our discipline and France conceded the first penalty five minutes later. Farrell's penalty put us ahead and he extended the lead with another three points to make the score 13–7 after 20 minutes; we were forcing France into errors at the breakdown. We were finally penalized for an infringement four minutes later. England had been on the front foot for most of the match, but France were resilient and then, just before the half-hour mark, Matthieu Jalibert narrowed our lead to just three points after he converted a penalty.

Two minutes later, France were ahead after scoring a sublime second try. Their hooker Julien Marchand took a long throw from the lineout which found Fickou with precision. The centre used Thomas as a decoy runner on the inside while he slipped the ball to Dupont who came looping around on the outside. Dupont fed Jalibert and, as our defence scrambled to get into position, his long pass freed Damian Penaud on the right wing to finish off the textbook move. Jalibert's conversion meant we were 17–13 adrift at the break.

Another Jalibert penalty after 49 minutes followed Itoje's first infringement of the game at a ruck. We were seven points down but our nerve held. Farrell punished French ill-discipline at a lineout soon afterwards and, with the score 20–16, we knew we could still win the Test. It was desperately tight and, while the game lost its free-flowing audacity, the closeness of the contest provided compelling drama. The French were resolute in defence but, with four minutes left on the clock, Itoje picked up the ball from a ruck and powered his way over the line with Cameron Woki and Teddy Thomas clinging to him.

The referee Andrew Brace initially ruled that the French pair had prevented Itoje from grounding the ball cleanly. But he and Joy Neville, the TMO, pored over the footage again, amid excruciating tension, before deciding it was a legitimate try. Farrell kicked the conversion and we won 23–20, with Itoje transformed from sinner to hero after a thrilling encounter.

It had been an immensely satisfying win because we made sure the 3 per cent difference went in our favour after playing a hybrid game with courage and conviction. Watson, Slade, Farrell, Sinckler, Itoje and Curry had all been outstanding, playing their best rugby since the World Cup, and our hybrid style took a big step forward.

'We always want to play like that,' I said after the game, 'and we're only disappointed that we didn't have 82,000 fans in here with us today. They would have got more than their money's worth and the RFU would have been happy. There's such competition for attention at the moment, so nearly every sport is moving towards being more entertaining and the laws are encouraging teams to play in a more entertaining way. We've always had in mind that we would keep developing our ability to attack with the ball in hand, passing and running, but still have our attritional set-piece game to fall back on. We're trying to get that balance right because the team's going through a transition. We've got to keep at it because we have a plan in place of where we want to be by the World Cup. Today was a first step but we can play much better.'

There had been a huge improvement, but I could not savour the victory for long because I knew what was coming next. Ireland would be very different and more difficult in our final game of the tournament in Dublin. I knew they would play a hard, niggly sort of game which meant we would not have the freedom to run and open up as we had done against France.

The media had flipped totally in the opposite direction. After telling us how bad we were against Scotland and Ireland, we were being hailed as a brilliant new England after winning such a good game of rugby. We were depicted as a wonderful team again that Saturday evening in south-west London, but seven days later the Irish would come at us with real ferocity. So while I told the players that they had done well, I stressed that they should avoid reading all the nice words coming our way. Something far harder was on the horizon.

A few days later I told the press that they were feeding 'rat poison' to my players. I pointed out that things start to go wrong when you 'listen to the poison that's written in the media, and that rat poison gets into players' heads. We try to spray all that rat poison that you try to put in . . . so we are always working hard to keep it out of their heads. It keeps me busy, mate.'

It was a comment that would not have raised any eyebrows in Australia, but it caused a storm in the English media. My quip about rat poison, however, carried a serious point. In praising my team excessively for the way we had played against France there was a real danger that the players would be seduced into thinking that they could do the same against Ireland. I heard that many of the articles and much of the punditry after the France game had posed a basic question: 'Why can't England play like that every week?' The answer was simple. No team is the same and all the good sides are set up to make your life difficult. Some games you just don't have the armoury to play that running and passing style we all love. The idea that Ireland would step back and allow us to play the kind of game which had beaten France was a poisonous thought that would weaken us in Dublin.

We trained hard in the week but some of the players struggled to raise themselves again. There didn't seem enough motivation playing for third place, and I felt that a few of them didn't give their absolute 100 per cent best.

Ireland were ready for us and we lacked the hunger and intensity of the previous Saturday. We also had few of the opportunities we had enjoyed against France where the ball was in play for about 35 minutes. Against Ireland it was in play for only 28 minutes. That's a 30 per cent difference, which is huge. So you can't play with freedom against Ireland. It's like when Premier League teams used to go to Stoke City. You know what they used to say about how hard it was going to Stoke on a wet Tuesday night. It felt like that in Dublin against Ireland. They kicked well and didn't allow the game to break open. Against a team like that you've got to be tough. You've got to be grinding. You have to stay in the fight. We weren't prepared to do that and we suffered.

The game was actually closer than the 32–18 scoreline suggested, but Ireland were unrelenting in their physicality and Conor Murray and Johnny Sexton dominated. This is part of sport because different teams play in different ways. The ability to stay calm, and stay strong, and play the game in versatile ways is so important. We had not been great against France, even though we were praised to the skies, and we were not terrible against Ireland. But it was telling that we were 3 per cent off the mark in a brutal match and we got punished. Parts of our game were just not right.

There were little things I saw in Dublin that will have an impact on selection. Some players were slow to get off the ground. They were lethargic moving back into position. They were not hitting as hard in the tackle as they should. These are small differences but, to the trained eye, that 3 per cent dip told me all I needed to know. We will need to refresh ourselves and rekindle that desire to fight harder for longer.

When you're not going in the right direction, you've got to look for change. People, above all else, change things. The plan was in place, but we needed players and coaches with deeper hunger and determination.

So the fight was back on to get better. I have always enjoyed the fight. Maybe that's down to my background in working-class Sydney, being the product of a mixed-marriage, and learning how to show plenty of grit to prove myself. But, as I've got older, I've learnt how to keep more of an emotional even keel. Years ago, if someone said derogatory words about me or my team, I'd be angry about it. Now, for the most part, I can let it go.

It had been a bruising tournament for England and, after it was over, someone asked me if it made me doubt my decision to stay on in the job. I answered with an emphatic 'No'. This is all part of the job. I want to be tested and challenged and, despite the adversity, I relished the struggle ahead.

A few days later I read a couple of lines in a book which really resonated. The book is about performing under pressure and the author spoke about the need to develop COTE – which stands for Confidence, Optimism, Tenacity and Enthusiasm*. It seemed a striking summary of how you need to be in a high-pressure

---

* From *How to Perform Under Pressure*, by Hendrie Weisinger and J. P. Pawliw-Fry.

situation. Even though you're not always confident before a big game, because you never know how your team is going to perform, you've got to portray confidence. You've got to be optimistic because, otherwise, your team will lose their nerve. You've also got to be tenacious because nothing comes easy in life or, especially, in elite sport. Finally you've got to be enthusiastic, because you need that energy and conviction and it's contagious. Enthusiasm breeds enthusiasm.

If you can produce COTE, you've always got the chance to turn things around.

I felt that sense of COTE surging through me just as much after we lost to Ireland in an abrasive battle as when, a week earlier, we had beaten France in an exhilarating game. It had been a problematic Six Nations, full of the adversity which imparts hard-won lessons. In a strange way I felt more optimistic about my team than I had done the previous autumn when we won the second of our trophies in 2020.

The cycle continued to turn. My leadership would adapt to the next stage of our development. As we searched for the next 3 per cent difference in performance, we would refresh, while keeping a key message uppermost in our thinking:

REMEMBER, IT'S NEVER AS GOOD OR AS BAD AS THEY SAY IT IS

- Assess transformation delivery versus goals in value terms

- Embed the changes made

- Remember the difference between being seen as 'a good team' and 'a terrible team' is usually around 3 per cent

- Answer the question: 'How good can I be now that things are going against us?'

- Identify which group individuals fall into: 1. calm and focused, 2. uncertain under pressure, or 3. looking to blame others. Remember the teabag test: you don't know what your players and staff are really like until you put them under hot water

- Develop COTE: Confidence, Optimism, Tenacity and Enthusiasm

11

OTHER VOICES

TALK TO OTHERS, ALWAYS REMAIN OPEN TO LEARNING

Leadership can be a very lonely business. It is solitary by nature because, when it matters most, you alone have to step forward and make the decisions which will help define success or failure. You pick a particular person to do a job for you, and if that choice doesn't work out you take the heat for making a mistake. The raised temperature replaces the icy edge that has often already emerged because anyone you have excluded feels hurt and wounded by your decision. They don't like you much. Neither do the experts looking in from the outside, people who are paid to express an opinion, because it is their job to pass judgement on you. You are there to be scrutinized and, with so much attention on you, that can feel isolating.

In the middle of a vast crowd, you are set apart. England's rugby matches are watched by millions of people; and at the end of a game you have to front up and answer questions as to what went right or wrong. You also have to stand up in front of your squad, who are elated or dejected, and find the appropriate words to ensure they stay clear-thinking despite the excessive emotion swirling around the dressing room. Occasionally, in victory, you can let go and share in the utter jubilation of a job well done. However, most of the time you are detached from everyone else so you can offer a more measured view. You have to stand alone to do this effectively.

When all the noise and clamour die away and you finally reach your room in the team hotel, the loneliness can really kick in. Players go over their own games in their heads at night, feeling regret or satisfaction, but they will concentrate on themselves. The head coach, or manager, has to think about every single player, as well as the overall position of the squad. He or she alone has the ultimate responsibility for making sure that improvement will follow. There is a weight of duty and expectation in the role that can deepen a sense of loneliness.

It has worked out differently for me. I actually enjoy the solitude of the job. I relish the fierce pressure of responsibility. I appreciate standing apart. I often feel alone, but I don't see that as a hardship. I don't even feel 'lonely', in the usual meaning of the word, because I chose to do this job. I came into the role with a complete awareness of all it entailed. I *want* that burden of duty and that sense of responsibility. If you make the choice to become a leader, then you have to accept the lonely and demanding nature of the role.

I talk to many young coaches and I always say that, before they get immersed in the complexity of coaching, they have to look to their family first. They've got to find a way to look after those they love the most that also allows them to do their job properly. You've got to prepare and plan and ensure that they are going to be all right while you're wrapped up in your work. Everyone in the family needs to be considered and given time to absorb how your work will affect them. You have to be honest and explain everything, while taking steps to ensure that everyone has the support they need when you are not with them.

Coaching, or leading a big company, is totally consuming. For many people the goal is to achieve a nice balance between life and work, but there is no balance if you're leading a high-performance organization. Your work becomes your life because you've got to be obsessive about it. It's more than all right if you don't want that. There are plenty of much nicer and more relaxed jobs out there where you don't have to be obsessive. Take one of those and get out of elite sport or big business. You will be much happier.

I'm not a good person to talk about this tricky work–life balance because I've often put a job ahead of my family. But I have got better about making sure that I give my family the attention they deserve when I am with them, and by ensuring they understand what I'm trying to do. If you're successful as a leader, there will be benefits further down the track for the family. But sometimes they come too late, when marriages have already broken down and the family unit has splintered.

I have been fortunate that Hiroko and Chelsea have been so understanding and patient. Chelsea is now an adult, with her own successful life in Australia, and Hiroko gets to spend more time with me when we take breaks in Japan or are based in England. After all these years she knows me inside out and we work well together. But I remind the young coaches that they need a very special partner to do the job in the way it should be done.

I am also lucky as my resilience and capacity to deal with the isolating pressures of coaching stem from my parents. We are all shaped by our mothers and fathers. They're the key influences for most of us – in either a negative or positive way. My father was a quiet man who only spoke out when it was important. He was very precise in his communication and always so level-headed. Dad was a typical Aussie but, because he came from a solid working-class background, and had been through the ordeal of World War II, there was often a seriousness to him.

My mother, Nell, was born to Japanese parents but she grew up with them in America. They suffered as a family after Pearl Harbor, when US citizens who were Japanese were treated as enemies. Nell and her mother were interned in a detention centre in California while, even more painfully, they were separated from her father. My grandfather was interned in a brutal camp in Arkansas, and they were only finally reunited years later. It was little wonder that he wanted to get out of America and resume life in Japan after that.

While my mother has always been hot-headed and even temperamental, expressing her emotions freely, she also has a great gift, even now in her nineties, to live her life without dwelling on negative issues. She endured so much discrimination in her past. There was terrible prejudice against the Japanese in America during the war, and she then experienced the opposite backlash on the family's return to Japan, when she was perceived to be an American. My parents met and fell in love with each other in Japan, where my dad was part of the occupation forces after the war, and there would be more discrimination when they moved to Australia to start a new life. My mother was abused and mocked; anti-Japanese sentiment was then as bitter as it was rife in Australia.

But my mother never harboured resentment or anger. To this day she never does. She always went out of her way to make sure she lived in the present, so that she could look after my sisters and me and make sure that we felt like Australians rather than damaged outsiders. There was something selfless and admirable in the way she set aside all her legitimate grievances and allowed us to grow up free of such troubling baggage.

I try and avoid her more volatile moments, but my mother set some really good principles for me that I still follow every day. I also always try to be as good a person as my father – and I never think I am. But I carry their work ethic, their determination and their stoicism within me. So I was very fortunate to be their son, because obviously you don't get to choose your parents. It boils down to fate, but having a solid family base and good parents helps so much when it comes to dealing with the challenges of leadership.

As you set out in a leadership role, look to others whom you respect for some early guidance. If you find the right mentors, or examples of leaders you admire, you will have a template to follow before you establish your own leadership style and philosophy.

As a player for Randwick in Sydney, I had two coaches who shaped me as a future leader. Bob Dwyer was tough, analytical, driven and ambitious. Jeff Sayle was the exact opposite. He just loved life, loved the team, loved looking after the boys. Everything he did was for the players, and he tried to ensure they made the most of life, and rugby, before, during and after matches. I've always tried to incorporate the lessons I learnt from both of them into my coaching.

Bob also gave me my biggest disappointment as a player when, as Australia's head coach, he chose not to pick me for the Wallabies. Instead he selected Phil Kearns who, at that early stage of his career, was only the reserve hooker at Randwick. It was tough for me but totally the right decision. Phil became a great Test player.

I was too small, and just not talented enough, to make it at Test level. It took me a while to accept it, but it ended up being one of my best and most formative experiences. I learnt another great lesson years later when I lost the Wallaby job in 2005. Again, I had to take responsibility for the harsh truth that I wasn't a good enough coach. I had to keep improving. Those lessons are still applicable to my work today – as is a third experience which taught me so much. I was a total outsider, and alone, when coaching Japan, but I saw it as a free hit. There was so much scope for me to start with a clean slate and be hugely experimental, innovative and courageous. It was lonely at times, but it gave me such an opportunity to show the world what Japan could do.

In lockdown we all felt more isolated and so I turned to discussions with other leaders, in different worlds to mine, to learn and improve. I spoke to Dave Brailsford, Gareth Southgate, David Moyes, Ron Adams, and others in Australian and Japanese sport. Our discussions were productive and helpful.

There is such freedom in these interactions. If you can speak freely, you will think more deeply. I can be honest with my fellow leaders in a way that I can't be on a day-to-day basis in my job. If I show vulnerability to the CEO of the RFU he will be thinking: 'Is he still the right bloke for the job?' You can't look vulnerable to your assistant coaches or the players. Any doubt or vulnerability could dent your ability to lead them. In contrast, open but private conversations with other coaches is liberating. It allows you to feel their empathy, and to show the same to them. Unless you have been in a position of real leadership in a high-performance programme, you can't understand the lonely demands of the role. They do.

One Monday night, early on in the 2021 Six Nations, I spent two hours – as I've mentioned – on an inspiring Zoom call with Ron Adams, the defence coach of the Golden State Warriors in the NBA, whose candour and insights are refreshing. Chance played its part in helping me talk to Ron. He went to the same college, Fresno, as an American coaching mate of mine. My friend knew Ron and I would hit it off and so he initiated the call.

We got off to a good start because he's from the same area in California, near Sacramento, where my mother was brought up on her dad's orange orchard. Ron also came from a farming family, and so he knew the little city, Lodi, where my mother was born. So we had that instant connection. He's a very socially conscious guy; he knew how badly the Japanese, including US citizens like my mother and her parents, had been treated inside America. We spoke a little about that and moved onto the Black Lives Matter movement and the impact the NBA has had in combating racism. Ron's head coach at Golden State, Steve Kerr, is one of the most informed and politically outspoken voices in the NBA. This led to our shared reflections on the subtleties of coaching young sportsmen.

Ron has been coaching for 52 years so he's seen it all. So much of what he said echoed my own experience. He explained how he had moved from being an authoritarian tell-them-all coach. Back then, in that environment, it was the right way to coach.

But players and society are different now. Ron and I discussed how we have both evolved and become much more connected in guiding players. At the right time you still direct them, but it is much more open-ended and you encourage them to take the lead. There is no less commitment, or seriousness, in your work, but Ron agreed that we probably offer more entertainment in our coaching environment than previously. Young players today need to be engaged and refreshed much more often. They are no longer content just to do the same old routine over and over again. It was striking how similar the NBA and rugby coaching sounded.

He is an intellectual coach who loves the art and strategy of our profession. As always, I find that the guys who love coaching are willing to share ideas much more readily than those who just see it as a job. We work in different fields, but I am primarily interested in how he manages his environment and connects with his players. We're just looking for different ways to present the same message.

Ron explained that he'd had a crack at being a head coach at Fresno University. He had mixed success, but he's a craftsman whose specialty is defence. He is also really good at forging a bond with players. Ron loves being an assistant coach and going to teams where he can help the head coach be successful. He told me a great story about the time when Steve Kerr was playing with Michael Jordan under Phil Jackson's coaching at the Bulls. Jackson relied on Tex Winter, a great old assistant coach, the tactical guy who honed their strategy. Tex arrived at the Bulls in 1985, a few years before Jackson joined the Bulls as an assistant, and he was already in his early sixties. When Jackson became head coach in 1989, he let Tex drive the strategy as he put together the attack system that would allow Jordan to be at his best. Tex was a key part of the Bulls dynasty, as they won six NBA championships. He then joined Jackson at the LA Lakers in 1999, and worked there as his assistant coach until 2004, finally retiring at the age of 82.

Kerr had seen how an older assistant coach could make a vital contribution. He was 48 when he was offered the role of head coach at Golden State Warriors in 2014 but, despite his fine playing career, he had never coached before. He was in a lonely and vulnerable position, and so among the first things Kerr did after he got one of the biggest jobs in basketball was to seek out Ron Adams – who was one of the most experienced assistant coaches in the NBA, and working then for Boston Celtics.

Kerr took Ron to a lovely restaurant in California. He ordered a very nice bottle of Pinot Noir and, when the waiter came out, Kerr asked Ron to taste it. So the waiter poured a thimble of wine and Ron tasted it. After a few moments he shook his head and said: 'No, that's slightly corked. Take it back.' Kerr said later he knew he had found the right assistant coach because he needed someone who would always tell him the truth. And Ron is, above all else, a truth-teller. He and Kerr steered Golden State to three NBA championships between 2015 and 2018.

It was also useful to me to talk to Ron about managing up. I still find it one of the most difficult parts of the job – having to liaise and deal with the corporate head of the organization which employs me. But I have got significantly better at it, and I really do understand now that it works to everyone's benefit if I keep Bill Sweeney, the CEO of the RFU, informed about our strategy and how we operate and manage it. It helps Bill stay fully in the picture and I am glad I finally learnt the value of this lesson.

When I was a young coach I would almost think it an injustice if the board above me wanted to know what I was doing. My attitude would be: 'Let me get on with it and do my job. I'm the coach.' I now understand that you've got to keep them informed. So I'll give Bill as much information as I can so nothing should surprise him. Bill has to trust me because, if you've never coached in elite sport before, how can you tell a head coach he's wrong? It would be the height of arrogance. It would be like going to the doctor and, after hearing his diagnosis, saying: 'You've got it wrong, mate. You might've studied six years at university, and practise medicine every day, but I know better than you.'

Of course, whether we're doctors or coaches, we all make mistakes. But you need people who have been educated in your field, and who have first-hand experience, to tell you that you've got it wrong. Most board members have not coached in any capacity.

That lack of knowledge gave rise to a saying that, in managing up, sometimes you have got to eat a lot of shit. Sometimes you've even got to pick the shit out of your teeth. That harsh little joke sums up my previous attitude to managing up. But it was a very limited view, and I'm glad to say I've now got a much more rounded and deeper understanding.

When I coached Saracens between 2007 and 2009, I attended a weekly meeting with the owner Nigel Wray. I would give him a summary of where we were and what we needed to do. It's different now with the RFU. They are a much more corporate organization, so they tend to communicate through board meetings. But I pass on all our team meeting notes to Bill so that he understands what we're trying to do.

I don't think I'm very good at managing up. I can be so consumed by the actual coaching that there are times when I think, 'Why should I do this?' But I know that the CEO and boardroom should be kept updated on a regular basis. Having this open dialogue is beneficial.

I had no complaints about the way I was being treated by the RFU and so, when Ron and I discussed how best we manage up, there was no whinging from me. I was just curious to learn how he and Steve Kerr dealt with the owner and the boardroom at Golden State. Ron was fascinating again. He explained how it is now much more difficult to manage up in the NBA. When he first started coaching in the NBA, almost 30 years ago in 1992, he and his head coach dealt with millionaire owners. Now they're billionaires.

Professional sport is driven by data analytics – and billionaires understand this tool. Many of them probably used data analytics to turn their millions into billions. So now that the owners and the boardroom members can study the data analytics of basketball, they think they know how to win. Data analytics makes clear what wins games, and that is a useful tool, but it becomes harder to manage the owners and the board. You have to spend time helping them understand that creating a winning team is a combination of data and coaching intuition.

So it was instructive to hear that even a coach as venerable as Ron Adams is having to adapt as he strives to manage up more effectively. He didn't hand down any pearls of wisdom to help me in liaising with the RFU, but there was an empathy and an understanding which meant I didn't feel lonely when the heat was at its most intense after the Six Nations. I could stay calm and relaxed while speculation swirled around me for a few weeks after the tournament. I can honestly say that I did not worry about the outcome.

I had a one-to-one review with Bill Sweeney and, as I had kept him up to date throughout the build-up and during the Six Nations itself, he was fully up to speed. I simply reiterated the challenges we had faced, the mistakes we had made, most of which were mine, and why I was convinced that we would emerge a much stronger squad after the disappointing results.

When the review was completed, Bill was supportive of me and the decision that I would remain in charge. In his statement he said: 'We were all disappointed to finish fifth in the Six Nations. Our track record and results under Eddie meant that we, the players and our fans had much higher expectations. Sport is all about fine margins, which is why every campaign debrief is invaluable in helping us to learn and improve. Eddie approached this review with a great deal of self-awareness and humility, allowing us to look at every aspect of the tournament to identify every small change we can make in order to improve.'

He pointed to some of the factors which had derailed us – including the lack of game time for many of our leading players, as well as the absence of so many coaches and backroom staff at key moments. Bill also acknowledged our indiscipline at the breakdown, but also the Covid restrictions that had prevented us from bringing new players into the bubble.

I held a media call soon after the review was announced and I was asked if I minded that a small group of RFU-appointed experts would now monitor my work. 'There's only one head coach, mate,' I said. 'At the end of the day, whether the team wins or loses, the responsibility is mine. I use a series of experts in and outside the game to come up with the best coaching environment. I welcome any good advice, any wisdom I can get. The only thing I know is that I took part in the review and I thought it was a good review. I didn't write the report. It is the RFU's. I'm the head coach. The head coach makes the decision.'

There had been more criticism of my coaching at Suntory and Sir Clive Woodward had another pop at me. He said that, with Japan being in our World Cup group in 2023, my consultancy role made 'English rugby look ridiculous'. I reckoned Ron Adams had more taxing challenges dealing with the billionaire owners of the NBA, so I responded calmly. 'I go round clubs continually to pick people's brains and obviously you share some information with them. I'm a coach, so I've also got to practise coaching. If you're a golfer you play golf, if you're a coach you coach, and I only get 12 weeks of the year to coach England so I've got to use my time in between to practise coaching and find better ways to coach.'

The criticism didn't make me feel lonely because I had other coaches to turn to with whom I could discuss our work. A couple of years ago I was invited to join a leaders' group, and that was another experience I valued. The group normally has a get-away, meeting up somewhere quiet to share ideas and experiences. In 2021, because of Covid, we had to do it via Zoom, but it was still enormously useful. These are outstanding leaders – the likes of Southgate, Brailsford and Moyes. Two hours with them threw up many new lessons for me. Southgate is such an intelligent and thoughtful man, while Brailsford is so super-sharp it's frightening. Moyes was really good too. He has a great sense of humour and so much humility. He spoke about the way he's had to change as a manager, and it was stimulating to listen to him open up midway through a season where he was doing excellent work with West Ham.

These discussions engender fresh ideas as to how you manage your environment, and sometimes they reinforce what you're already doing. That can be useful when there is a lot of pressure and outside noise. So I would urge all leaders, no matter how big or small their job, to talk to people in similar positions in other fields of work. It makes leadership far less isolating.

The conversations with others also worked well in the Operation phase of the Experiment stage of the leadership cycle. They helped me concentrate on the need to:

- Review and improve

- Re-plan, re-execute and then move at pace

Arsène Wenger is usually part of the group, but he was not available on this last occasion. He is immensely impressive. I had been a Wenger fan for so long that, the first time I met him, I was thrilled to have the chance to go and see him at Arsenal's training ground in London Colney. I watched him at training and we spoke afterwards, but he was by then carrying the weight and loneliness of 20 years in the job.

He was honest in admitting how much he missed David Dein who, as vice-chairman of the Arsenal board, had brought him to the club in September 1996. Dein was his confidant and biggest supporter at the club, who also took on the weight of boardroom decisions, and both Arsenal and Wenger missed him terribly when he fell out with the club and left in April 2007. Arsène mentioned him four or five times in our conversation and the implication was that, without Dein, he took on too much and almost had too much power. He had to take charge of every aspect of the club, rather than just the first-team squad.

When we met again a few years later, he was totally rejuvenated and inspirational. I asked him to come and speak to my squad in 2018. We were a year out from the World Cup and, as in early 2021, a bit out of kilter. I just felt the players needed to hear a different voice and so I invited Arsène to join us. He came in very elegantly dressed, wearing a crisp blue suit, white seersucker shirt and smart shoes. Arsène sat in the front of the room in a lounge chair, crossed his legs, and I was not sure how our 45 players would respond to him. They had been training hard that day and it was a hot August night. Arsène speaks quite softly and when he started I was thinking: 'I'm not quite sure how this is going to go.'

He was magnificent. For 45 minutes he captivated the room with the clarity and intelligence of his thinking. He is also such a warm and engaging man that the players were swept away – just as they had been when Sir Alex Ferguson spoke to them before the World Cup the following year. I've since met Arsène on numerous occasions. I always wonder if I really deserve to be sitting at the same table as him because his intellect is way above mine. Every time I come away feeling re-energized and full of new ideas after an immersive experience in his company.

Louis van Gaal, the former manager of Ajax, Barcelona, Manchester United and the Netherlands, is another favourite when it comes to meeting top coaches from other fields. He was brilliant company and has a really good appreciation of the strategic aspects of coaching a team as well as the psychology of leading players. I am drawn to so many top European football coaches because, working in such a competitive environment, they operate at an incredibly high level. Look at how many great coaches there are in Holland, Germany, Spain, Italy and Portugal. Only the best rise to the very top.

When you meet such coaches, you realize that the environment in which they work creates a desire for them to be the best coach they can be, and to improve constantly.

My own desire to learn from – and engage with – other coaches in different sports has always burnt brightly. In 1998, during my first year of coaching at the Brumbies, I went and saw Wayne Bennett. Ten years into a famous 30-year tenure at the Brisbane Broncos, the great rugby league club, Wayne was already the guru of coaches in Australia. He is ten years older than me, and when I met him the gulf between our levels of experience and success was vast. We got together in the Broncos gym and he said: 'I'm going to tell you a few things today, son. You might remember them in the years ahead.'

He started doing weights. So I'm following him around doing weights as well. Wayne's a tall, skinny guy, but he is strong and he trains hard. He was bench-pressing big weights and he said: 'Always remember what the mother and father couldn't change, you can't change either.' He was talking about the character of a player and it rang true. But, all these years later and having learnt so much, I also think you can change their behaviour for a period of time. I've had success with players who are difficult to manage, and I have been able to change their behaviour for periods of time. Now, that's not to say you can make those changes permanent, but you can definitely get something out of players for a spell – even a sustained one – before they fall back into bad habits. So much depends on the right environment.

In *The Last Dance* we saw how Dennis Rodman, the epitome of a problematic player, thrived for the Chicago Bulls. Phil Jackson, as head coach, had to make allowances for him, as when Rodman disappeared to Las Vegas during a crucial part of the post-season, but he found a way to get the most out of him when it mattered. But the environment was everything. If Michael Jordan and Scottie Pippin had not been there, would Rodman have found the discipline he unearthed that season to become a valuable resource for the team?

I remember a question Wayne Bennett asked me that day: 'Can

you coach decision-making?' I was still very green as a coach and I jumped straight in: 'Yeah, I can.' Bennett looked at me quizzically before he replied: 'Well, I've been coaching 22 years, mate, and I've got no idea. So I don't know how you have.'

Although he is right in some ways, I have also learnt that there are ways of having a positive impact in the area of decision-making. Neil Craig and I had a recent Zoom session with some of our coaching mates in Australia. Craigy is big on having lots of one-on-ones with players, as I am too, and one of the Australian coaches said: 'Well, I don't, mate. But they know that I care about them. I also get the right staff in to give them that one-to-one communication, but I don't do it myself.'

It showed again that there's no right or wrong way to get things done. But you've got to care about the players. You need to show them that care if you want to improve them. I normally avoid using a word like 'authentic' because it seems a cheap buzzword. But the word was used a few times in our coaches' discussions and, in this context, it rang true. Players always smell bullshit. They might be young but they always sniff it out if you're trying to con them. You have to be yourself when you show them that you care. You also need to understand people. Only then will you be effective in helping them become better decision-makers.

A good example for me would be Andrew Walker, an Indigenous Australian who played international rugby in both union and league. When I finished my last year of playing at Randwick, I was 31. Andrew was 17. I was the second team captain then. I used to pick him up and drive him to the game. He'd bring along his girlfriend and their baby. Andrew had become a father at 16. He was an unbelievable rugby player and reminded me of my great old mates Mark and Glen Ella – but he was even faster and stronger than they had been. He just had this fatal flaw. Andrew was always in trouble, always late. He ended up leaving rugby union at 18 and going to league. Back then, such a move was seen as the mark of a traitor. But he was absolutely brilliant in league too and, a few years later, in 1996, he was good enough to be picked for the Kangaroos.

The only problem was that he'd played the last game of the club season and had disappeared. Imagine that? This young bloke is picked for his country and they can't find him. Phil Gould, his coach at the South Sydney Roosters, is a famous commentator now. Phil looked all over for Andrew and he couldn't find him anywhere in Sydney. Finally, he tracked him down to the south coast. There's a big park in the middle of this little town and Andrew was right there, drinking beer with his mates.

'Hey Phil', a bloke in their drinking crowd said, 'do you want Andrew?'

'I sure do', Phil said. He's just about to tell him the big news when the other bloke says: 'Well, you can't have him. He's doing business with us. So the only way you can have him is if you sit down and have a drink with us.'

So Phil sat down with them. He ended up having to drink with them for three hours before Andrew was ready to go. Phil got him back to Sydney to play for the Kangaroos on the weekend. He knew he had to adapt to Andrew to make it work.

I recruited Andrew from the Roosters to the Brumbies soon after that. I knew how brilliant he was as a player – if wayward as a person. Phil's story didn't scare me off. But, once he was with us, our manager at the Brumbies would have to ring Andrew ten times a day to find out where he was and when he would get to training. He lived on a farm outside Canberra and he was a handful. He'd come to training without any gear. His family had moved into his house and they had taken all his kit. If his elders came down, he had to entertain them and he would go missing.

But Andrew gave us two years of unbelievable rugby at the Brumbies and he played seven Tests for Australia. We were able to modify his behaviour through a lot of love. We also employed Glen Ella, another Indigenous Australian, to look after Andrew. Glen did a fantastic job with him. We got Andrew playing great rugby. He loved the boys, and the boys loved him. It was fantastic for a while and it proved you can get the troubled boys on the right track for a period of time.

I thought often of Wayne Bennett and Phil Gould when Andrew was driving us mad with his antics and thrilling us all with his rugby. Wayne had been right. We couldn't change our player's long-term decision-making but, with a little guidance from Phil, we found a way to show him we cared. I learnt so much from a great coach in Wayne, as well as from a thoughtful coach in Phil, and a blend of their different styles and insights worked with a troubled genius of a player in Andrew Walker. It was a reminder that we should:

TALK TO OTHERS, ALWAYS REMAIN OPEN TO LEARNING

- Review and improve

- Re-plan, re-execute

- Customize the advice you get to suit the situation

- Move at pace

- Accept that being a leader can be lonely and demanding

12

A CLOSE EXAMINATION

STUDY THE INDIVIDUALS, THE PROCESSES, THE ORGANIZATION

The leadership cycle is unending but, after a difficult period, close examination tends to be more intense. However, it should actually remain at the same level. The course of examination needs to be used consistently and in a measured way throughout the cycle. We review all the working parts of the organization – from individual players and coaches to the overall strategies and processes. We reflect on all areas and decide where we need to improve or to change. We apportion time to professional development. We plan and we move ahead.

It's human nature for leaders to push harder to get the organization out of a little dip. No one likes the pain of difficult times, and one way to feel more proactive is to increase your discretionary effort. For me it will be as simple as wondering whether I should start getting up at 5 a.m. rather than 5.15? That extra 15 minutes could give me the impetus I need as we strive to move to a new stage.

Self-examination is the starting point for any management review in this Experiment stage of the cycle. Am I sending out the wrong messages to the players, or modelling outdated attitudes? Have my own working practices and decision-making

skills been as sharp as they should be? I always try to get feedback
from those I trust, but looking at myself, as forensically as I can,
is also fundamental. You have to lead yourself first before you
examine those working under you.

It is obviously important to review and reflect on the leadership skills within your team. So much attention is heaped onto
the captain in Test rugby, but the more I consider it, the more
I believe it's about the entire leadership group and how they
work together. It was different years ago; on one occasion, I
even went down the 'Mike Brearley' route when picking a captain.

Brearley had first been appointed skipper of the England
cricket team in 1977. Ian Botham had replaced him as captain for
a brief spell but, by the summer of 1981, Brearley was back to
cement his legendary status as a leader. He returned as captain
after two Tests of the Ashes that year, with Botham's confidence
shot and Australia 1–0 up. Brearley transformed England. They
won the three remaining Tests, with Botham as Superman in the
incredible comeback at Headingley. Brearley had proved himself
a consummate leader yet again.

Brearley captained England in 31 of his 39 Tests, losing only
four matches and winning 17, and yet his batting average was a
modest 22. He was an intellectual, having obtained a first-class
degree in Classics at Cambridge, followed by a post-grad degree
in Moral Sciences, but Brearley understood and empathized with
people above all else. As the Australia bowler Rodney Hogg said,
Brearley had 'a degree in people'. He also had a lightness of
touch – if ever he was criticized for a decision, he would simply
smile and say: 'You never know. The alternative might have been
worse.'

Brett Robinson was my Brearley on one occasion. He was still
captain of the Brumbies as the Super 12 season ended in 2000.
Brett was an outstanding leader. Absolutely first class, a bright
boy, good with people, committed to the nth degree. But a young

George Smith had emerged as a back-row sensation. Brett didn't play in the semi-final of the Super 12 because he was injured. George flourished in his absence and he was a key player as we beat the Cats 28–5.

We faced the Crusaders in the final. We had finished six points clear of them in the regular season and in the final league game we beat them 17–12 in Christchurch. But they were coached by Robbie Deans and Steve Hansen, and they had a really experienced side captained by Todd Blackadder and packed with All Blacks such as Andrew Mehrtens, Reuben Thorne, Greg Somerville, Leon MacDonald and Daryl Gibson. I had a difficult decision to make. Brett was fit again. He would not be able to match George as a player but I decided to bring him back as captain. I thought it would be more destabilizing to leave him out.

So I went down the Brearley route, believing that Brett's qualities as captain would compensate for the drop in playing quality when he replaced George in the back row. That's not to discredit Brett as a player. George Smith was already a great player at 19. He was still a great player at 38. George is one of rugby's all-time greats. But before the Super 12 final, in what was then my biggest-ever game as a coach, I left George on the bench. I opted for the primacy of the captain ahead of a teenage prodigy. It was a leadership decision rooted in logic, but I can see now that it might have been the wrong choice. I had put too much emphasis on the role of the captain and we lost the final 20–19 in agonizing circumstances. I brought George on as a replacement and he scored our only try. It made me think that, on reflection, I should have played him from the start.

I should have trusted the entire leadership group we had at the Brumbies rather than relying so heavily on Brett as my captain. We had so many natural leaders and they had been developed by the diverse nature of their education and upbringing. George Gregan had done a business degree and he ran a cafe as a thriving venture. Steve Larkham, with his IQ of 150, had a computer studies degree. Joe Roff had studied resource management. Rod Kafer was one of the smartest players I've ever coached, and he helped create our new system of attack. There were so many others; we had this broad range of people with different skills.

They had grown up learning how to prioritize their time as they had to balance their studies with rugby. So they had life skills and experiences which broadened their attributes as leaders. A year later, after Brett's retirement, and as George Smith shone in the back row, we won the Super 12 with a dominant performance in the final. Gregan gave a spellbinding speech as captain before we demolished the Sharks 36–6, but the leadership group ran the show. Our troubled but brilliant full-back, Andrew Walker, scored 21 points as the group kept him on track.

It is much more difficult to develop a leadership group these days because the modern player has so much less life experience. From the age of 15 or 16 he gets given a schedule at the start of every day which he follows to the letter. We make sure he is stimulated, but those key prioritizing skills which all leaders need are not given enough opportunity to develop.

This is a challenge for every major team in international sport – we strive to develop leadership skills in players who have generally emerged out of an academy system which has kept them in a bubble, away from real life, since they were very young. We are looking for ways to fast-track their leadership skills but, essentially, it's a long development process. It takes a lot of thought and care; and it's not easy. Sometimes we make progress and sometimes we slip backwards.

The onus of responsibility should not just centre on the captain, but I understand why the role is a source of fascination. Owen Farrell is developing well as a leader. He had quite a smooth run after he took over from Dylan Hartley in the English summer of 2018, and his first really big test as captain came during the 2021 Six Nations. He's quite an aggressive leader, and captains of this type can find it difficult to adjust to the nuances of the role. They have to develop their softer skills – to empathize with their teammates and bring them together into a cohesive unit and, also, to manage the referee.

We call them 'soft skills' but they're actually bloody hard. Clarity of thinking, communication, composure, diplomacy, empathy, sensitivity and understanding others are sophisticated and often elusive skills. Some of the best CEOs in the world are weak in these areas and they have to bring in consultants and pay millions to instil these soft skills into their organization. Neil Craig and I talk about it a lot. He's 65 and I'm 61 and, although we've been working in high-performance sport for decades, Neil is much better than me in terms of soft skills. But he always stresses that he can learn so much more. So we need to be patient with our young leaders. It's easy to tell your captain to go out and have tough conversations with his teammates, while showing plenty of empathy, but you need to understand the complexity of his task.

We also only have the players for short periods, so it is tricky to maintain continuity. But that does not mean it is impossible to develop the soft skills a great captain needs. We try to give Owen the right advice. Will Carling and Steve Borthwick, as former captains of England, understand the pressures of the role more than most. They have been of real value, and Will is now Owen's main point of contact. We've helped Owen gain access to Cameron Smith, who is one of the great captains and rugby league players in Australia. He led Melbourne Storm for 15 years, winning the NRL Premiership on three occasions between 2012 and 2020. Cameron has also played 430 NRL games, which is more than anyone else in Australia. He played 56 Tests for the national team and captained them until his retirement from international rugby in 2018. Owen, with his rugby league background, understands the magnitude of everything Cameron has done as a leader, and so they shared some useful conversations.

Neil and I also work closely with Owen, and he has people away from the England camp who he trusts and talks to all the time as well. But Neil made a really good point when he said that, as a support group, we've made the mistake of having too many people, too many ideas and too many conversations with Owen. He's got enough information to digest now.

Owen asked Neil if they could have a Zoom call midway through the 2021 Six Nations. They would normally meet for a coffee, but Neil was stuck in Australia. Owen wanted to talk about the way the tournament was unfolding, his captaincy and also his game because he had not played a lot of rugby. He understood that as captain he needed to perform at a very high level and that the team was struggling and in need of his leadership. Neil made some very astute comments. He reminded Owen that he has to lead himself before anyone else. Neil also said it was time for Owen to concentrate on the advice that made most sense to him. He needed to stay true to how he wanted to lead England – and remember that the captain's first job is always to be the best player possible.

He said that Owen should talk to just one or two people he really trusts about leadership. If anyone else wanted to share their thoughts about captaincy he should tell them to back off in a respectful manner. He now just needs to practise being a leader as much as he can and stick to his core principles. It was a really valuable suggestion because, sometimes, in our desire to help, we can overload individual players.

We can assist Owen most by developing his lieutenants into better leaders and by using smarter strategies so that, in training, he can practise being a captain under pressure. If training games are calm and perfect rather than full of pressure and chaos, how is Owen going to get better in dealing with difficult situations, whether they involve teammates' intense emotions or responding to a bad refereeing decision?

Sometimes we design training so that there are fewer players on a particular team being led by Owen. The pressure builds on that team and then we might also make sure that a number of decisions go against him. This allows him to work on his mindset. It obviously can't be the same as playing in front of 80,000 people, while millions watch on TV, but it allows a debrief as we see how he has done in adverse circumstances. We'll ask some simple questions. How do you think you handled it? How did you prepare? What do you think you did really well? What didn't you like?

It's a continuing process and we will constantly review the role of captain and of the leadership group.

We need careful thought, a lot of internal discussion and a clear call of judgement. Those same review techniques need to be applied to every single position in the squad and the coaching team. The easy option is to do nothing and stick with the current situation. It might also, in this case, be the very best option, as Owen is developing all the time. I have great confidence in him, but we can help him most by improving the leadership group around him in the next two years.

His lieutenants since he took over have been pretty clear. If there is an issue with the forwards, Mako Vunipola or Jamie George will talk to the players. George Ford would take charge if we needed to sort our tactical play with the backs. If there was an issue around the breakdown, Tom Curry would sort it out. Maro Itoje can lift them if their energy starts to flag. They all take that responsibility. But they can all do more, and some will be under closer review than others.

We need more in the leadership group who can develop the relationship side of performance. Since early 2019, we have spent a lot of time trying to develop connection and cohesion with the playing group. It's the power of the tribe to look after each other and bind closely together. We need players willing to make sacrifices for the England tribe and, to generate that commitment, our leadership group requires both hard and soft skills.

The longer you're together as a squad, the more there is a danger in thinking: 'I'm entitled to be here. Everyone thinks I'm pretty special.' They never say it out loud, but you know that's what they are thinking.

When you become part of an elite organization you should not regard it as an end point. It should only be the starting point. To thrive within that company or team you need to raise your standards and keep evolving. There are some companies where, at the highest levels, you have up to 18 rounds of interviews and psychometric tests to see if you've got what it takes to be put through that process. It's really tough and cuts away any sense of entitlement.

The same principles apply in the military. If you want to get into the SAS, you have to endure a brutal training regime. The people who survive it get selected. If you wilt then you're out. Test rugby is not that different. It involves that same brutality and intensity.

The right examples are out there. What did Richie McCaw write in his dairy at the start of each new day? Start again. He then underlined those two words.

That attitude needs cultivating. Some of our younger players are fantastic; some of our older guys are fantastic. Other players have to be taught that they are involved in a constant process of review and improvement.

Maro Itoje has what it takes. He has an enormous work ethic and an intense desire to be at his best. Maro is at it the whole time. But there are other facets of his role that require work. There were lots of calls for him to be named as captain of the British and Irish Lions in South Africa in 2021. Alun Wyn Jones rightly got the job instead. That seemed sensible to me. I might be wrong, but I am not sure Maro is a future England captain. He is going to be one of the great players, but Maro is very inward-looking. He drives himself rather than anyone else. He doesn't usually influence people off the field. Maro might be able to develop this skill and relate to people even more effectively, but he has work to do here. He has the intelligence to do it and so no door is closed to him. At the same time, no door is automatically open to him either. We'll just keep reviewing his role and his contribution and see where it slots into the process and the organization.

We've sent Maro to acting classes, which is having a beneficial effect. He speaks more influentially now, and I am hopeful he can develop more communication and leadership skills. Acting brings Maro out of himself. We don't want to quench his inner drive, but we will have made huge progress if we can tap into it in different ways so that it transmits to his teammates. The acting classes are a practical step to helping Maro and others share that internal fire and magic which makes them special. We're always looking to see if we can develop these traits and find the right mix of leaders.

Examining all the individual players and coaches, as well as our interaction together in this stage of the cycle, continues the review process. But as we approach the end of the Experiment stage, it is a reminder that hard choices always need to be made. There are numerous players in the England squad who might have played their last international. Nothing is certain, but we are moving ahead and not everyone can keep pace. Some older players, as well as some of the younger boys who don't quite have the right stuff, will be gone. Others might just need time away from the squad to regain the hunger.

I have got better at making these tough calls. Back in 2005, in my last year as Australia's head coach, I was guilty of staying too loyal to some older players. I was thinking that they had done a great job when we reached the World Cup final in 2003 and they were too good to be axed. So I did nothing. I allowed them to play on in the hope they would regain their edge. Instead, I should have dropped some permanently. With some of the other players, though, on reflection I think they just needed to freshen up and regain their sharpness. I didn't need to cut them all off permanently. Sometimes you can leave players out and then bring them back to gain a good result. Failing to do that meant we went on a long losing run which cost me my job.

I learnt a good lesson from that painful experience. When I took over Japan in 2012, I left out all the senior players initially. They had to fight their way back into the squad. We suffered as a consequence, and I lost my first five games. But the environment in Japan allowed me that opportunity to teach an immediate lesson to our senior pros for the long-term benefit of them and the entire squad. In a much more ruthless environment, you wouldn't still have a job if you lost your first five Tests as head coach. I did the right thing and it proved that I would be loyal to committed and excellent performances, rather than to individuals simply because they had been around for a long time.

We've gone through it twice now with England. In 2017 that squad had basically been together for six years. They had done four years before the 2015 World Cup and then two more with me when we won the Grand Slam, swept the Wallabies 3–0 away and lifted another Six Nations. But the wheels fell off and we lost a string of matches before I made the changes we needed. I don't know whether I kept some of those players too long or not. It was the same thing again in early 2021. Was I too loyal to some players? We'll wait and see.

There is such a fine balance in striving to maintain cohesion when change is so important to your development. That's why we talk about sports-science and the art of coaching. The first can analyse the physiology of athletes and pinpoint some of the reasons for their achievements and setbacks. But we are dealing with human beings, so sports-science cannot provide a simple formula that will guarantee sporting glory. Science cannot tell when you've got to push a bit harder, or pull back, or change your personnel and tactical approach. You have to rely on the more subtle art of coaching and management when it comes to finding the right balance of what you need to do with individuals and the group. It comes down to judgement.

Earlier this year I was in the car when a radio show hammered Gareth Southgate for his team selection. The pundits and the listeners all had strident views on who he should be picking and most of them were saying that Southgate really didn't know what he was doing. He was too conservative a coach to maximize the attacking talent in his squad. I thought about the times I have spoken to Gareth and how much he impressed me on every occasion. I would not pass judgement on his squad because he knows so much more than me. He has all the know-how, combined with the hard data and the evidence of his own eyes as he talks to the players behind closed doors and sees them in training, so he is always going to know more than me and all the commentators. Five months later, when he steered England to the final of Euro 2020 with such assurance, I wondered if those same critics reflected on their earlier misjudgements of Gareth and his methods.

So much is always happening within the inner sanctum of your squad that no one on the outside can even begin to fathom. There is always conflict and disappointment when players, or staff, are being reviewed by you as their leader. Before every game, in club or provincial rugby, you've got 15 players who like you at that moment. You've got eight players on the bench who are ambivalent. Then you've got another 20 players, or however big or small your squad is, who think you're an idiot. You would have spent a chunk of the week trying to show them how much you value them. When they don't get picked, they feel you really don't care.

That constant process is the same when it comes to national selection. You have 30 players in a Test week and at least seven of them don't like you at all just before the game because they're out of the match-day squad. So how do you keep them on the right track? I'll give you an example from the 2019 World Cup. We had 31 players. Fifteen started and they were happy. The eight finishing players, on the bench, did not feel the same degree of happiness. So we went out of our way to have one-on-one discussions with them about their role. There were another eight players who felt much more on the outside because they would have no direct role in the match itself. So we held specific training sessions for them and I would lead at least one of those because I wanted to show how much I cared about them. We'd meet with them one-on-one and had a special lunch for them on the day of the game to show them how much they meant to us. We also presented each one of them with a jersey, the same jersey the other players got, in recognition of their contribution.

I know Gareth does similar work behind the scenes with his fringe players. It was telling that, in the immediate aftermath of England beating Ukraine 4–0 in the quarter-finals of the Euros, the first people he mentioned in his post-match interview were the four players in his 26-man squad who had not set foot on the pitch in the previous five matches of the tournament. He made them feel included. But I bet if you spoke privately to those four players, or the eight in my World Cup squad who played no role on the field when it mattered most, they would admit their lingering disappointment. It's a natural and constant process which you have to try and manage as best you can.

I remember one of the funniest selection meetings I had was with a bloke called Peter Ryan. He was a very good rugby league player who did well for Brisbane Broncos. We signed him for the Brumbies and he was decent. But before one game I said to him: 'You're out, mate.'

Ryan looked at me for a long time and then he said: 'You're an absolute prick.' He said it with such force that I thought he was going to hit me. Instead he said: 'Now I'm going to prove you're a prick.' He walked straight out of the office. A few hours later we trained and it was meant to be a light session. But Ryan was smashing blokes and showing me just how much he wanted to play. I loved it. I thought he offered a great example of a player using his anger over his non-selection to try to promote the team. The other players might not have appreciated it at the time, but Ryan made our team tougher and harder.

Those combative and emotional guys are much easier to coach. They put everything on the table and you can use it in a positive way. The trickier guys to coach are those who sulk or have conversations behind doors. I much preferred being called a prick by Ryan because he said it to my face and then went out there and poured all his energy into proving me wrong.

Attention also needs to be paid to the coaching group. The individuals within it, and the cohesion of the group, requires constant examination. England's coaching leadership has evolved and devolved. From 2016 to 2019 we went from being a very passive, directed group that I dominated. I wasn't happy. I wanted to be challenged far harder by the group. I wanted healthy conflict and fierce debate so that we could push each other as coaches. By 2019, we had a very good coaching staff which was robust but respectful of each other. Every single coach was engaged in the decision-making process, but that took four years to develop.

Then, after the World Cup, we had an inevitable change of personnel. Steve Borthwick and Neal Hatley eventually moved on to become head coaches at, respectively, Leicester and Bath.

Scott Wisemantel returned to his family in Australia. These were understandable reasons both professionally and personally. They all left with my blessing after they had done special work with England. We're in the process of evolving a new leadership team for the coaches and, just as with the players, it's going to take time. But I know we will get the right group in place before the next World Cup, just as we did in 2019.

I'm always interested in staff changes. We've got a higher proportion of women on our staff than previously and it creates a better environment. Out of our current staff of 25, we have four women covering key roles such as logistics manager, sports psychiatrist, massage therapist and media liaison. It reinforces the importance of diversity to every successful organization. Having women on the staff has brought a different view and a better edge to the team. Twenty years ago, coaches would have disagreed. They would say the presence of women would make the environment too soft. We were all wrong. Women bring a depth and perspective to high-performance sport that is a pre-requisite for success. Players need to open up and reflect, and there is no doubt that having women on the staff aids this process.

I first learnt the value of having female staff when I was with Japan. This might seem strange as Japan can be a very sexist society. In traditional Japanese life a woman would have served tea, put slippers out for her husband and been a very subservient presence. But fortunately all societies evolve, and I was able to bring in a young Japanese woman to work as our team psychologist. She was not subservient in any way, and when we were discussing the attitude of some of the players, she made the telling point that I needed to look at myself first. I knew she was right when she said I walked around camp looking grumpy and unapproachable. I was intimidating some of the players and I needed to bring a lightness to our interaction.

We weren't going to take her to the World Cup because she'd just had a baby. But she had such a positive impact on me and all the players that we changed plans. The players drove it because they came to me with a direct request that she join us for the tournament. They had come to rely on her and trust her when they voiced their doubts and fears. She had a massively positive impact on the players. So we had to organize a babysitter for her during the first three weeks of the World Cup and, again, she added immense value to our mental preparation.

Of course, not every leader or company can afford to bring in an outstanding psychologist. So when you are examining issues of stress, doubt or fear you should always start with yourself. You're only human, so you will be subject to negative emotions. But there are ways of dealing with them. First of all you need to understand these feelings and how they affect you. You then need to manage the conditions and your immediate environment.

For me it's simple. Come up with a routine and stick to it as one way to look after yourself. I recently spoke to an AFL coach and he suggested I listen to a podcast with Hugh Jackman, the Australian actor. Jackman spoke about the fact that he has such a strict routine when he performs. He doesn't drink alcohol or go out after work. He monitors what he eats and how he looks after himself. Every morning he and his wife read a book for half an hour. He then meditates for another half-hour. Then he exercises. He is strict in following this regime because it helps him combat stress. And in any high-performance role you have got to find a way to manage your stress. When do you make the most mistakes? When you're under stress. So you need to find calm and composure to maintain the clarity of your thinking. You've got to find your own way of doing it because it's vital you control the stress levels for your health and also for the sake of your performance.

When it comes to darker emotions, some people are moti-vated by a fear of failure. Others take a lighter approach as they are motivated by being optimistic. In our review process we carry out spotlight personality tests on the players. They either gravitate towards success or towards failure. When I say failure, it's the fear of failing which drives them. So again, there is no right or wrong way. But for each player we try to pick out where they are on that spectrum. It changes from time to time, but the key facet is developing relationships with the players and trying to nail what they need. Do they need a bit of a push or do they need more support and encouragement?

Doubt and fear are present for everyone. We're all fearful of losing our job. We're all fearful of people not thinking we're good enough. We doubt that we're doing the right thing or making the correct decision. That's human nature, but you need to be in control of these emotions and use them in a positive way.

It's more dangerous when you become successful as a leader. You can become fearful of losing your status in the coaching hierarchy. The temptation for some is to read what is being written or said about them. That path is a dead end. Imagine if I started reading Sir Clive Woodward in the *Daily Mail*, analysing what I should do next. Some people listen to the loud-est dog in the yard. But you're going to go even further off track then.

They can make assumptions about you and your players. But those judgements are based on pure guesswork from an outsider. You should not pay close attention to them when deciding the course you need to follow.

You just need to keep a clear head and, in your own way, always do the following:

STUDY THE INDIVIDUALS, THE PROCESSES, THE ORGANIZATION

- Avoid the temptation to examine the organization more closely after difficult periods; examination should be consistent and measured throughout the cycle

STAGE 4: WIN
[OVERCOME FAILURE]

13. The Science of Learning
[STRATEGY]

- Review the current and future environment and the climate
- Maintain a clear line of sight between strategy and delivery

14. Red Teaming Transformation
[PEOPLE]

- Plan the next tranche of transformation – to refresh or rebuild

15. A Clean Sweep
[OPERATION]

- Review performance and identify trends
- Target continuous improvement

16. Chemistry and Diversity
[MANAGEMENT]

- Tackle the marginal improvements
- Realize all opportunities
- Address all tactical issues
- Drive out minor imperfections

13

THE SCIENCE OF LEARNING

BORROW IDEAS FROM SOMEONE SMARTER . . .
BE AN IDEAS THIEF

I spent two days being transfixed and educated by Doug Lemov in the summer of 2021. We have a similar background because, like me, Doug was once a teacher who became a principal. He is now an educationalist and the author of books such as *The Coach's Guide to Teaching* and *Teach Like a Champion* which has sold more than a million copies.

As we moved into the Win stage of the leadership cycle, I knew we needed to freshen up our strategic thinking. I was right to believe that Doug could do this by helping us consider our teaching, coaching and leadership roles in new ways. All eleven of our coaching staff – from the rugby coaches to the strength and conditioning guys to the analysis experts – were on our Zoom call with Doug. They were all blown away by what we learnt during those two days.

Doug told a story about when he first started teaching. He asked one of the senior teachers: 'Why do we teach like this?' The teacher replied: 'Because that's how we've always done it.'

This left Doug feeling dissatisfied and, because he is so curious, he decided to study how the brain absorbs knowledge and he soon developed a more scientific approach to teaching.

I've been coaching for over 30 years and, in all that time, I didn't really consider how the brain works. I was stuck in oblivion, even though I understood that the brain matters more than anything in elite sport and life. Relentless physicality, in the end, is no match for the brain. And yet I ignored its inner workings for decades.

To summarize in simple terms, Doug explained that we've got two types of memory. We have a working memory and a long-term memory. The reason we practise so relentlessly is to bolster our long-term memory so we can perform under pressure. Our working memory enables us to be clear and uncluttered. It allows us to absorb and understand what's going on in the present. Doug pointed out that it takes six-tenths of a second to have a thought. But you get just three-tenths of a second to hit a baseball. So the ability to hit a baseball transcends logical thought and it explains why most people can't explain why they do things really well in sport. But it's a combination of what we practise, and what we store in our long-term memory, and our ability to be clear in the moment.

I had never understood how the brain functions with any real clarity until then. That's embarrassing, isn't it?

Doug takes these simple facts and applies them to the principles of teaching. As coaching, at least for me, is an extension of teaching, it was fascinating. I felt like an eager schoolboy both days we spent with Doug. I've never seen anyone run a two-hour Zoom presentation with such precision and engagement. He made sure everyone remained totally focused and in tune with the conversation. Doug would present ideas and then split us into pairs to discuss them in bursts. 'Tell me what you've got,' he'd say after 30 seconds. The next time he would say, 'Right, you've got 30 seconds to do it by yourself. Come up with a thought.' Then we would split into groups of three. He kept changing and he always maintained the tempo and our levels of concentration. It was brilliant teaching.

He showed us a video of Denarius Frazier, a maths teacher in New York, at work in class. It was illuminating to see this tall, skinny, geeky African American teacher with long dreadlocks walk around the class, absorbing data about every student's progress while reinforcing his individual relationship with each of them. The way he taught his subject was incredible; his energy and engagement with the students was inspiring. He also created a culture where it is OK to make mistakes. Every time a student made an error he did not look disapprovingly at the kid. Instead, Denarius Frazier had this wonderfully warm little way of saying to the class: 'Who agrees? Who disagrees? Who can build on it?' It's just a really immersive learning environment. He also encourages this clicking sound with their fingers if they agree. The class is concentrated but humming.

All our best work environments echo these practices. They might not be as explicit as that, but they are important parts of driving a good culture. If you're in a strategic review meeting it can be very tedious and feel useless. But if you get it right, you'll see that everyone will be looking at the person who is talking. They're giving energy to that person. When you see a disengaged group, their eyes will be down when someone's talking. Instead of listening properly they're writing or doodling. But you're striving to bring out that extra 3 per cent in your group. Learning new teaching skills always helps.

After our second Zoom call with Doug, we went out and coached the under-20s. I encouraged the coaches to experiment, as a reminder that you've got to practise new coaching ideas and begin building your long-term memory of everything you have just learnt. The coaches were all so enthused that four of them emailed Doug the very next day. As he is such a warm and inclusive bloke, he sent us an unpublished chapter from his next book about teaching. That spirit of sharing knowledge makes our work so much easier and more interesting.

There is a possibility that we will invite Doug to join the start of our World Cup campaign, or even before that, so that he can spend a week with us and improve the way we operate. We take our cue from the best companies in the world, who always put emphasis on continual improvement. To use one example: why did Toyota go from making sewing machines to being the biggest car company in the world? Their insatiable desire to keep getting better drove them.

'*Kaizen*' is a Japanese word which means 'continuous improvement' or 'change for the better'. It has become a business philosophy that Japanese leaders share with all their employees. Kaizen is the enduring theme at Nissan. Kaizen holds the same resonance at Uniqlo where, if you work for Tadashi Yanai, you know you're going to work your socks off. My old friend Tadashi is going to be at you all the time to be better.

Kaizen is at the heart of everything you want to set in place as a leader. So you need a certain amount of humility to keep on striving to get better and to always be searching for people who are much more knowledgeable than you. If you've got that attitude, there's a good chance that the people underneath you will also be curious.

On Doug Lemov's Twitter page, he is smart enough to admit in his bio on the masthead: 'Most views borrowed from someone smarter'. This echoes Pep Guardiola, who agrees that you've got to be 'an ideas thief'. You need to acquire knowledge and insights and lessons from thinkers and innovators and then adapt and turn them into your own ideas and practices.

This is why coaches today are so much better educated. We have wonderful opportunities to learn because there's so much more information out there to help improve our teaching, coaching and leadership.

The way we set up our interaction with Doug reinforced how important it is to network. I was in Japan helping Suntory when a New Zealand coach at another club came to me for advice, telling me he was about to get the sack. He is a good man and a good coach, and so I went out of my way to try and help him, telling him about *The Coach's Guide to Teaching*. He said: 'I know Doug Lemov. I'll put you in contact with him'. Within a couple of weeks I was back in England and we had the first of our Zoom calls with Doug and our next stage of learning was under way. It reminded me that curiosity opens up opportunities to learn so much.

A week later we had a session with Vincent Walsh, who is a professor of human brain research at University College London and a leader of the Applied Cognitive Neuroscience Group. His specialist interests are brain stimulation, adult learning, sport and performance, numerical cognition and sleep. Vincent is obviously seriously bright and ground-breaking. As he says on his UCL home page: 'The 21st century challenges humanity to think across traditional subject boundaries. The ability to integrate across disciplines is what makes the difference between the merely intelligent and the intellectual. We need to begin to educate a healthy disrespect for boundaries.'

He came into our camp and talked about the science of learning. He broke it down into 15-minute presentations with three points every time. He gave it real meaning, using excellent principles, and we reinforced it in groups of four. It was yet more invaluable learning for our leadership group as we reviewed our strategic approach in the Win stage of the cycle.

In my own role as head coach I've also been working one to one with a forensic scientist. He has made me value my gut instincts with a new clarity. Gut feel, in deciding a course of action based on everything you encounter in a particular set of circumstances, is such an asset in both his work and my own. He suggests it is based on all the experience that you've accumulated over the years. You're always seeking the best combination of proven information and your gut feel. We have been talking informally about these issues for six months. I'm always trying to add another tool to my box of knowledge, but we will only be able to say it's been a good fit if we win games.

Leadership is not about finding something new. It's about finding new ways of doing work that has proved to be successful in the past. The core principles never change.

You need good people and hard work. You need to create a good environment. And you need to be able to keep it fresh and engaging all the time. Great leaders are always able to do this.

There is also so much to be gained from bringing in educated, intelligent and unbiased people. All organizations develop a certain amount of bias because you want to be part of that team. People from outside don't have that bias. Most of all it pays to bring in people that are smarter and better than you are to add to the environment.

I'm always looking for better ways to coach and to teach – and listening to the input of successful thinkers offers clues for that constant improvement we're all seeking.

You need this help to cope with all the contingencies of coaching at the highest level. It's a very complicated and demanding job. You need to be able to see right into the heart of what is happening around you while, at the same time, looking ahead to the goals set out in your vision. The good coach has to see around corners and to identify problems beneath the surface. There are so many unpredictable twists and turns, so many unknowns and intangibles. You have to live with uncertainty and scrutiny.

It helps to have a good support system around you and some truth-tellers to balance your leadership. It is also important not to get carried away by either defeat or victory as you maintain a clear line between strategy and delivery. Without that necessary balance, you can either overplay your success or catastrophize your problems.

The clichés of sport, and life, suggest that it is easier to learn valuable lessons after defeat or failure. But you need to reflect hard after every win and every loss. Whenever you perform, the same truth pertains. Mistakes are made and, at the very least, there is a potential that things could go wrong at any stage. As a leader you need to try and anticipate these problems before they occur. You should be mining for future conflict ever harder and more deeply after victory.

When you suffer a loss, the problems will be more obvious. You need to look more searchingly for areas of improvement after a win. But, even in victory, you should understand that nothing will have been flawless about your performance. The ability to put away the scoreboard, and just look at your work with the clinical gaze of a scientist, is one of the most difficult challenges in sport. It is part of the science of learning in high-performance leadership.

Of course, you have to savour the winning moments in the immediate aftermath of victory. When I took over from Rod Macqueen as head coach of Australia, he warned me about the loneliness of the job while urging me to – as he said – smell the roses along the way. You have to enjoy the job and so you must relish the wins. But never linger over them for longer than 24 hours. Give yourself a day, at the very most, to soak it all up, but then get back to serious work and look hard to establish where you can make the biggest improvements and eradicate the worst problems. They are already there, believe me, just beneath the surface of your shiny new winning score. It is the same in every sport and all forms of business.

When you're on top, and business is booming, you have to observe your players or staff even more vigilantly. They need to understand that if we don't hunt for markers of improvement when all seems to be going well, we will already be slipping behind because our rivals will be working harder to catch us. You have got to inspire everyone around you to believe they can become even better. If you see anyone in the organization looking settled and comfortable, you must find ways to prod them into greater action. If you're not able to do that, you're doing them a disservice, because the hidden problems will simply grow. You need to give them the opportunity to keep pushing forward by telling them how good they really could be with even more dedication. It's important to try and create a picture of where they can go. Make the impossible seem possible for them.

All great teams have to go through disappointment. I have never seen any special side skip this step. And, once you've come through it, the length of the cycle of success varies. It seems to me that Northern Hemisphere sport has shorter cycles of success than Southern Hemisphere sport. You see it in rugby and cricket. The media scrutiny might be a factor, but the seasons are also longer over here. The players are weary. We have just seen our players go through back-to-back seasons, with no pre-season, and while this has been caused by Covid, there is always less time to regenerate and refresh in the Northern Hemisphere.

We had to take this into account in 2021. But there were deeper problems within the England squad. The Saracens core had cracked completely. Their power had dissolved, and we were trying to find the right people to fill the vacuum. This was a key reason why we had been through this sticky period. I used to teach Economic Geography, and we studied the 'hegemonic class', which dominates the political or social context. It applies to elite sport too, and it's always fascinating to establish who runs the leadership group amongst the players. Saracens had ruled the hegemonic state of English rugby. They controlled everything but, after they were relegated, there was space for a new power base. We are still waiting for it to become fully formed.

We had a bit of a shake-up after the World Cup, which broke up the Saracens core a little. George Kruis, for example, went to Japan. We had leaders who were more representative of the squad. But then we lost senior players from other clubs, most notably Courtney Lawes (Northampton), Jack Nowell (Exeter) and Joe Launchbury (Wasps). They were all injured and the balance tilted. Saracens took control again. Owen Farrell, Jamie George, Elliot Daly, Mako and Billy Vunipola carried us through 2020. But the Six Nations in 2021 showed that we need to find a new balance to take us forward.

It is an uncertain but an exciting time. As a coach, when you review the current and the future environment and the climate surrounding the team, this is the most interesting period. You're like a chemist searching for the right mix as you throw in a variety of ingredients. Most successful teams in Test rugby are based on one or two clubs. In 2003, the England side was driven mainly by Leicester and Wasps. When South Africa succeeded them as world champions four years later, they were built around the Bulls and Sharks. They occupied the power base and John Smit, as captain, had the gravitas to pull them together. Siya Kolisi did it just as effectively in 2019 when he united the different factions in the Springbok camp. They established a strong enough base for the team to operate. All teams are like this, and how they forge this cohesion is intriguing.

As I've mentioned, I think Tom Curry, from Sale, can come through as part of the new leadership base. He's young and he is improving all the time as a player and a person. It's an exciting time for him. Maro Itoje will take more steps forward. Owen Farrell will be there. They will lead the group, but they need two or three others around them. We haven't quite established their identity yet, but by 2023 all will be in place.

In the interim we need to understand the shifting patterns. Every time you have success you have got to be looking out for looming problems. Try to build into your organization the capacity to get out of trouble quickly. You do that by developing the resources of your squad so that, collectively, they can handle the difficult situations. So our issue in this stage of the cycle is that the team is going through a process of change. And the difficulty is that, when coaching England, you don't get any respite to rebuild. People don't accept that you should be allowed the time to do this in a steady way.

The pressure and the scrutiny are relentless – which is why, at the outset of each new stage of the cycle, it is essential to have your strategy firmly in place.

Establishing a new power base when I took charge of Japan was difficult. I came into the Japan job having coached Suntory for three years. At the time, the two dominant clubs in Japan were Suntory and Toshiba. It helped that both my first two captains were Toshiba players. That offered a balance, because it meant the players did not feel as if Suntory were running roughshod over the national team.

My strategy meant that I was also prepared to challenge the status quo, and the players I took on hardest were the senior members of the squad. Normally in Japan, because of the hierarchical tradition, the leaders take on the weaker players. The hegemonic state stays intact. But I tore that up. I knew Japan well enough even then to understand the need for discretion. When I confronted the senior players, I did it in one-on-one exchanges between me and them. This meant that they didn't lose face and I got a result out of those guys by changing their behaviour.

When I first coached Japan in 1996, they won the Asian championship without any foreign players. I also got them playing fast, fluid rugby, which was a replica of the Randwick style when we were the best club side in Australia. I always thought you could win at international level playing running rugby, but it becomes much harder when you're working at the top tier of the game because defence is so dominant. We tried to play that brand of rugby with the Wallabies and it wasn't as successful as we would have liked. But it made sense with Japan because they have smaller players.

In my second tenure as head coach, from 2012 to 2015, we found the right balance in terms of personnel, and we built a Japanese playing style which was created through the methodology of tough training. The leader always has to set the direction, while having the end in mind, but all through the cycle you're building relationships between your leading personnel. You need to ensure that there's mixing and continual communication and interaction.

I have learnt a lot from Masanori Mochida, the president of Goldman Sachs in Japan. He has stressed the art of cohesion, and ways to develop it, and his words carry even more weight because his own story is singular. Masanori has been at Goldman Sachs since 1985. In 2001, after 16 years at the firm, he was offered the chance to head the company in Japan. He initially resisted, because he was a brilliant investment banker, maybe the best in Japan, and he was consumed by chasing deals. Masanori had the instinct to find the best deals and the ruthless composure to close them. It gave him immense gratification, because everyone knew he was the king of the deal. It was similar to being the striker who scores most of the goals in a football team, or a try-scoring glory-hunter among the backs in rugby. Masanori was almost addicted to the deal and so he reacted with extreme reluctance to the offer which had been made to him by Hank Paulson who was then the CEO of Goldman Sachs.

Paulson went on to become the US Secretary of the Treasury and so he was a man of some substance. He told Masanori how disappointed he was in this response. As Masanori remembered in later years: 'Hank told me that it was time to stop thinking about myself and to start thinking about what I could do for the firm. I was mortified. And, upon reflection, I knew he was right, I was being self-centred in not accepting the role. I did accept it eventually and, to be honest, I've never changed so much in my life as I did then. It was from this experience that I learnt that in order to change and grow to your full potential, one must always let something go.'

Masanori gave up individual glory for the collective good. On the outside it might seem as if becoming the leader of Goldman Sachs in Japan was a moment of personal vindication. But, in reality, it sparked a realization in Masanori that he needed to focus on the group rather than himself. He poured everything into developing and strengthening all facets of the company. His strategy is clear and, in a recent interview, he laid out his philosophy of leadership.

'There is no such thing as over-preparation,' Masanori stressed. 'In my experience, the key to success is all about confidence. Confidence is born of painstaking preparation. There are no shortcuts or fast-tracks. Practise until you reach the point of tedium. And then prepare some more. That extra mile will set you apart from your competition. To succeed, you don't need a sky-high IQ score; you need staying power to see things through. In my experience, the people who are most successful are those who set goals and stick to them. That's not to say that you shouldn't be open to new opportunities. Being receptive to feedback is also important. I often encourage people to share any negative feedback they get from performance reviews with their colleagues, and ask their advice. It's the surest way to grow.'

Masanori walks the floor at Goldman Sachs every day. He understands how important it is to monitor everything and make sure that communication and relationships are strong while always being on the lookout for problems. We have discussed it often and share a belief that, as a leader, you need to mix it up. Always try to get a laugh at the start of the day, make it relaxing, so it feels more fun than serious, and then get working. Make sure that people interact and that groups mingle with each other. Just as Masanori does at Goldman Sachs, I avoid having a head table – or a coaches' table. At meal-times I like the coaches to join the players. Chris Robshaw told me he had never seen that from a coach before and he liked it. It just seems natural to me.

I remember having lunch with Guus Hiddink when he was caretaker manager of Chelsea and he operated in the same way. He is such an engaging character that all the Chelsea boys would come over to say hello while we were eating. He would also walk the floor, and the whole room was filled with this energy that he transmitted. His track record as a national manager was exemplary and he did special work with South Korea, Australia and Russia. I understood why Chelsea kept going back to him when they were in turmoil and between managers. Guus bound everyone together. He was also very good at understanding what his team could do and then producing the tactical clarity to help them thrive. Such simplicity is a form of brilliance, and it enhances the effectiveness and unity of the team.

In the spirit of this chapter, I'm going to pinch a saying from Arsène Wenger. One of my two-hour meetings with him remains among the best professional experiences I have ever had because he's such a lovely philosopher. He's a wise man, as articulate as he is smart, and he made yet another telling point. He said the style of the team is a compromise between the ideology of the coach and the potentiality of the players. There was such truth and clarity to that phrase. It was yet another example that I should always:

BORROW IDEAS FROM SOMEONE SMARTER . . . BE AN IDEAS THIEF

- Review the current and future environment and the climate

- Maintain a clear line of sight between strategy and delivery

- Find new ways of doing work that have proved successful in the past; the core principles of leadership never change

- Always look for better ways to coach and to teach – listen to the input of successful thinkers

- The key to success is confidence; confidence is born of painstaking preparation

14

RED TEAMING TRANSFORMATION

COURAGE IS NEEDED AS YOU TRANSFORM YET AGAIN

'Red teaming' emerged as a regular presence in military preparations in direct response to the events of 9/11. After the planes flew into the Twin Towers and the Pentagon in September 2001, causing shock and devastation, US military officers were determined never to be caught off guard again. They transformed their preparation for worst-case-scenario situations by introducing specialized 'red team' strategists, who played the part of their deadliest enemy as they looked to expose the weakest areas of the US defence operation. These mock infiltrations would help the military fortify themselves against future assaults.

It was not a new strategy. During the Cold War in the early 1960s, the US military relied on the practice of pitting one team of strategists against another in a form of artificial conflict. The red team were meant to replicate the Soviet threat while a blue team, representing the United States, would try to defend their systems. As the strategic struggle between the teams was meant to take place in the most arduous of circumstances, a 'worst-case' situation, the red team would be given an unfair advantage and additional information designed to leave the blue team in difficulty. They would have to find ways to plug the holes and rectify the problems before they were overrun by the reds. Those lessons could then be applied to intelligence and surveillance.

The dismantling of the Soviet Union changed the dynamics of

intelligence gathering and there was less rigour before 9/11. Numerous warnings were missed or ignored but the rise of Al-Qaeda shook the US military into action. They began to develop specialist red teaming courses to train select groups in the art of imitating enemy attacks. There is a set pattern to these operations. A dedicated red team brigade, representing the invisible 'opposing force', almost always beats the blue team. It is then the task of these trained red team specialists to go through the entire process with the blue team and point out where they made mistakes which they cannot repeat in real-life combat.

Before they found and killed Osama bin Laden, the CIA used a crack red team to test and probe the intelligence obtained as well as the proposed strategy to capture or execute him. In a similar way, the Federal Aviation Administration in the US relies on red teaming to carry out simulated terrorist attacks on major airports. Governments and technological giants such as Apple and Microsoft use constant red teaming checks to sharpen their readiness for cyber warfare or insidious hacking of their systems.

We have adopted red teaming strategies with England's rugby team. Mostly, we use it when preparing for difficult games we are supposed to win. We try and predict how the game would look and feel to the team if we don't play to our potential, while imagining the opposition playing at a far higher standard than normal. We might also consider a red team situation where we are reduced to 14 men, the officials seem against us, or we are facing a hostile environment in other regards. We're trying to create psychological models in the heads of the players. It helps them work out what they need to prepare for if our plans go awry and they are suddenly under immense pressure. It can be a very useful methodology and I like to use it with the coaching staff as well. We try to predict what a bad coaches' box would look like – if we're playing against Scotland, for instance, and they're beating us at the breakdown. We then try to decide what we need to work on to ensure that doesn't happen.

Certain games have encouraged us to turn to red teaming. In the

English summer of 2018, we went on tour in South Africa and lost the first two Tests after holding commanding leads. At Ellis Park, the Springbok fortress in Johannesburg, we were ahead 24–3 after 18 minutes but by half-time we trailed 29–27. We lost that first Test 42–39. It had been a special game of rugby, but blowing such a healthy lead was painful. A week later, in Bloemfontein, we scored two tries to be 12–0 ahead after 13 minutes. But in a mirror image of the Johannesburg Test, we were 13–12 down by half-time and ended up losing 23–12. We lacked leadership and composure.

Nine months later, in an even more infamous meltdown, we ended up drawing a Six Nations game against Scotland at Twickenham. After half an hour we were 31–0 ahead and the Scots were on the rack. Scotland scored a try before half-time and some of our players took offence when I told them at the break that we needed to tighten up. They took that as a sign I was being negative. And, because some of our players like things to be nice and comfortable, they dropped their bundle after I pointed out that not everything was as rosy as the scoreline suggested. The senior players weren't able to pick them up and that exposed a chasm in the team. Some of the players were too sensitive and lost control as the game tilted in dizzying fashion. We were 38–31 down with a minute left before George Ford snatched a draw by converting his own try.

Those results were the driving force behind our decision to use red teams. We didn't do much of it before 2018, but that has changed since 2019. Red teaming doesn't provide all the solutions, but it helps the process of thinking how, if things aren't going well, we can adapt quickly.

There are definitely times when we artificially create problems or conflict if I think things are running too smoothly. You need this sense of discomfort in your organization. It can't burn the organization, so it can't be completely uncontrolled, but a restlessness helps ward off complacency. But you need to realize that complacency and entitlement is always around the corner. There is no simple way to get rid of it.

This is where red teaming helps us. We say, 'Right, if we're not at our best in this game, what's going to happen? What are the newspaper headlines going to look like? How do we overcome problems in the game to avoid that situation?' The Scotland draw turned out to be a fantastic learning experience. I was very unhappy that we had got into such a mess, but the lessons we learnt – and the red teaming we did from then on – helped so much, and we made the World Cup final later that year. But we had to dig deep because the problems had been buried.

Red teaming is transformative. It helps highlight these issues before they rise up and throw you totally off balance. We try and explore all possibilities and prepare ourselves for them.

It's not really a new concept in rugby. We were doing a form of red teaming back in our amateur days at Randwick. There was no Netflix or Amazon Prime or social media back then and life was pretty simple. We had work and family, sport and our mates. I know that we discussed the game a lot more then, in a socially congenial setting, than players do now. Players today have other distractions and they regard rugby as work. As soon as training and meetings are over, they are immersed in other facets of modern life. They also don't drink much, not in the way we did in the 1980s and 1990s, and so they put rugby away and disappear into their insular bubbles.

We did it differently. Over many beers after training, a few of the more vocal players would start speculating aloud on the upcoming game and debating what we would do in all kinds of different scenarios. When I reflect on it now, it resembles the kind of red teaming we do today – because, for us, red teaming is just another opportunity to talk about the game.

As a coaching group we have to create these red team situations for the players because they won't talk about the game in depth on their own. I'm not being critical of them. It's just the reality of life today. You watch parents take their kids to the playground these days. The first thing they do is get their phones out so they can check their messages or social media. Thirty years ago, when you went to the playground, you were playing with your kid as soon as you got there. It's just different today.

There is also a more professional kind of red teaming, when we expose the squad to work with the RAF and the army's special forces. Frank Dick, the famous UK Athletics coach who worked with Daley Thompson when he was so dominant as an Olympic and world champion in the decathlon in the 1980s, comes into the England camp one day a week to monitor the environment. He is still brilliant at what he does, after all these years, and he has a diverse coaching background. Frank also worked with Boris Becker in tennis and with Katarina Witt, the double Olympic gold-winning ice-skating champion from the 1980s. He's very well-connected as he works regularly with the RAF and has also opened up opportunities for us to speak to people in the emergency services and on BP oil rigs.

Our interaction with BP helped us understand the value of set routines and being very rigorous when preparing for unforeseen crises. The emergency services taught us a lot, but perhaps the main point was that you often need to work with a team that you've never met before. You've got to quickly come up with a solution and sell that solution to new people, whether in fire brigades, police units or healthcare settings. You need to get them rapidly onto the same page as you and, later, you have to debrief all involved. That continuum of moving from a pre-briefing to managing a crisis to the debriefing and the lessons learnt helps our own red teaming exercise.

The military operations are obviously very precise, and their instructions are concise, which helps us to understand the process. But our situation in elite sport is more fluid – and tangled – so we have learnt more from the emergency services in terms of being able to think and react very quickly.

I don't really see such exercises as red teaming. It's more about widening the breadth of experience of the players so that they can cope with different situations. Red teaming, at least to me, is specifically about concentrating on aspects of a game that could go wrong and then coming up with solutions.

We usually do a red team exercise at the start of the week. We have a concept called Set the Tone, which underlines how we want to behave. It dictates our mindset for the week. For example, we might be playing Ireland at the end of the week. So we might start by looking at what would happen if they keep beating us in the air. We'll break the team up into groups of four and they'll go away and discuss it. Why would it happen? What would it look like? The other groups work on the solutions. So you're creating imagined problems and practical solutions. It's a mental rehearsal that should result in the players being able to come up with effective answers if this troubling situation occurs on the field.

You have to have the mindset that a crisis is always coming. If you imagine the crisis then you're planning and preparing for it. And, if you're prepared, you've got a better chance of getting out of it quickly. In every high-performance outfit, whether in business or sport, there are peaks and troughs. Everyone enjoys the peaks but your ability to get out of the troughs quickly is far more important. And even when you're on a booming crest, the possibility of a looming dip is always there. There's a nice English expression that says you should always fix the roof of your house when the sun's shining. That's why we use red teaming. We're always asking ourselves: 'When is the next crisis? What will it look like? Have we prepared for it?'

You need that mentality to cope with the adversity that is never far away.

In the People phase of the Win cycle it is important to follow three basic principles:

1. Stay calm

2. Stay strong

3. Remain open-minded

It is vital, as you work out whether you need to refresh or rebuild, that you retain a clarity of thinking. This is not possible without composure. You need to detach yourself from the scoreboard, or the balance sheet, so that your perceptions are not clogged by short-termism. The results, and the profits column, obviously offer one immediate insight into your current position as an organization; but they only tell a partial story. If everything is going well on paper, this is the time to really drill beneath the surface to establish how much longer this is likely to last. And, if you are struggling, you need to hold your nerve and work out how best to transform the weaker areas of your team or business.

You need strength, too, to remain true to the vision you set at the start of the cycle. For England the vision remains the same. It is still about us striving to become the best rugby team the world has seen. Clearly, this is a few years away, but the aim is to realize that vision in the autumn of 2023 at the World Cup in France. We are still on course, but we begin again. The vision is unchanged, but we seek a fresh start through transformation while the cycle keeps turning. It never stops. You keep moving from one stage to the next. It's like the cycle of evolution. You win, you adapt. You lose, you adapt. But you need to ensure that the cycle always has momentum moving forward. So you have to ensure your own cycle of evolution transforms and you adapt in a way that leaves you stronger than you were before. Human beings have managed to do this, amid conflict and confusion, because there are enough smart people out there to imagine and engineer our development. But they are always building on the work and the ideas of others who came before them.

So never close your mind to external thinking. Pick out the right information and the right people as you work out who can and who cannot help you. Listen to their experience. Read their thinking. Talk to them and ask questions. Gather the information and then revisit your plan.

Refresh or rework or rebuild.

The media likes to convey everything in a linear way but, as you are dealing with human beings, there are always ebbs and flows. Everything is a cycle. Success follows failure. Failure follows success. You keep moving through it and each time you want to be just a little bit better.

There is a fine balance in transforming a team positively without causing long-term damage to it. Maybe the right term is evolution. We continually evolve as people. Look how much technology has evolved over the last 25 years. Teams evolve. They evolve and transform to being close to their optimum state. And then, in a natural process, they change and decline and a new form of transformation is needed. I see England's dip in 2021 as a process through which we emerge from difficulty into a much stronger position – as we did in 2018.

Everyone thought we had a great team in 2016 and 2017. In my first 16 months in the job, we won a world-record-equalling 18 Tests in a row. But I knew 2018, where we lost five consecutive Tests, was coming. We weren't that good when we matched New Zealand's 18-Test winning streak. There were flaws and cracks in that team which 2018 exposed. But I also understood that we were not as bad as the critics suddenly said, and that we would use that little slump to solve a number of issues.

We are going through the same again in 2021, but we can't use exactly the same measures of transformation. The process remains, but it's a different situation with different players. Back then we had a lot of players – Dylan Hartley, Chris Robshaw, Danny Care, Mike Brown and James Haskell – who were over 30. So we were dealing with a transformation that entailed breaking up an ageing team. The problems we have now are mainly hunger issues. Some of the players have had success with England, and success with their clubs, and they aren't prepared to be as hungry as they were previously.

They are different issues, but we solve them with the same principle of transformation and change. But there is always a gap between those players you are moving on and the new group that still needs to be bedded into the team. Occasionally you will get lucky and there will be a ready-made replacement. But the gap between the less hungry, or the ageing, player and their replacement is usually sizeable. It takes time for the new player to close the gap and, in the interim, your results will suffer.

At this stage it is hard to know if any of those who have lost their hunger will turn it around and emerge revitalized in a new season. They might be voracious again and persuade me to give them another chance but, at the end of the Six Nations, there were five players who I thought were unlikely to play Test rugby again. But you never know. People change. Situations change. I will keep an open mind, but for the autumn series in 2021 we will have to work some miracles. We will have one week to prepare for that series and so much will depend on the state of the players when they come into camp. Around 40 per cent of the squad will still be recovering from the British and Irish Lions tour of South Africa, which was dented by Covid, and it's hard to predict how they will react to that ordeal. It's part of the usual struggle over here, in the Northern Hemisphere, because of the deluge of games. As I said earlier, it is so hard to sustain success here and I have not seen an international team do so for more than two years.

It's different for the All Blacks. When they go back to Super Rugby in New Zealand it's not their bread and better. They are contracted to the All Blacks, as their primary source of income, and if they don't do well for their Super Rugby side, they will be rested. Here, our guys play for their club side every week. The clubs want to squeeze everything out of them. I understand because the clubs invest a hell of a lot of money into paying the players' salaries. But the workload causes so much wear and tear and it blunts the hunger of the players. They can become trundlers on the conveyor belt of club and international rugby.

Before central contracts were offered, the England cricket set-up produced countless steady and canny medium-pace bowlers, but was not so impressive in developing real quicks. The nature of the wickets had a big role to play, but the attritional routine of playing so much county cricket was a bigger factor. To survive such arduous seasons, English bowlers had to temper their speed and output. They bowled within themselves, intelligently and economically, but they also came to rely too much on the conditions to help them. There was a dearth of fiery quick bowlers.

Test match rugby has a similar effect on our players as constant fast bowling has on cricketers. You have got to come in, go hard and fast, and bounce off the back fence, and do it all the time. That makes it difficult for the players as they really should be given little respites from rugby. They have done it differently in New Zealand. Giants of the game in Richie McCaw and Dan Carter weren't just flogged into the ground, as they would have been here, and they were sometimes allowed six-month sabbaticals where they could get away, travel and rest, then recharge and revitalize their games for the following World Cup. Players can't do that here because they wouldn't be paid.

In New Zealand they still pay their best players when they take time to transform themselves through a break. Beauden Barrett takes six months off and plays in Japan. He refreshes himself and, while he is paid by a Japanese company to play for Suntory, he is still on a New Zealand contract. He'll go back and play for the All Blacks. He will feel transformed and probably be a better player for the change and the experience.

Do you think any of our boys could do that? If Anthony Watson needs six months away from the rugby hothouse after a long season that has been topped off by playing for the Lions, is Bruce Craig at Bath going to keep paying him? Of course not. That is the big difference between rugby here and in New Zealand. It's a problem because rugby is increasingly becoming so intense. If you're not 100 per cent at it, then the game finds you out.

The development of your team or company is often scarred by acrimony and dissent. You need courage as a leader to quash the strife. Personal animosities need to be put to one side, and you start doing that by identifying them quickly. Whether you're in the classroom, the dressing room or the boardroom, you need to look around and work out who is going to help you and who is going to hinder you. Who are going to be the influential voices? Who are going to be the problem-makers and who will be the problem-solvers?

Sometimes there is a clash between teammates or your staff members. You might need to bring them together to sort it out or you might separate them and talk to each one about their individual responsibility to the team or the organization. When I went to Saracens in 2006 as the caretaker Director of Rugby, they had won just four out of the previous 16 games. I had Kieran Bracken, an England international, at 9, and Glen Jackson from New Zealand at 10. Glen is a good mate of mine and, like most Kiwi backs, he wanted to run from everywhere. Bracken wanted to play a traditional tight English game. They couldn't get on and the atmosphere was sour.

I spoke to each of them individually and worked out their specific role and responsibility. Then I told them that, for the team to survive, they simply had to work together. I said: 'You don't have to like each other. But you've got roles to play and if you stick to them we'll be a much better team and the club will be OK.' We then took them out for a drinking session and that broke down a few barriers. They talked about their problems with each other and we ended up winning four of the next six games.

It's the same in a company. If there is a problem between your workers, you've got to resolve it quickly. The longer you let it fester, the more it poisons the atmosphere, which then clouds your vision. Modern work psychology often suggests that people should own their own problems and others shouldn't interfere. But people don't necessarily have the ability to find the solution. So you have to step in and find it for them. You've got to be prepared to be wrong and then return with another suggestion. You usually find some resolution.

In August 2017, soon after the successful tour of Argentina, we had a pre-season training camp. The Lions players were back after drawing the series, but I could sense we had entered a period of uncertainty. Manu Tuilagi was playing rugby again after a long period out following a serious cruciate ligament injury. But Manu still had some growing up to do. After a weekend of light work, we had one more day of our three-day camp left. The boys knew that the Monday was an important day as it would feature our only hard session of contact training.

I took the whole squad out for a meal in Teddington and it was a relaxed evening. As I treated them as adults, I didn't set any curfew after dinner. I just expected that everyone would settle down for an early night once we got back to the hotel. But Manu and Denny Solomona, a promising wing, decided to head out once we had dispersed. They rolled back into camp in the early hours of the morning, and it did not take long for me to hear of their drunken antics.

It was the first lapse of discipline in the squad since I had taken over, but I would not accept it. I sent them packing immediately. They went home with sore heads and embarrassed expressions. Manu was an important player for me, and Denny was just setting out on his international career, but I treated them exactly the same. I also made it very clear that it was totally down to them, individually, to find a solution to their problem. They would have to prove to me that they deserved to be reinstated.

Manu was able to change his behaviour and come back with a new maturity. Denny, sadly, seems to have dropped out of rugby at the very highest level. He has had personal problems and mental health issues. Denny eventually admitted to drinking too much and making poor choices. He had quite a difficult upbringing when he grew up as a Samoan kid in Auckland and life was not easy. We always try and support such players, but sometimes the problems can seem overwhelming. You end up losing some really talented individuals. Manu was different. Marriage and fatherhood calmed him down and he became such a serene presence for us from then on.

There were other problems, and we had a bust-up between

Mike Brown and Ben Te'o before I announced the final 2019 World Cup squad. Both of them had done well for England, and Mike had been one of my best players in 2016, but they were on the fringes of selection for the final squad. I probably wouldn't have picked them anyway, but when they fell out I made a decisive call. They would not be selected and the break with both of them was swift and clinical. I could be brutal for the sake of clarity and team spirit.

Organizations are always defined by their leadership. We are constantly asking ourselves the same question: 'How you can create strong leadership?' But the leadership model we have now is different to the model of 30 years ago. Leadership then came purely from the top down. Now, leadership moves from both the top down and the bottom up. I was in Japan and I went to a meeting to hear Tadashi Yanai speak to his staff at Uniqlo. Eighty Uniqlo store owners were there and Tadashi implored them to be courageous. He stressed how much he needed them to develop ideas for their own individual stores. It was not good enough for them to wait for head office to filter down ideas. They needed to generate courage and innovation and he would meet them in the middle with his own injection of fresh ambitions and plans. It was an example of how business has changed and that, rather than being run by a dictatorial head, you need the base of the pyramid to be creative and robust.

Tadashi showed courage in setting the tone and being willing to relinquish control to allow the store owners to flourish for the benefit of the entire organization.

Courage is always a prerequisite before transformation. When I took over as head coach of England and set about transforming the squad, I needed to be bold and courageous in appointing Dylan Hartley as our new captain. He had been criticized repeatedly for his behaviour and he was seen as a bad role model. Look at him now. In his retirement he has secured his place as a statesman of English rugby. He had a great record as England captain and he conducts himself well in the media. Dylan is willing to talk openly about difficult issues – discussing the dangers of rugby while retaining his obvious love and respect for the game. Dylan has a voice now that is respected and listened to closely. But when I took him on as leader, he was still perceived by many to be an uncontrollable lout. He changed those perceptions because he is intelligent, and responsibility helped him to thrive. My courage in choosing him paid off.

I also showed courage in a phase of transformation in my second season with the Brumbies in 1999. It was my first big job as a professional coach and, succeeding Rod Macqueen, I did not make many changes in my opening season. We came tenth that year after the Brumbies, under Rod, had finished second in 1997. We were getting absolutely belted by the New Zealand teams and it wasn't much better in South Africa. In April 1998 we lost 34–3 in Cape Town to the Stormers. It was such a bad defeat that late at night, back in my hotel room, I sat on the bed and cried. I felt helpless and lost. It was only when I forced myself to get out of the room and go for a walk on the beach in Camps Bay that I found the right balance again.

I thought: 'We're going to change this. We just need to find a way to get out of the mess.'

I steadied the ship but, more than anything, I needed time. When you're building an organization, you've got to work out its style and identity. You need to have the courage of your convictions and to ignore the outside noise as always. There was a lot of noise back then. I coached from an open box at Bruce Stadium and when I walked to the dressing room at half-time, I had to pick my way through the crowd. The fans let me have it:

'Go back to Randwick, Jones. You're hopeless,' and, 'You've got no bloody idea, mate' were two of the kinder insults I remember.

But I knew we could transform the team. Ideas were beginning to form in my mind. It then became an issue of finding the right people to drive them with me – and finding the right people who would be soldiers for me. The pressure was building but I was given some stark advice.

Steve Nance had joined Rod Macqueen with the Wallabies; he was a tough strength and conditioning coach. He had won three Premiership titles in rugby league with the Brisbane Broncos, and he had the respect of great coaches like Wayne Bennett. Steve took me aside in 1998 and he said: 'Mate, if you don't do well next year, it's probably the end of your career.'

I knew he was right and so I valued what he told me next. Steve urged me to trust my instincts and really take charge of the Brumbies. I had allowed the organization to drift because they were a success story before I came in as head coach. But they were also an ageing team, with that creeping sense of entitlement in some players, and I had done well to begin rooting it out. I had cut the dead wood away and Steve could tell I had a chance to do something special if I showed enough courage when completing the transformation. Change is always a precarious business, and I might have run out of time and options before I could get the Brumbies playing the rugby I envisioned in my head. But, as Steve said, if I was going down then it was best I did so while coaching and leading in the way I wanted.

Soon afterwards, I remember sitting down with Rod Kafer, Steve Larkham and George Gregan at a cafe in Kingston in Canberra. I said: 'Right, how are going to beat these blokes? Physically they're better than us. We have to play differently.' So we began to talk. We came up with a strategy to outmanoeuvre the New Zealanders and the South Africans. And then, in the third phase, we would have our best attackers up against their worst defenders. It was a simple strategy, but the process of how we would make it work was complex. It needed so much courage and hard work.

Larkham and Gregan went off to play for the Wallabies. Kafer hadn't been picked for Australia yet, and so he and I began working on a blueprint together. We ended up transforming rugby for a while because we created a style that no one had seen before and which, eventually, everyone wanted to use. We were outmanoeuvring teams and we didn't kick the ball and it changed everything. It led to our reaching successive Super 12 finals and becoming champions.

I instigated the change, and set the vision of transformation, but the players were central to our evolution. They took ownership of the strategy. You have to involve the team in the ownership process. We're looking to do the same with England, so that the players can own our style of play and our problems. They need the courage to become problem-solvers and leaders rather than just followers. But before you make such changes it helps to remember that:

COURAGE IS NEEDED AS YOU TRANSFORM YET AGAIN

- Plan the next tranche of transformation – to refresh or rebuild

- Create discomfort or restlessness to ward off complacency

- Employ 'red team' strategies to challenge plans, organization, and responses to unforeseen crises

- Stay calm

- Stay strong

- Remain open-minded

15

A CLEAN SWEEP

IF YOUR PREPARATION IS RIGHT, LEADERSHIP IS LOGICAL

You're always trying to develop leadership. It's the key part of any organization. How can you uncover more influential leaders? Leaders who set the tone. Leaders who will be role models as they drive and regulate the team. Leaders who will question and challenge you and each other. Leaders who are consumed by the cycle of learning and improvement. Leaders who want to win while improving on and off the field.

The absence of such leadership in the England team had been glaring in 2021. Neil Craig, Will Carling, John Mitchell and I spoke about it consistently, examining every crack and flaw, as we prepared to shake up the group with a real statement of intent in the autumn. Will acts as mentor to the leaders, and he shared my concern about the drift and lack of development amongst the group led by Owen Farrell and including Mako Vunipola, Maro Itoje, Jamie George, Tom Curry, George Ford and Elliot Daly. We both felt that we needed a change and a shift away from a selection where most of our best players were trusted with leadership roles.

Sometimes it just doesn't work this way. Sometimes, and this often becomes more evident in the Win stage of the cycle, your best players are not guaranteed to be your best leaders. When I compared the Operation phase of our performance in this most recent Six Nations with our efforts five years earlier, during the

2016 series against the Wallabies in Australia, I saw the clear differences. The core group had cracked in 2021. A power vacuum had emerged as hunger and desire ebbed, focus fractured, and chemistry was lost.

The opposite was true in 2016. We had the right captain, an effective and healthy mix of leaders in the senior group, and striking proof that the best players were not always best placed to steer the group. Dylan Hartley was not a great player. But he was a great captain and, on that tour, he was exceptional. Dylan was still new to the job, and he was full of energy and purpose. Even more impressively, he was at his most disciplined as he curbed his fiery temper and showed how skilled he was at the difficult art of bringing people together, and keeping them together. The ability to do that should never be underestimated. It is the cornerstone of leadership.

The players really liked him, partly because we all knew he was a bit of a rogue. But everyone also knew he gave everything to the team. My interaction with him just flowed. We didn't need to do too much formally on a one-to-one basis. Dylan's not a formal guy. So we stuck to informal chats which often lasted only three or four minutes. We would meet up before breakfast, or eat together, and whip through what we needed to do that day. Who's going to lead it? What's our main aim? Who needs a bit of coaxing or a bit of a chase-up? It was short, sharp and to the point; and we had many meetings like this through the course of each day.

It was another sign that, as the overall leader, you've got to identify the best meeting format for each person. You are better off catching some people on the run. There are others who you need to sit down, have an agenda, give them a lot of time to consider ideas and suggestions. Owen likes to think about things much more than Dylan.

Dylan would say: 'Yeah, we'll do that' or, 'What about if we try it this way' or, 'Yeah, got that. Let's go.' With Owen I give him things to think about before a meeting and allow him time to respond.

It's one of the most important forms of communication – understanding and respecting how each person needs to receive information and how best they can reply to you with feedback.

We were fortunate in 2016 that Dylan had so much help among the lieutenants. Chris Robshaw, James Haskell and Mike Brown were such diverse characters, but each brought an element of leadership in his own way. Robshaw had been England captain for four years and he was a diligent professional and role model. Haskell was a huge character with a deep hunger to succeed that was supplemented by his desire to make everyone laugh. Brown was more introspective, but he was so driven that he raised the level of intensity. Owen and Mako added a great deal too, and so Dylan had at least five leaders below him who could share the load.

Australia were the clear number two, behind only New Zealand in the world rankings. They had reached the World Cup final the previous year, helping to knock England out of the group stages and, under the coaching of my old Randwick teammate Michael Cheika, they were on a roll. Most of their best players were just the right age, and they played fast, fluid rugby. They were rippling with confidence, and I knew we were going to have to fight like hell to match them. We ended up fighting harder than probably any team I have ever coached. We also got some luck and we rode it.

In terms of our play on the field we were still finding our feet. We had won the Grand Slam playing a hybrid style of rugby. Against Australia it was obvious we would have to defend well and then be clinical on the counter-attack. There wasn't a conscious effort to change our style then, whereas now, in 2021, we're trying to develop a different kind of rugby.

The challenge for us on that tour was massive. England had never won a series in Australia and so we had to be bold and courageous. We got it right from the very outset.

We met up in this funky little art deco hotel in Brighton. It was close to the beach and the players loved it. In setting the tone of the tour, I introduced the concept of Bodyline, because I knew it still resonated in Australia. In the 1932–3 Ashes, England's captain Douglas Jardine set the vision even before they reached Australia. He planned a brutal but very clear campaign in which England's fast bowlers, led by Harold Larwood, would target the bodies of the great Don Bradman and his fellow Australian batsmen. It was aggressive and uncompromising – which were two of the characteristics we needed to utilize against the Wallabies. The fiery physicality of Bodyline provided just the right template.

Most of the players had never even heard of Bodyline. So I gave them a few film clips and background information on Jardine and the strategy that helped England win the Ashes 4–1. Then we repeated the meeting, but the focus this time was on what it was going to take to beat Australia. It hit home and, afterwards, Joe Marler came up to me and said: 'Look, I can't give you that. I'm not in the right spot.'

Joe's honesty is searing, and he opened up about his mental health and how hard it would be for him to be away from his family. I admired his courage and respected his candour. I agreed that he needed to put himself and his family first. They mattered more than a rugby tour. But at the same time I also thought: 'We've got a good group of people here. When a player can have the honesty to do that, we must be doing something right.' I felt we were on track because the more you can paint pictures in people's heads, the more chance you've got of getting the right reaction. And the right reaction is either applying yourself to the task or saying it's not for me. This is what you need in any high-performance activity. If you can't commit to it 100 per cent, you can't be in it. It was such a good sign that one of our senior players was candid enough to say he needed to step down rather than give me part-time commitment.

No other England side had beaten the Wallabies in a series in their own backyard. There was a reason for that – part-time commitment. When I coached Australia against England in 2004, they came out as world champions. But, more significantly, they came out for a holiday. We saw them on the Thursday night before the only Test and they were out drinking. Maybe that was rooted in the past approach of the English where, at the end of a long season, you go to Australia and your mood is softened by the fact it's almost always warm and sunny. English teams on tour down under had this attitude of 'we'll dig in and we'll try hard in the actual matches – but let's have a good time the rest of the tour'.

I knew we would be different in our approach, but you always have to guard against complacency. We had won five successive matches in the Six Nations, and so – as ever – there was the looming threat of complacency. Group complacency and individual complacency both need to be curbed. You need to fight them every step of the way.

We got the vision right, with the Bodyline theme, and we also got the planning right, so there was the correct balance of recovery, rest and then hard training for the first Test. It's always a tricky balance with England in the summer because the Premiership final means you get one group of players for ten days before the tour – and another group for only five days. To get these different players in sync, after an exhausting club season, is not easy. But we got it right. We went to the Gold Coast and had a few days off. Then we went to a really nice training centre, which I'd used before, and it was perfect. We trained at twilight and, with kangaroos running free across the training fields, it was picturesque.

Our two young tyros, Sinckler and Genge, were like runaway trains. They had both played fewer than ten games each in the Premiership, and they were as wild as the kangaroos gambolling past. That wildness was one of the reasons I picked them. Sincks and Gengey wanted to hit players hard and rip the ball away from them. They added an edge to training.

We had a really good preparation, and off the field our messaging also went well. Cheika had been named as coach of the year in 2015, and we made a song and dance about that. I kept name-checking his award and it got under his skin. It was just a bit of fun but I think it unsettled him. There was also a hoo-hah about me being an Australian coming home but, in truth, it was a bigger issue for the local media. I've lived my life all over the world, often out of a suitcase, and have always been an outsider. I was returning to a country where I was never one of the establishment, and so it wasn't difficult.

When we arrived in early June 2016, I was picked out to have my bags scrutinized at the airport. It amused me. 'I went through immigration and got shunted into the area where you get checked,' I told the waiting media. 'That's what I'm expecting, mate. Everything is coordinated to help Australia win. They're second in the world and they've got the best coach in the world. They're playing in their own back yard, so they have to be strong favourites. Our record in Australia is three Tests won since Captain Cook arrived. It's not a great record, is it?'

I was smiling and in control of the messaging. Dylan picked up on that combination of danger and humour when he pulled a great prank on the boys. A lot of them were terrified of the marauding Aussie creepy-crawlies, and one night, when they were playing cards, Dylan came hurtling into the room. He was yelping and holding a snake by its tail. Most of the boys ran out, screaming even louder than their captain, and there was hilarity among the braver souls when they realized that Dylan was holding an authentic-looking plastic snake.

We needed colder leadership in the first Test, which was played at the Suncorp Stadium in Brisbane. It is the toughest ground in Australia and we were reeling in the opening quarter. We conceded two early tries to go 10–0 down. The score could have been 17–6 after 28 minutes when a third Aussie try seemed to have been scored after Farrell, at 10, and Luther Burrell at inside centre failed to close a huge gap between them. Bernard Foley left them for dead and only the intervention of the TMO saved us. The replays showed that Burrell had been blocked by Rory Arnold, the towering Aussie lock. I didn't care. I had seen enough.

In the 29th minute I made a harsh leadership decision. I yanked Luther off the field and replaced him with George Ford. Owen switched to 12, where he would offer a much more robust defensive presence than Luther, while George could run the attack as England fly half. It was a necessary tactical decision but, for Luther, it was quietly devastating. I knew how humiliated he would feel because a coach almost never substitutes a player in the first half, but that call defined my view of leadership. It had painful ramifications for Luther, but I had to pull the trigger for the good of the team. Luther was struggling defensively, and we also needed a bit of control because the Wallabies were slicing us apart. We were bleeding and in trouble.

I rolled the dice; but my gamble was rooted in coaching logic. The benefits of my decision were soon apparent. It helped that Owen kicked a third penalty to cut their lead to a scarcely credible 10–9 margin. Haskell then marmalized David Pocock with a perfect and legitimate hit that would have impressed Douglas Jardine. Our confidence and cohesion grew. We looked more solid and more creative, and a Jonathan Joseph try put us ahead. Another penalty each meant we were leading 19–13 at half-time. Our planning and preparation, combined with a ruthless substitution, had transformed a dire situation.

That first half of the first Test was an example of how you operate in the Win stage against long odds and difficult opposition.

It also offered yet more proof that, as a leader, you need to quickly admit when you have been wrong and make the appropriate change. You must be prepared to make controversial and difficult decisions if your team or organization needs them. Convention and tradition should be put to one side, and you should instead follow the path indicated by your clear-eyed assessment of the situation.

Resolve and desire, commitment and skill rippled through the team after the break, and we won a famous victory, 39–28. It was the best England had played since I took charge. But it was only the start. I stressed how much further we needed to go to win the remaining two Tests.

I was still gratified by the mentality we had shown. Eight months earlier, when being dumped out of a home World Cup, England had cracked. They could have won both the games they lost in that tournament, against Wales and Australia, but they lacked the on-field leadership when it mattered most. They blew the match against Wales at Twickenham and then simply imploded a week later as the Wallabies ran away from them to win 33–13.

Many of the same players were on the field in Brisbane, but they had a new captain in the inspirational Hartley, and a different vision and strategy. Most of all they now felt mentally, physically and tactically equipped to handle the Australian onslaught. As a leadership group, the coaches had put them through rigorous training while lightening the mood around the camp at the same time. It is not an easy combination to maintain, but we did it.

We wanted to win all three Tests. You've got to have the courage to say it. As a leader you should never be anything but honest in that regard. If that's your ambition, express it clearly. I know it's a very un-English thing to do, and anything that resembles brashness doesn't sit well with the media here. To me it's obvious to say you want to win every Test you play.

But those wins don't come easily. In the second Test, in Melbourne, we produced what the BBC described as 'one of the great defensive displays in the history of Test rugby'. I was more circumspect and, after we had just 29 per cent of possession and 26 per cent of territory during the game, I said: 'We had to defend and play off scraps. That's how we executed the game.'

We soaked up the pressure and our three big leaders – Hartley, Robshaw and Haskell – led the way. England made over 200 tackles, nearly four times as many as Australia, and with such immense defence we were able to win 23–7 with tries from Hartley and Farrell.

*

You can't replicate the intensity, but we had built belief in a group of players who were able to withstand everything Australia threw at us. I wanted us to celebrate the moment but, at the same time, I also stressed: 'We're not going to be satisfied unless we win 3–0.'

There was much room for improvement in our attacking play and this quest for betterment inspired the players. They had been written off as losers, and now they had a chance to make history. The narrative around the team had changed completely. They loved the tour and in the third week we went back to my old stomping ground in Sydney, to Coogee Beach, so that they could relax in the surf before we went again. My former Randwick coach, Jeff Sayle, dropped by for a few beers, and we brought in Andrew Johns, the great Aussie rugby league player.

A Fox journalist sounded appalled after he had seen some of our boys at the beach. 'Do you think your players should be eating ice-cream?' he asked. I thought it was pretty hilarious.

It was a tough but engaging last week of the tour and a reminder that you've always got to manage your performance triangle. The peak display is at the apex of the triangle, while in the two corners you have the learning that stems from hard work and the enjoyment that comes from relaxation. You're always trying to get that triangle to be equilateral. If you move it a little too much towards either corner, you will be off-kilter and your performance will suffer.

It's one of the most important facets of leadership – finding the right balance between the rigour of hard work and the release of relaxation. If you get it wrong, it is very hard to regain equilibrium. But if you're bang on target with both corners of the triangle, your performance will be humming and there will be no better feeling than being part of that team.

Our best performance on that tour was probably the third Test. We were out on our feet. Exhausted. But England fought through it and were able to stick in longer than Australia to win the game 44–40. We also scored four tries and it showed again how quickly rugby teams can change. Eight months after facing

New Zealand in the World Cup final, Australia had lost a little fight. They wouldn't recover from losing a series at home 3–0 for a very long time.

We looked transformed after winning the Grand Slam and a clean sweep down under. I knew we had the nucleus of a good team, but as usual we had to keep growing. That is the hardest part of Test rugby, because we don't get much time to influence their careers. We have a maximum of 11 weeks a year with them. So in that truncated period, we're always trying to nurture good habits and develop leadership. That helps them to keep growing in environments which are not quite as demanding or as stimulating as Test rugby. We were ready to move on to the next stage of the cycle.

Five years on, we're going down a different pathway, where our team has to break up before it can go forward again. We're doing this a little bit later in the cycle. But the base beneath the break-up will be more solid than it was before. We have the foundations in place and the changes will not be as disruptive. Our big limitation, as always, is time. We feel it even more so now, because of Covid. How quickly we can move the team on has to be balanced against the ravaging impact of the pandemic.

After the Six Nations in 2021, we were also subject to the usual limitations of English rugby. I could not meet with any of our leadership group because they were back with their clubs. We could swap the odd text but they were restricted to the 'How are you doing, mate?' basics because we don't get any access to the players outside of international weeks. Some clubs tell us, as England coaches, we're not even allowed to visit their grounds. We have to accept it.

If I need to see Owen Farrell, I need to get permission from Premiership Rugby. It's the way the game has been run here since rugby turned professional in 1996. Years ago, when I coached the Wallabies, it was different. I could keep in close contact with John Eales, my first captain. I have no complaints about the way rugby is run in England. I knew what I was stepping into when I took on the job; there have been no surprises. You have to be prepared to work within these boundaries.

I could have been really pissed off at the way I had been hauled through the mud. But I don't mind if people say you deserve it if you come fifth in the Six Nations. That's true, but there are factors and issues which need to be taken into account. So I just see this as an opportunity from which to learn.

Twenty years ago, I would have let anger get the better of me. I would have been gunning for people and fought hard against the criticism. But I can let it go easily now. I don't hold any grudges. You learn to control what you can control, and ignore everything else. Again, it helps to talk to others in a similar situation in elite sport.

I spoke to a basketball coach the other day. He's 68 and he had coached in China for 12 years. He told me this amusing story, which offers insight into coaching in China and in some areas of elite sport. The coach was given $2 million to fly to America to buy a player. He gets out to the US, invites players to a training session that is doubling as an audition, and one guy who is six foot nine inches tall stands out. He's the best of them, and so the coach talks to his agent and says: 'I'm going to offer you $500,000.' The player and the agent are delighted and they sign the agreement. Everyone is happy.

The coach flies back to China on the team owner's private jet. He meets the owner soon after he is back and tells him about the player and the deal. 'I want you to go back and sign him as a $2 million player,' the owner tells him. My mate looks at him like he is crazy but the owner is emphatic. So he flies back to the US on the private jet and calls the player and his agent. They are worried but they agree to meet. Worry turns to surprised elation when they hear that the offer is going to be improved to $2 million. When the coach gets back to China, the owner is delighted. 'Fantastic,' he says. 'Now we can make the announcement. We have a $2 million player.'

This coach is now working with a new club in Melbourne. He has a new owner. These days all basketball owners assume they know how to coach the game because they can all access data analytics. This owner in Australia also watches NBA highlight reels which are full of great athletes, at the height of their powers, sinking three-pointers from all over the court. So the Aussie owner tells my mate he wants their side to play a game dominated by three-point shooting. But Australian basketball, at least compared to the NBA, is a bit like mud wrestling. You've got blokes playing in T-shirts. Blokes straight out of pub leagues. They're big, fit boys but they aren't especially skilful. Australian basketball is a physical, ugly game. The coach reminds the owner of the realities: 'I can't play like that in this league. I've got to find the right way that suits the skill set of the players we've got.' He's still struggling to win the argument.

Don't think this is an unusual story in sport today. We're battling with this all the time, and we need to remember that most sports administrators aren't trained for the role. As a coach, I see myself as a professional. I have worked hard and accumulated a lot of experience along the way. But a team owner or a sports administrator can feel like an expert a few weeks into the job. I'm sure it happens a lot in business – you might have a senior management or an ownership group who are not aligned to your vision of the team. You've got to find a way to manage them while operating with pragmatism and professionalism.

In terms of my situation with England, which is obviously different to that experienced by my basketball coaching friend, so much is about picking the battles that are really important. I learnt the value of this in Japan. When I was a young coach in Japan, if I didn't get a positive answer, I'd want to know the reasons. As discussed earlier, the Japanese will always say yes, but you know if nothing happens after a second yes, it's really a no. There is much hidden communication in Asian communities that you need to understand. The lessons absorbed in Japan have helped me in England, where people won't always say outright what they mean. They'll say something more subtle, and they expect you to pick up the key message within those layers of meaning.

In this stage, however, I focus instead on the practicalities of the role, which include preparations on match day and team talks in the dressing room. These are always more low-key and pragmatic than the romanticized ideas many people have of these rituals. They are merely operational aspects of the Win stage of the leadership cycle.

On match day I am up early, around 5.30 a.m., and I have a long workout. I push myself a little bit harder than I normally would. I usually follow it with a long steam bath. So I'm basically wrung out by about 9 a.m. There is no space for any tension then. I either go off for a coffee or return to the room and have a cup of tea. I then go over my notes for the game and check all my thoughts about the individual players and coaches. We'll have a midmorning meeting and I'll share my key notes with everyone. I'm usually back in my room from about 12 and it's a quiet time for me then. I will read whichever book I'm currently immersed in and I will jot down any points of inspiration which will help my thought patterns for the day. Before we meet up again to head for the stadium, I will have another steam bath to keep myself calm.

I am usually pretty good because we have prepared hard and I feel we're ready. I have also learnt how to keep control of my emotions.

It's vital to be composed in front of the players.

I think a lot of rugby fans have got the wrong impression of the modern dressing room before a big Test. Their perceptions are often rooted in the *Living with Lions* video – when cameras were allowed into the 1997 British and Irish Lions dressing rooms before the Tests against South Africa. It was entertaining viewing, but it was far closer to the great eras of amateur rugby in the 1970s and 1980s, rather than the much more measured atmosphere you will see in the England dressing room in the 2020s.

In the amateur era, and let's not forget that the game had only been professional for a year when the Lions beat South Africa in 1997, the kind of speeches that Jim Telfer made were more common. They were very emotive and highly charged, because coaches had players for far less time and they played fewer games as well. They needed to really fire up the team.

I remember some powerful moments as an assistant coach with South Africa when they won the World Cup in 2007. Before we left the team hotel for our opening match of the tournament, against England, who were the defending world champions, Jake White made a speech as head coach. It was a good speech, but similar to my style in not being excessively emotional, and I thought: 'Yeah, they do it the same way we do in Australia.' But then one of the management team got up and he spoke in stirring fashion about the fact that South Africa needed new heroes. You could feel the energy in the room. It lifted and crackled and the players were really engaged.

We then caught the bus to the Stade de France. It was a hushed journey through Paris and then, about five minutes before we reached the arena, they put on this Afrikaans song about the Boer War and how the English had killed so many Afrikaners. You could feel the tension on the bus lift, and change. There was real intent in the players' faces, especially the Afrikaans boys, and they went out and beat England 36–0.

When these things are done well, they can be incredibly powerful. But you need to pick the right time, the right moment, to do it. Their sports psychologist, who had organized it, was a really clever man, always smart in finding little cues to prompt the players and create the right story.

I tend to avoid them with England, but I do remember the third Test against Australia in 2016. In the dressing room in Sydney, I had a balloon filled with water. About 80 minutes before kick-off, the players were ready to hear my pre-game speech. Instead of launching into a long talk, I threw the balloon against the wall. It made a huge splash as the water gushed out and the empty balloon sank slowly to the floor.

'There you go,' I said. 'That's Australian passion.'

The Wallabies were desperate not to lose a home series 3–0. So they would come at us with a torrent of passion. We had to cope with the raging onslaught for a while and then, eventually, that passion would evaporate like the water drying on the wall.

Sometimes those intense and fiery dressing-room speeches are still needed if the players are a bit flat. But 90 per cent of the time everything is calm. We allow the players to prepare in their own way. Some like to listen to music on their headphones, while others prefer getting ready by following their own quieter, private rituals.

Think about it from the players' perspective. They hear around 35 or 40 pre-game speeches a year. So it's just not going to work to spike their emotion every time. You need to find different ways to help them get ready.

I actually think the pre-game speech begins right after the previous match, when you start planting ideas in their head. Then you talk to them all week leading to the match. It's continuous, and sometimes the emotional spike can come early in the week rather than right before a game.

I remember a romantic pre-game talk given to us at Randwick by Jeff Sayle. We had been through a tough period, because a number of our best Wallaby boys were out. Sydney University were top of the league and they were expected to beat us because they had Nick Farr-Jones, Peter FitzSimons and other players who belonged to Australian rugby royalty. We were just working-class blokes at Randwick and we were under the pump.

But it was a beautiful day and Jeff said: 'Boys, today the sun's shining on your back.'

He paused so he could look at all of us in the dressing room and then he continued: 'I opened the first page of the book with passion. I opened the second page of the book with passion. I opened the last page of the book with passion.'

That was all he said, but the simplicity of his message, making you feel good about the sun on your back and the intent of how we wanted to play, ran through us. We went out and hammered Sydney Uni. Jeff's speech set us up perfectly – but you only remember the winning ones, don't you?

I got my message across very clearly in two World Cup semi-finals. In 2003, when Australia beat New Zealand, and again in 2019 with England, I made sure the players understood exactly what they needed to do beat the All Blacks. With the Wallabies it was all about outsmarting them, keeping the ball and not giving them possession. In 2019 we focused on the way we were going to go after them and dictate the play.

In the 2015 World Cup, the pre-game messaging before Japan beat South Africa was also simple. Small Team v. Big Team. Joke Team v. Champion Team. It resonated in the players' heads and they were determined. The great speeches are when you get your team to play above themselves. Those three games stand out because we weren't meant to win them. We had to play above ourselves. That's when you know you're really coaching well, because it hasn't really been down to a speech. It's all down to the preparation.

So that's why before most games I say very little that is startling. The preparation has all been done. It's just a case of reminding them of the key points.

The same applies at half-time. Players are under enormous stress and they're physically fatigued. You need to allow them to recover and to calm down when they come back into the dressing room at the break. As coaches we will consult briefly with the senior players while everyone else gets a drink and sits down for a little rest. We're working with them to find the best solutions for the second half. This is where the game has changed so much in recent years. The old dictator of a coach shouting out a team doesn't work any more. We want to decrease their stress while increasing their focus and awareness. The idea that a coach changes the course of a match at half-time is now a redundant way of thinking. The partnership between the coach and the players is far more important. You've got to work together.

In 2019, against New Zealand, I just had to remind them to keep doing what they were doing. Don't get bored with it. When you're on top, as we were at half-time, you can be seduced into doing the easy things instead. We agreed to keep doing the hard things. We kept running hard and direct. We kept defending with intensity and energy. That half-time team talk was not inspirational. It was obvious. I understood this truth again:

IF YOUR PREPARATION IS RIGHT, LEADERSHIP IS LOGICAL

- Review performance and identify trends

- Target continuous improvement

16

CHEMISTRY AND DIVERSITY

FIND A DIFFERENT CHEMISTRY WITH A FRESH PERSPECTIVE

Will Carling and Ellis Genge are diverse characters. Ellis is a rough-and-ready 26-year-old prop-forward who grew up on a council estate in a tough area of Bristol. Will is 55, a former public schoolboy and army officer who, playing at centre, became England's youngest-ever captain at 22. In contrast, when he was 21, Ellis was sent packing by Bristol, who had grown tired of his various off-field problems and the ill-discipline which blighted his early years in rugby. Will endured intense media scrutiny throughout his playing career, and was hounded by the paparazzi in London in the 1990s. Over the last five years, Ellis has developed his character in the gritty environment of Leicester, where he eventually shaved off his mullet. He had earnt 28 caps for England by the end of the 2021 Six Nations. Will won 72 caps between 1988 and 1997.

They sat down together in the summer of 2021, and their conversation was yet another reminder of why I persuaded Will to join our management team in late 2018. He understands that a connection with the past is meaningless for young players if it is not linked to the here and now. If Will spoke only about how rugby had been played in the 1980s and 1990s, what would he teach the team today? He brings credibility because the players know he has practical knowledge of the demands of captaining and playing for England. But it is to his credit that he is reluctant ever to mention the past, unless they specifically ask him about it, and he prefers discussing the squad now.

When we were preparing for the summer Tests against the USA and Canada, Will surprised Ellis with his passion for the current England squad. He told Ellis how emotional he felt whenever he watched the boys play. Ellis looked at him and, eventually, he said: 'Are you joking?'

Will shook his head firmly and said: 'I mean it. I'm churning inside and my heart rate goes through the roof when you run out because I love it. I was a fan when I was a boy and I loved it when I played. It's no different now I'm 55. You wear the shirt that I would still love to wear – but I can't. So, Gengey, you boys really do it for me now. I want you to do so well, so badly.'

Gengey stared at Will for a long time and then he said just one word: 'Fuck!'

It was a statement of how taken aback, and touched, he was by Will's commitment to the extremely young team we would send out to play the USA and Canada. The obvious sincerity of Will's little speech was powerful because he does love being around the boys and watching them play for England. He is hugely proud of them when they win, and he is determined to help them improve and become even more successful. Will believes we have a richly talented group of England players, and good men, who have a serious chance of winning the 2023 World Cup. His conviction forged a real connection with Gengey.

Will knows, having mentored our leadership group, that we need meaningful change in the next two years. We need a different mix of leaders, and a much more diverse and proactive group to drive the squad to another level. It's one of the reasons he talks about strengthening our foundations by calling in some of the great players of the past to engage with our squad today. He wants to bring in Jason Robinson and Martin Johnson to talk to the boys. He wants them to hear the sheer passion that pours out of Phil Vickery when he talks about playing for England, and what it means to him. If you bring in the right people, you can forge a connection between the past and the present which will strengthen our current players.

Before I selected my squad for the summer of 2021, I steeled myself for a mucky interlude. A combination of the Lions tour and the continuing onslaught of Covid was always going to complicate life. After such a long club season, which saw some open-ended and high-scoring rugby that culminated in Harlequins surprising many people by winning the Premiership final after beating Exeter 40–38 in late June, many players were missing. A large group had been called up to the Lions, and many had been involved in the Premiership play-offs.

It would be another period of transformation, but the vision remained uppermost in my mind. We would continue planning towards 2023 while being on the lookout for young players who could potentially make it to the World Cup. If we could find a few new players, as we did with Sam Underhill and Tom Curry in 2017 when we went with a weakened squad to Argentina, we would have a hugely successful summer. But there were so many variables – not least the fact that we could not actually go on tour because of Covid. We would play the USA and Canada at Twickenham instead.

Amid the flux and transformation, I had initially planned on including only a couple of older players. Courtney Lawes and Kyle Sinckler were earmarked for the role that the likes of Robshaw, Hartley, Ford, Brown and Care had done in 2017, when they were so selfless in encouraging and bringing on the youngsters in Argentina. But Lawes and Sinckler both ended up going on the Lions tour after all.

I was happy to focus on a new crop of young players – most of whom had never come close to England selection before. There were exceptions. My plan for the Six Nations had been to include Harry Randall, of Bristol, at scrum-half. I liked the look of him, but an ankle injury intervened and kept him out for a couple of months. I was keen to see how he would do in the summer. I was also interested in the likes of Marcus Smith, Max Malins, Charlie

Ewels, Alex Mitchell, and others who had worked really hard at their clubs and improved. I would also be closely watching a couple of players about whom I harboured doubts both on and off the field. It would be a learning experience on our path to transformation.

The final summer squad carried little resemblance to the group which finished the Six Nations. Twelve England players were with the British and Irish Lions, and I decided to rest George Ford, Ben Youngs, Manu Tuilagi, Jonny May, Mark Wilson and Billy Vunipola. My 37-man squad included only 13 capped players – Henry Slade (38 caps), Ellis Genge (28), Sam Underhill (22), Charlie Ewels (21), Dan Robson (12), Joe Cokanasiga (9), Lewis Ludlum (8), Ollie Lawrence (6), Joe Marchant (5), Paul Hill (5), George Furbank (3), Beno Obano (1) and Ted Hill (1).

Twenty-four of them had no experience of international rugby at senior level – including all three hookers in Jamie Blamire, Curtis Langdon and Gabriel Oghre. So I knew I would have to prepare the younger players to cope with failure. The bulk of them were between 20 and 23, and many would be new to elite-level training. Instead of having nice-looking sessions, where everything works well in club rugby, they would face a 30–40 per cent failure rate in all we would ask them to attempt. It would be important to pull back a little to give them some success. At the same time we needed to be disciplined about the process.

After the Six Nations, I watched a lot of club rugby and I travelled around the country to meet the potential squad picks. With each meeting I aimed to keep it relaxed and informal as it would be a new experience for the young player. I usually suggested a cafe for our chat as I wanted it to be away from their club while also avoiding anywhere that might seem imposing.

I also wanted them to see a clear pathway ahead, and so I used Genge and Sinckler as great examples for young players breaking into the summer squad. I reminded them that, while they didn't play a Test on that 2016 tour of Australia, Gengey and Sincks had come in, trained with serious intent, fought hard, and by the end of the tour they were in a really improved position. They had gone on to build significant careers. Sincks was on his way to becoming a two-time Lion. Gengey would be one of my leaders this summer and he has since become the captain of Leicester Tigers. They were the perfect role models – and who would have predicted that five years earlier when they were such raw newcomers?

There was a real opportunity for this next wave of talent, but we would be testing them to see if they had the desire and the hunger for the 2023 World Cup. I wanted players who would be determined to go to France to win the tournament, not just make the squad, and so this summer together was seriously important for them and for us as a coaching group. I wanted to find and develop young players who could handle being in a much more intense environment than they were used to, and deal with the pressures of Test rugby. Could they add to the mix we've already got? Could they fit in socially and competitively with our established players?

All these attributes are vitally important, because the vision we had set at the start of the cycle was unchanged. We aimed to build a team that could become the greatest of all time. That remained our target, and part of fulfilling that goal is bringing good young players through. The great thing about these Generation-Z players is that they are generally able to be themselves. There would be more nerves for them, obviously, but the boys who are confident tend to show that self-assurance pretty quickly. And those who are less sure of themselves find ways to adapt. They're much more open in expressing their feelings than players of my generation.

So for me it's an exciting time – because when you're coaching young players, you don't know where you can take them. The challenge is to find out how far they can go. How much can you improve them? Each new player is different, and the freshness of their impact is invigorating. My enthusiasm for coaching is always high, and I was thrilled that I would do much more direct work with the young players than in a standard international camp.

I was also intrigued by all we would discover in forming a new leadership group. This was the area where we were struggling the most, and we needed to find a different chemistry with a fresh perspective. There had been many times during the Six Nations when we backed off even trying to drive the leadership development of the existing group. They were struggling to find form after playing so little rugby, and it would have been wrong to berate them for becoming so passive as a leadership group. They were working so hard to regain their playing confidence.

There was less debate than normal – and they would often become inward and suggest that everything was 'OK' and 'fine', when they knew deep down that was simply unacceptable. I felt for Owen because he would always front up and respond, but the others often looked to him for a reaction. It was all a bit one-way; by the end of the tournament I knew we needed a more collective brand of leadership.

It is a consuming job, captaining England, and the scrutiny and the judgement spills over into the family and personal life of a beleaguered skipper. Will did the job for a long time, for seven years, and he talks powerfully about the demands of the job. While he will always be proud to have been England captain, he regrets that his leadership role scarred him and his family.

Will might be a posh bloke, but he forged a toughness of spirit that allowed him to lead an England team full of grizzled hard men, who were much older than him, for so long. That toughness emerged again in his work with England. Most of the time, Will plays the role of the supportive mentor, a man who listens and is capable of great empathy. I might seem abrasive to some of the players, but they can talk to Neil and Will and be encouraged every step of the way. Will is also straight and honest. He won't show sympathy if it is undeserved.

Occasionally players have gone to him after a game, when I have called them out for failing to perform, and they have said something along the lines of: 'Will, the way to get the best out of me is to put your arm around me and tell me how good I am.

That's what I need this week. Wouldn't that be the way you would be treating me if you were captain?'

If the player has not performed, Will does not let him get away with it. He can be very blunt when he says: 'Mate, if I was your captain, I would be very clear. We lost that game on Saturday and we now have to fucking win this weekend. I don't care whether you feel down. If I was in charge I would kick you up the arse and tell you to stop sulking. You keep telling me you're a leader. Well, go out and show me. If we win on Saturday and you play in the way I know you can play, I'll put my arm around you and say: "Brilliant, mate." But I'm not about to put my arm around you now just because you're having a moan. Put that bottom lip back in and get back to training.'

The players take the point and perform as they should. So Will remains a Test match animal. But, as a leadership mentor, he could tell that Owen was not being supported enough by the wider group. We needed to become a much more cohesive and rigorous unit.

Just as the team is never complete, so the leadership group is always a work-in-progress. Our group had been dominated by Saracens, which made sense. Saracens had been the dominant club team in Europe, so it was rational to expect them to lead the national side. They gave us some great players but, like everything in life, groups and individuals all have their own course to run. Nothing lasts for ever. So it comes down to judgement and knowing when is the right time to make a change and bring in the next group of players and leaders. It could be later this year or next year. We have until the World Cup to get this right.

Whether or not we kept most of the core leadership together, or broke it up and made something new, we needed rejuvenation. I had underestimated the simultaneous effects of Saracens' relegation and a global pandemic on certain members of the team and their subsequent performance. But the summer offered me a chance to refresh, transform and build again.

There were going to be plenty of changes within the coaching group too. We needed a new attack coach to replace Simon Amor, and a skills specialist to take over from Jason Ryles, and John Mitchell wanted to return to day-to-day coaching in club rugby. John had done very good work for England, but I did not stand in his way when he decided to take up a new role in late July 2021 as the attack coach at Wasps.

We were interested in Martin Gleeson moving in the opposite direction, from being Wasps' attack coach to joining the England set-up, but for the summer series I was happy to bring back young Ed Robinson for another consultancy series. Ed would help me with the attack before he also joined Wasps in the autumn. So there was a great deal of fluidity and movement.

I didn't mind because we were in the midst of building new groups on and off the field. In terms of the coaching set-up, we had started a project called Fresh Eyes, which is to bring a new perspective to the team. If you keep on looking at the same problem in the same way, you'll get the same results over and over again. So we want fresh eyes in the form of different coaches and different professionals from different sports.

I recently reread a book on leadership written by Jack Welch, the former head of General Electric, and he stressed the importance of fresh eyes coming in to scrutinize your organization. Carlos Ghosn was brought down by his own arrogance, but when he transformed Nissan, he did so by bringing a fresh perspective. Traditionally, Nissan's management team had just picked graduates from Tokyo University. Ghosn tore that up. All future applicants had to blank out their university on their CV so that Nissan would select individuals on merit rather than status. We needed the same impetus from the views supplied by fresh eyes – and two years out from the World Cup felt like the ideal time to start the process.

There was such freshness in our summer camp. The injection of new young players, and a totally different leadership group, was transformative. We introduced a key theme at the very start which set the tone: Can you find your personal best? How many players in the world have actually achieved the best they can be?

The players addressed the gap that exists between where they are now and where they could end up if they fulfilled their potential. We stressed that it all comes down to being driven, and how hard you have to work to become a great player. Their talent was enough to get them into this squad, but desire and hard work would, in the coming years, turn them into the best player they could be at their very peak. We spoke about sportsmen – from Ronaldo to Tom Brady – who define this search for their personal best.

We ran a different schedule because we had such a young squad. Every morning we would get together at 8.20 a.m. and go through plans for the day ahead. They embraced it, worked hard and had a good time together. They were fantastic, but of course it only takes one player to change the mood in such a dynamic and fluid environment. It's your role as a leader to fix potential conflicts before they fester. We brought one player into camp and we immediately started to have problems. So we got rid of him within a matter of days. That old saying remains so true: one bad apple can rot the whole barrel.

But we got the exact leadership group we needed for the summer. It began with another of our central themes for the campaign – chemistry is rooted in diversity and respect. Diversity has become one of the most important aspects in creating a thriving organization today, and it only really flourishes if you drive respect for people who are different to each other. You need to understand and accept – in a respectful way – these different backgrounds, ideas and patterns of behaviour in order to establish outstanding relationships with people within the group. When that happens, you create a chemistry which really gets things fizzing.

We had such an effective and creative sense of diversity and respect amongst the leadership group, and the resulting chemistry was the exact opposite of the flatness we had experienced through much of the Six Nations. Ellis Genge led the way in a forceful and direct style. He was full of emotion, and he could be both aggressive and empathetic, which is an unusual but extremely useful blend in international rugby. Beno Obano was more discreet and personal. He worked behind the scenes, building trust and supporting some of the newest boys. Henry Slade, the most capped player in the party, was deeply respected for his knowledge and insights and the way in which he trained. Sladey was an excellent role model. Sam Underhill played a similar role, while Dan Robson was outstanding socially – bringing the boys together and developing cohesion off the field. Lewis Ludlow, who I had chosen to be captain, was the right glue player to hold everything together. He was very good in allowing the other leaders to use their strengths, and he found a way to help gel together a highly effective leadership team.

They were all very different people, with not too much in common, but they created a winning blend. Gengey can be pretty rough and tough. He speaks his mind and there's not too much soft-soap in what he says. But he could do that in a powerful way because the players respected where he had come from and what he had achieved. They weren't offended if he called them out and urged them to do better. Maybe in previous teams some players could have been upset by that approach. But we had the chemistry to make it work. Obano and Robson kept it upbeat, and Sladey maintained a calm and professional air. Ludlow was not a dominant figure, but he kept things organized and used the different strengths of his lieutenants. He was very good at delegation and inclusivity, and offered a reminder that there are diverse ways to be a leader.

It also reinforced my belief that, in Test rugby, you now need a leadership collective rather than a domineering force as captain. Martin Johnson was the undoubted leader of England's World Cup-winning squad in 2003. But he relied heavily on the other leaders in that group. Lawrence Dallaglio, Phil Vickery, Will Greenwood, Matt Dawson and Richard Hill all offered different attributes in terms of leadership. In a more modest setting, in games against the USA and Canada this summer, Ludlow was the captain, but he had five generals around him.

Everyone thinks the captain should have all the answers. Far from it. He can't be watching all aspects of the squad on and off the field and play Test rugby as well. The load has to be shared, and the summer leadership group did this superbly. There was a lot of debate, even healthy disagreement, as they came up with fresh ideas and moved forward together as a unit.

I also really liked the inclusivity they generated. The younger boys settled in so fast because with the senior guys there was no sense of arrogance or entitlement. Genge, Slade, Underhill, Robson and Ewels put themselves on the same level as everyone else. They treated every player the same and there was none of that, 'Wait till you've got a cap before you speak to me, mate' nonsense you can get in some underperforming teams. They were open and inclusive, demanding and encouraging. The chemistry, built on diversity and respect, flowed.

Our summer of quiet rejuvenation coincided with England's football team, under Gareth Southgate, reaching the final of Euro 2020 where, in familiar agony, they lost to Italy on penalties. But so much else was different about England, who were impressive both on and off the field, and it offered conclusive proof that Gareth had transformed the culture and credibility of the team.

I first met Gareth in 2017 when he came to one of our training sessions with Tracey Neville and Lisa Alexander, who were then coaching the GB and Australian netball teams. Gareth was no different to how he is now – very serious and very curious. He was hungry to learn as much as he could and see if any of our ideas could be applied to his own work. Gareth was extremely studious, but warm and open to new ideas.

I think he has one of the best jobs in the world – but, as always with the great positions, it's also very difficult. Managing England's football team is a wonderful opportunity, but it's challenging because of the weight of expectation and scrutiny bearing down on you. Gareth has always tackled it with a constructive methodology. He instils clarity and cohesion, and I think he is hugely impressive and very smart. He also refuses to be distracted or swayed by the outside noise.

Gareth has skilfully driven a campaign of togetherness where the media and the entire country feels like they're part of the team. I could sense that when seeing how my young players reacted to the tournament as they watched the games together as a group. They were just ordinary fans, swept along by the compelling story that Gareth and his players had developed. England's multimillionaire footballers were humble and united, socially conscious and principled. Even when there was a racist undertow to a minority of fans booing their informed decision to take a knee before each game, and when their young black players were subject to appalling racial abuse after missing in the penalty shootout, Gareth and his entire squad reacted admirably. They were inspiring and an example for my young squad to follow. I said as much to the media before the Euro 2020 final, and our own last game of the season against Canada.

'Gareth's a humble, curious, very well-educated coach. The thing that impresses me most is that, for a young coach, he carries himself with a lot more experience. We all watched the semi-final with a lot of interest and intense supporting. The English have the right to go nuts. It does seem that, in England, sport does tend to galvanize quite a diverse community. That stands out.'

I also discussed Gareth's transition from an England player who missed a penalty in the Euro 96 shootout, in a painful semi-final defeat to Germany, into a deeply respected national manager. 'That's one of the reasons we're all involved,' I said, 'because there's always another chance, always another opportunity. It's the drug of coaching, and the drug of sport, that makes you want to be involved. They keep showing that penalty choke of Gareth, don't they, and now they've got other shots of him, which is fantastic.'

The media picked up on the fact that Gareth had used some of my ideas – such as boosting the role of substitutes by calling them finishers. But I pointed out that it works both ways and we had used some of his techniques in our camp. 'We saw their recovery where they are all on the unicorns. We just had a recovery session out here with a Canadian theme, so we had axe throwing and chopping down trees, and doing all sorts like that.'

We were still building cohesion while relaxing and, before our first games against the USA, I had made a similar point amid the familiar limitations of Covid. 'It's reasonably restricted, but we had a "hot dogs and Budweiser beer" night. That's the closest to the USA we're going to get. The restrictions are still there but we've tried to encourage the players to enjoy themselves as much as possible.'

The media were keen to press me on my decision to appoint Lewis Ludlow as captain. He led Gloucester in the Premiership but had never played for England before. This seemed to cause some surprise. 'I had no understanding you had to have a cap to be captain,' I said in reply. 'We select the captain on the basis that he is the best leader of the team and that's why Lewis has got the nod. From our observation, we found Lewis to be the most effective club captain. He is a clear communicator, a good and sincere person. He is the best person to captain England on Sunday.'

There was also much interest, predictably, in my selection of Marcus Smith for his England debut. I had been impressed by the way he had improved since I challenged him a year earlier to become the best he could be. I was happy to give him his chance against the USA. 'He is a bright young talent,' I told the media. 'I happen to be a friend of his godfather who I met in Hong Kong. He told me about Marcus. Ever since I saw him play, I definitely knew he had some talent. But there are plenty of boys with talent. You need more than that. Marcus is now showing it. He has worked hard, come up with a game that is in its infancy but it's exciting for him to get the opportunity on Sunday. He is ready now because there is a greater degree of consistency about his game. His decision-making has improved, his effectiveness in defence has improved. But he is a very young 10. A number 10 is a bus driver and a conductor. He's got to make sure that everyone's playing together, and pick the right route, and it's no different for Marcus.'

The same applied to everyone I picked to play against the USA. 'I need to keep a completely open mind about how many of these players will come through. If we can get four or five who can go on to be the best in their positions, it'll be fantastic for us. This isn't a temporary team, this is England playing USA. Everyone who wears the shirt has the chance to own that shirt.'

We beat the USA 43–29 and scored seven tries. Joe Cokanasiga got two and Underhill, Lawrence, Blamire, Smith and Randall, also went over. Smith kicked four conversions. The downside of playing together for the first time meant we conceded four tries. But I was happy enough, and picked out Marcus Smith and Harry Randall as well as Freddie Steward, who was colossal under the high ball at full-back. 'We were looking for something a bit different from them and they gave it to us. Harry was inventive. We wanted him to put some pace in the game and he did. Marcus really did his job well and served his outside backs. He'll only get better.'

He did, alongside the entire team, and even though Canada were pretty weak, we powered away to a 70–14 win the following Sunday. There was a hat-trick of tries for both Jamie Blamire and Adam Radwan, and we scored four more with Marcus Smith racking up 18 points. It was a golden afternoon for Marcus. He had a ticket for the Euro 2020 final that night at Wembley but, as he left the pitch, he found out that he been called up as a replacement for the Lions in South Africa.

'I can't believe what is going on,' Marcus said in his post-match interview. 'To play for England a second time is special and a day I will never forget, and then I got pulled down the tunnel. I thought I was in trouble . . . but I was then given the good news. I was shaking and I don't really know what to say. I did have a ticket for the football, I still think it is going to come home, so when I land I hope for good news. It was always my dream to represent the Lions. I am massively overwhelmed. I will have to sit by myself for ten minutes tonight. I will try and take it all in but I don't think I will until I get out there.'

It was all good fairy-tale stuff, but the real tests for Marcus are still to come. 'We're pleased for him,' I said after the game. 'It's a great learning opportunity for him. He'll play with some good players against some good teams. It will aid his education process and speed it up a bit.'

Marcus had made real progress and we felt he was in a very good place when he left us for the Lions. But so much will depend on him keeping his feet on the ground in a new season. He's going to be a pin-up boy because that suits the English media mentality. They like the fact he's slightly different and seen as an X factor type of player. It's easy to be seduced, but Marcus is from a good family and he's got a good manner. He just needs to keep working to get the best out of himself.

There had been so many positives from the two summer Tests. We were delighted with the attitude and the effort of the players, and with the team leadership. We benefited from the collective leadership we are going to need as we move forward. We also have five or six players coming through who look as if they will not wilt when tested under pressure. We didn't know a lot about them before, but we can now see that they are good characters. That's important because, when you're picking a World Cup squad, your top 26 guys will play in the tournament. When we go to France in 2023, we will take 33 players, so that means seven guys might not get a game. They have to be your character guys – the players that are prepared to work and remain good people around the camp even when they are disappointed. In 2019 we got that right with Mark Wilson, Ruaridh McConnochie, Piers Francis and Lewis Ludlam. They didn't play much but they offered a lot to the squad. We need to get that right again next time.

The 2021 summer also proved you have to meet young players halfway. You've got to be conscientious about explaining your expectations and their responsibilities. But it's important not to tell them *how* to do it. That's a big difference from coaching 30 years ago. It means you are allowing them to go away and come up with the solution. And that's the right way, because players these days are much better educated than they were previously. I had dinner with a couple of them at the end of the camp, and they were talking about the history of the Soviet Union. They watch so many Netflix documentaries and so they've got good general knowledge – and they apply that desire for new information to their training preparation. You want them to stretch themselves.

The third lesson of the camp was how important it is to pay attention to your learning environment. We worked hard on making sure every meeting was full of understanding and clarity. We only made a couple of key points every day. The more stressed the players were, the less information we gave them. We made sure they absorbed new ideas at the right time.

It had been a summer of transformation and progress. We might not have settled on discoveries as obvious as Tom Curry and Sam Underhill after the Argentina tour in 2017, but plenty of players caught the eye. So much depends now on how hard they work on their game to correct their weaknesses and improve their strengths.

I liked Jamie Blamire, the young hooker from Newcastle, because he's got something about him. You saw the celebrations of the other players when he scored his tries. They were happy for Jamie and that tells you a lot about him. He had played fewer than ten Premiership games, but he works hard and he's very assertive in his own quiet way. He can really add to the squad. I also liked the look of Gabriel Oghre, another young hooker from Wasps. He's of Nigerian descent and he hasn't played much rugby at the highest level, but he's always bubbling, always got a smile on his face, and is such a pleasure to have around the squad.

Smith, Randall, Steward and Radwan also stood out among the newcomers. But we owed so much to the leadership group and to the stalwarts in Genge, Slade and Underhill. If we had played a third game, I would have felt sorry for the opposition, because we had just started to click and really fly as a team. But we had been through back-to-back campaigns and the senior players were exhausted. They deserved a break after a summer of rejuvenation and lessons in transformation. They would return with renewed energy, and even stronger belief in our vision, because we had managed to:

FIND A DIFFERENT CHEMISTRY WITH A FRESH PERSPECTIVE

- Tackle the marginal improvements

- Realize all opportunities

- Address all tactical issues

- Drive out minor imperfections

- Understand and accept different backgrounds, ideas and patterns of behaviour

- Seek out fresh eyes to bring about transformation

STAGE 5: REBUILD

17. The Cycle Continues

[STRATEGY]

- Decide your scale of change. Refresh or rebuild?

[PEOPLE]

- Rebuild (if required)
- Align resources
- Deliver fundamental changes

[OPERATION]

- Rebuild–Experiment–Win [Overcome Failure] again at a tactical level

[MANAGEMENT]

- Focus
- Resolve the areas that are sub-optimal

17

THE CYCLE CONTINUES

**MANAGE BEHAVIOUR, MINE FOR CONFLICT,
MAP YOUR PLACE IN THE CYCLE**

The leadership cycle is unending. Our high-performance environment demands a constant search for evolution and improvement. This explains why we are never content and we are never comfortable. It is harsh and it is relentless. But the challenge to coach, operate and manage in this singular world is fascinating and rewarding.

Another season had ended but, in July 2021, there would be no holiday for me. I had too much to consider, plan and implement. We had been through two of the most surreal campaigns in my 25 years as a professional coach. Covid had swept the globe with devastating impact. We were all affected by the long-lasting shock of a global pandemic. Beyond the lockdowns and bubbles, as well as the empty arenas and the periods of self-isolation, the ongoing uncertainty in economic, social and psychological terms was profound. I felt the impact, as did everyone else around me. My team, and our sport, reeled from its consequences. But so did every other sport, team and coach in the world. Even those who tried to dismiss it, or refused to be cautious or vaccinated, could not escape the insidious spread of coronavirus and its deadly variants.

In early March 2020, the Six Nations tournament had had to be postponed. It was eventually completed in late October. Club rugby in England and Europe had gone into lockdown for five months. Even when the Premiership resumed in August 2020, it would be played behind closed doors until the following May. Clubs were losing around £1 million a month. The wide-ranging implications of shutting out spectators for international games in the Autumn Nations Cup in late 2020 and the Six Nations in 2021 will be felt for years to come. The RFU, which funds a large chunk of English rugby, derives 85 per cent of its income from England selling out Twickenham. The losses during this period exceeded more than £100 million.

But in elite sport you live by the mantra of worrying only about issues you can personally control. Everything else is uncontrollable and, as a leader, I have become better at focusing on the specific areas I can influence. We had learnt to prepare and to play rugby under the shadow of Covid and, despite a proper off-season for the first time in two years, I spent July and August continuing my work. The world had changed but my leadership doctrine remained.

You reflect. You review. You start planning. You begin looking ahead. You also apportion time to professional development. What areas do I need to improve in? How can I facilitate that improvement? A coach is like a player. When the season ends you usually have a break. Then you move into pre-season work where you get ready for renewed competition. So it's the same cycle again. But I chose to continue without any time away. The consuming nature of my role demanded such dedication, and in fact the summer Tests had felt revitalizing.

In mid-July I reached for a pen and lined pad of paper. I wrote the words *The High-Performance Challenge* at the top of the page, and then produced a simple little sketch. There were four words which I joined together in a circle, with arrows leading from one to the other. They resembled a bicycle wheel, with the word Leadership written in the middle. At the top of the cycle, at twelve o'clock on an imaginary clock face, we had a word linked to three other words – one at three o'clock, one at six o'clock and another at nine o'clock. Arrows leading from one word to the other made a circle. The four words defined my cycle of leadership:

1. Vision

2. Structure

3. People

4. Culture

Beneath the small drawing I made three notes in bullet-point form:

• Manage people

• Mine for conflict

• Map where you are in the cycle

It was a reminder to myself that leadership centres on the performance environment. We are trying to create an environment where we maximize the performance of the people in and around our England camp. The leader's job is to create a vision, and then from that vision you put a structure in place. They are symbiotic, because the structure then enables you to implement the vision, as long as you have the right people around you. The right people enable you to drive the culture and behaviour you need to fulfil the vision that started the cycle.

In the diagram I wrote the phrase 'Motion for Growth' in a box, which I then linked with an arrow to the three Ms . . . manage, mine and map.

It made clear that sustainable growth, which is vital for the development of the leadership cycle, depended on MMM. Management, mining and mapping.

The driving focus of the leadership cycle is growth. It means that you cannot stand still or ever consider the cycle to be complete. You are always striving to get better, and to do so you need to constantly mine the environment for pitfalls and problems. As we have discussed, even when you are on a successful run, there is no doubt that the potential for conflict lurks beneath the surface. You need to find it and resolve it and move on, and the best way to do this is to manage the people within your organization. As you walk the floor you can monitor their behaviour and overcome trouble before it spreads. At the same time, you need to map exactly where you are in the cycle and, if you have fallen behind, it is imperative that you redouble your efforts to get back to where you should be on the path to success. You have to try continually to be on top of the cycle, managing and mining it all the time, even though your work is never over until you decide to walk away and do something less demanding.

This process applies to any high-performance environment. But it is especially true of elite sport. You reach a point where it seems as if everything is running smoothly and you're moving in the right direction – but that can be dissolved the very next day. You never conquer it, but you're always trying to get ahead of the curve and stay on top of the problems.

In terms of our leadership group, we have had some good periods, and some bad periods, under both Dylan Hartley and Owen Farrell. We are now rebuilding the leadership group for the next World Cup. It's two years away but we will be managing, mining and mapping this area of the squad until the very end of the tournament on 28 October 2023.

As I write this in late summer, during the Rebuild stage of the leadership cycle, I have not settled on anything before the autumn Tests in 2021. I have 12 players I'm looking at closely, and from which I will select a leadership group of five – one of whom will be Owen. But we need to see who will be fit and available and who is in form when I make this next leadership selection.

One of the key ideas we're considering is making the leadership group a fluid entity. The traditional idea is to pin everything on one figurehead but, as outlined in the previous chapters, I have begun to move more towards the idea of collective leadership among the players, with diversity and flexibility being central to our development. The chemistry generated by the summer group for the Tests against the USA and Canada was far more powerful than relying so heavily on a captain who has to shoulder so much responsibility.

I have been reading and thinking a great deal about the difference between engaged leaders and entitled leaders. You can start off as being a highly engaged leader, keen to inspire and galvanize your team, but then you can become an entitled leader where you are motivated more by the power of the role. We've got to make sure that we keep our leadership group engaged. It's fair to say that, since the 2019 World Cup, we've slid a little down the path of entitlement. We have to pull it back to the pathway of engagement.

I will consider how best to do this but, as the established leadership group has cracked, we might use the November internationals as a trial period to see what we need to change. I might decide, instead, to stay with what we've got. But the process of examination and judgement will be ceaseless. We are considering various options, including one of Will Carling's ideas around the leadership programme. Will has suggested we might use Deloitte to support us in doing some psychometric testing of the leaders.

After the 2021 Six Nations, we agreed that we have to give them more leadership skills, by educating them and engaging with them more constructively to drive sustained development. Will said: 'Why don't we look at one of the big companies who do this on a regular basis?' Deloitte were mentioned and, like most corporate businesses in England, they like rugby and want to be involved. So we're moving down that track.

It will be tricky because we're in quite a unique situation. The only other example I can think of in elite sport is the Australian cricket team, when the leadership group was shattered after Steve Smith and David Warner were found guilty of involvement in the ball-tampering saga against South Africa in March 2018. Smith was the captain, and he was aware that Warner, one of his trusted lieutenants, had encouraged a young player, Cameron Bancroft, to use sandpaper as a way of scuffing the ball to aid their bowlers. When they were exposed, all three were banned from Test cricket for a year. Tim Paine, the wicketkeeper, was brought into the team and became the new captain. After a year, Smith and Warner were recalled. I am sure Smith is again playing a leadership role, but it is in the background because Paine remains the captain.

Our Saracens players were caught up in controversy, but the onus of responsibility for breaking the salary cap belonged to their club. So while the players were not punished officially, they were hurt by the club's infamy and relegation from the Premiership. They lost money on their contracts and so much playing time. Our leadership group was rocked and we now need to repair the fractured chemistry or rebuild the entire entity. As the overall leader, I've got to make a crucial judgement on what the squad needs.

It is also clear to me that, in English sport, diversity is going to become even more of a crucial factor, and we want to address this both publicly and internally. Society needs – even demands – that sport should set the right example. Alongside Gareth Southgate's England football team, we have made a significant contribution to diversity in sport. Our squad is much more representative of England as a multiracial country than it was previously and, in making a difference, we have been aggressive in our selection. We have picked on merit and, as a consequence, diversity has flourished.

In England, as in many first-world countries, there is a lot of hidden racism. I think we can do so much more and be even better role models. So we will continue down this road because it's of great importance to the squad and to society. The leadership group clearly needs more diversity – and I mean in a sense which extends beyond just racial inclusivity. We need a fluid and engaged group, drawn from a wider variety of backgrounds. The summer selection proved the validity of this view.

The clock is always ticking, but I've got until the World Cup to get it right. No coach ever has enough time, and we are always clamouring to get everything in place long before the biggest tournament in our sport kicks off. But the Springboks won just 45 per cent of their Tests in the build-up to the last World Cup. Nothing ever clicks seamlessly, and it is impossible to be precise as to when your vision will come to fruition. I am certain, however, that we are on the right path. We will make the necessary changes to the leadership group at the appropriate time.

In terms of my own leadership, I am constantly assessing and evaluating all that I do. Just as Ron Adams holds Steve Kerr to account at the Golden State Warriors in the NBA, so I rely on Neil Craig to be my truth-teller in regard to my own leadership errors and flaws. We are hopeful that Neil will be back in camp for the autumn of 2021 but, in his absence, Will Carling and Simon Scott have occasionally filled the gap.

Will stays clear of selection, and so that means there is a clear demarcation in terms of his work with the group. He is there purely as a bridge to the past and as a leadership mentor. But when it comes to discussing the leadership attributes or deficiencies of the group, then Will is not afraid to tell me when he thinks I've made a mistake. During our rare disagreements, I value the honesty of his response. It explains why I also invited Simon Scott to assess my management style.

Simon is a management consultant who was in the Marines. I met him about three years ago at Pennyhill Park and we enjoyed each other's company. Simon was keen to come in and have a look at how we operated, and I suggested when he did so that he should make observations and suggestions regarding my leadership. We soon settled into a mutually beneficial arrangement, where Simon comes in around four times a year to offer another fresh perspective. It's a pretty informal working relationship.

Simon receives no financial reward, and so he has complete independence and the ability to be honest. He has said it is an opportunity for him to learn in a high-performance sports environment, while I certainly benefit from the wisdom he brings.

His key observation is that I need to work constantly on becoming less blunt in my engagement with the other coaches and the players. The language we use now is empathetic encouragement – using a softer approach, rooted in respect for someone else's position, while suggesting they might consider doing it in a different way. Simon felt I had plenty of empathy, but I can express myself too directly. If you're too blunt in today's environment you can cause stress – which then affects the performance of the people around you. Of course, elite sport remains an often unforgiving business, and so there are times when you need to cut right to the heart of a problem. You can't waste time on verbal niceties when you're facing defeat. But you are always striving for the right balance between the need for blunt honesty and the need for empathy. I am working on my softer skills and I think I am improving.

Simon's very detailed and organized. He writes everything down and brings a real rigour to his assessment. Will is more fluid, and he will talk openly rather than write lengthy reports. They provide a diverse blend as they observe the leadership group, my fellow coaches and me with contrasting styles of scrutiny. They offer a reminder that, as a leader, you always need fresh eyes to look at your environment and the way in which you carry out the three essential Ms – managing behaviour, mining for conflict and mapping your place in the leadership cycle.

As suggested throughout the previous pages, my leadership know-how is also developed and enhanced by regular engagement with other coaches. One of the most enjoyable is with a small and tight-knit group of Australian coaches that includes Neil Craig, Luke Beveridge, the head coach of the Western Bulldogs, the Australian Rules football club in Melbourne, Brian Goorjian who coaches the Boomers, Australia's national basketball team, and

Ange Postecoglou, who now manages Celtic in the Scottish Premiership.

They are all impressive blokes. Luke led the Bulldogs to their first Grand Final victory since 1954 when they won the title in 2016 – after he had inspired a real turnaround in their fortunes. In August 2021, Brian coached the Boomers in the Tokyo Olympics. When he became national coach just weeks before the Games began, the team was already being led by three NBA players. Patty Mills of the Brooklyn Nets comes from Canberra and he spearheaded the players' desire to dictate the team culture. Brian was happy to let this unfold because Mills, an Indigenous Australian, was a strong leader who, with the backing of his NBA teammates, established how the team should train, work together and foster their identity. They were solid and powerful values and the NBA trio, with their high standards, drove the team. Bryan read the situation and, with great wisdom, he decided there was not enough time to implement any of his own ideas. He allowed the players to keep leading.

It was still tricky because, before joining the group, he had only met the players on Zoom. But once he was embedded in the job he found the right moment to take charge. The Boomers played great basketball in the semi-finals but they lost narrowly to the USA. After the game the team was devastated. The locker room looked a mess, with kit strewn all over the place. All the high standards had vanished in the aftermath of defeat. Yet they still had another game to play – the bronze medal match against a very good team in Slovenia.

Brian delivered a blistering speech. He reminded his players that they had come into the Olympic Games with gold-standard values. They could no longer win gold but that did not mean, for one moment, that they should allow their standards to slip. It was time for them to reinforce that gold-standard quality as they strove to leave Tokyo with a medal-winning performance. The players were very quiet and Brian was not sure of their reaction.

Just before 1 a.m. that morning there was a knock on his door. The towering figure of Patty Mills said, 'Coach, you were right. It's not over. Let's go for this thing.'

The Boomers were galvanized and they went out and blitzed Slovenia 107–93, with Mills scoring 42 points. They had also made history by winning Australia's first ever Olympic basketball medal. It's a great story about how a leader has to read the room and the temperature of the team – and know when to take over.

Meanwhile, Ange Postecoglou was born in Greece but he grew up in Melbourne and managed the Australian national football team, the Socceroos, from 2013 to 2017. He took them to the 2014 World Cup in Brazil and he also steered them through a successful qualification group for the next tournament. But a few weeks after Australia's 2018 World Cup place was secured, Ange opted to return to club football with Yokohama F. Marinos in Japan. He helped them win their first J-League title in 15 years when they became champions in 2019. Ange was appointed Celtic's manager in June 2021. It's a challenging position because, after being Scottish champions for nine successive seasons, Celtic's hopes of an historic tenth title were shattered by their bitter rivals, Rangers, managed by Steven Gerrard.

In July, during one of our fortnightly sessions, Ange offered an insight into the high stakes he faced. His first game in charge was a Champions League qualifier that would have been worth £40 million to the club if they had got through against the Danish side, Midtjylland. But when we spoke a week before the first leg, he had only six fully fit first-team players. Celtic drew the game 1–1 at home and were knocked out after extra time in the away leg. That put immense pressure on Ange, even before the Scottish season had started, and as all of us were becoming busy again, we took a little break from our group meetings.

We obviously couldn't help him with his Champions League preparation, or the first three months of his Celtic tenure, which would decide whether he would be given time to rebuild the club in the way we knew he could, but you pick up so much from these forums which you can apply to your own work. It might just be different ways of saying things that make it fresh for the players. Using someone else's words or training techniques can sometimes light a spark in your players.

The Rebuild stage of the leadership cycle also allows time to introduce ideas from other disciplines. In the late summer of 2021, I resolved that the new season would see us bring back tactical periodization as a training technique. It had been immensely useful in the past but we had drifted away from it. We needed to return to its core principles to revitalize us still further.

When I took over Japan, their average losing score against Tier One countries was 85–0. So John Pryor, the strength and conditioning coach who was my solitary assistant, helped me consider every possible concept to improve our training. I was becoming more and more interested in football, and intrigued how the top European teams could remain so consistently good throughout a long season of 50 or even 60 games. I was amazed at their ability to sustain their excellence so long because rugby teams traditionally go up and down. I sensed that such consistency must be rooted in training.

So we looked at tactical periodization, which many leading football clubs were using. JP is quite an academic guy, and he did most of the more sophisticated reading, while I concentrated on finding contacts for people working within the field.

We had an almost perfect laboratory to work on tactical periodization with our Japanese squad, because we had the vital ingredient of time and players who had an enormous appetite for work and who would be compliant. So we started to experiment and work out how best to maximize this new strategy. Traditionally, fitness training in rugby had been run independently of skills training, because it gives you clear indicators of each. But they were already very fit and we wanted to train as many rugby skills as we could utilize. We wanted the Japanese to play a rugby version of Barcelona and the Spanish national team's tiki-taka style of possession football, which is characterized by short passing and fast, fluid movement as the ball is moved from one channel to another by nimble and skilful players. It is coordinated and cohesive, moving and passing the ball in synergy, like orchestra members in harmony with each other.

Tactical periodization had been invented by Vitor Frade, at the University of Porto, and John and I went to Qatar to meet a Portuguese disciple of the technique. It was fascinating and we were inspired to create our own methodology. We experimented a hell of a lot and we cheated a little bit because we instituted additional early morning sessions at 5.30 a.m. where they did independent strength and conditioning work. It was a hard sell to the Japanese, because they come from a late-night culture where they don't get up early in the morning. We were ordering them to wake up at 4.30 a.m. so they could be training hard an hour later. But they did it, and we soon moved them on to two S&C sessions in the morning. On top of this they did focused tactical periodization work to enhance their performances.

Through trial and error, and a lot of failure and pain, we came up with a system that worked really well for the Japanese. We helped them reach an incredible level of fitness, which meant they could outrun and outlast anyone at the World Cup in 2015. We also fulfilled a clear picture of playing as if we were the Barcelona of rugby. Tactical periodization was the bedrock.

So, as we moved deeper into England's Rebuild cycle in 2021, I decided one of our great challenges going forward would be to bring a new version of tactical periodization to the team. I knew that this meant I needed to find the right coaches who would be prepared to break tradition to coach this way. It's hard because most coaches have been successful working more conventionally and they are reluctant to switch to anything radical. This is a difficult concept, because you have to be so disciplined about the way you train and keep referencing your style of play in training. But I believe tactical periodization is the most effective way to train a team. As I refreshed my thinking, I had a long call with Raymond Verheijen, the Dutch coach, and we worked out how we could apply his form of football periodization to our tactical periodization. Out of the disappointment and failure of the Six Nations, we were making fresh progress again.

The pursuit of perfection, at least in the leadership cycle, is a dangerous illusion. I've learnt that it leads you down a blind alley. Rugby is such an imperfect game. As the game becomes more chaotic, the idea of 'perfection' is the ability to adapt rather than to chase the impossible dream of doing everything perfectly. In a 100-metre sprint it might be possible to run the perfect race. But you cannot produce the perfect game of rugby.

I came closest to 'perfection' in my first year as a coach when I coached Randwick's second-grade team. I had a real focus on three-phase completion. I also had a very good team and we used to do this drill at the start of our three-phase completion. We nailed it most of the time and won the league easily. We then won our play-off semi-final and, in the final, we were ahead 36–0 at half-time. It was almost perfect three-phase rugby. But the key word is 'almost'. We fell away in the second half and we won 42–0. It gave me a taste of what you could do in rugby, but we have to remember that this was second-grade rugby and we were much better than the opposition.

You can't play perfect Test match rugby. Of course I'm still trying to coach a perfect game where, rather than playing utterly flawless rugby, you dominate every minute of the match. It's never going to happen but, when it matters most, the 2019 World Cup semi-final is as close as you're going to get. The scoreline didn't reflect our domination of that game, but the performance was hugely satisfying – and it's rivalled only, for me as a coach, by Japan's defeat of South Africa.

I've seen players in my teams touch on a form of perfection in certain games. Wendell Sailor in my Australian side's 2003 World Cup semi-final win against New Zealand was almost unstoppable. The All Blacks couldn't tackle him, and every time Wendell had the ball we were on the front foot and put them under huge pressure. Richie McCaw and Dan Carter played games like that. Fourie du Preez came close to it when South Africa just lost the 2015 World Cup semi-final to New Zealand. Jonny May has touched on absolute magnificence in some games for England. Tom Curry will do so in the future.

Perfection is an illusion, but defeat and mistakes bring a clarity of thinking. I know that I am a better coach now than in 2019. If a coach or leader has worked only in a successful environment, then he or she will only have been in the job for a very brief period. They won't have learnt much. I want to learn from people who have actually been exposed to adversity, who have had to reflect and then fight on. They might feel badly about themselves or the mistakes they have made, but I am more interested in how they respond and get back up again.

The experience of losing a second World Cup final and, more importantly, my capacity to reflect on these lessons, deepens my knowledge. I have also learnt so much about coaching, because the subsequent circumstances of the team have become much more difficult. I've had to evolve and use my skills to adjust and to appraise where we need to adapt. It's been difficult, but I'm getting closer and closer to the right solution. I am working on doing it in a way that won't do too much damage to the team.

Rather than chasing perfection, you need to accept that whenever you change your team, you cause some damage. But if you don't change your team, you will probably damage it more deeply. So you are trying to balance this fine art of leadership all the time.

It has helped me to use the values, principles and methods which have shaped this book. I believe they apply to so many aspects of leadership, whether in sport, business or any other high-performance field. As I have improved over the previous two years, I have discovered again the following core truths:

- Building another high-performing team demands a ceaseless cycle of activity

- My England squad needs continuous improvement

- There has been a rigorous process of rebuilding and refreshing

- I have applied strategic, transformational, operational and managerial thinking

- I have moved across all three levels of thinking, while also applying tactical insights and having clear communication with my assistant coaches and the players so that there has been growth even amid adversity

- I have had to draw on all my years of leadership experience – and relied on the lessons of both victory and defeat

- I have engaged consistently with other coaches, absorbing new ideas and methods, and broadened my understanding of leadership

- I have set our vision

- I am building the appropriate structure

- I am searching, constantly, for the right people to coach and to play for England

- I am working consistently on the Three Ms . . . managing, mining and mapping

- We are building, experimenting, winning and rebuilding relentlessly

- The cycle is unending and so we continue, hopefully improving all the time

If you are an outstanding professional pianist already, with a great natural talent, how do you become one of the greatest pianists in the world? A simple answer is by continually practising the piano with rigour, by performing at the highest level, by listening to other musicians, by learning from other pianists and by practising some more. There are obviously so many intangible mysteries which aid the process, but the fundamentals remain the same.

Practise, perform, listen, learn and practise some more.

I believe it's no different in leadership and elite coaching. You need to practise, perform, listen, learn and practise some more. The art of practise can never be denied. How do you become a great coach or a great leader? You need to practise coaching and leadership.

I love rugby and I love coaching. And so I am going to take any opportunity I get to practise coaching in my spare time. I love going back to Suntory in Japan and I love the ten-day spells I have to refresh myself by doing nothing else but practise my coaching with a group of players who are always eager to work and to learn. I learn even more from them at these practice sessions – especially when the chance arises to work with Beauden Barrett.

A Bob Dwyer phrase still rings in my head today. He said: 'The best coaches in the world are the best players.' He meant that, if you want to become a better coach, learn from the best players. Every time I talk to a leading player, I learn more from them than they learn from me.

In England there has been much criticism of me coaching Suntory, and working with Beauden. But for me the best thing is that Beauden, one of the world's great rugby players, is comfortable enough in himself, as I am in myself, to talk about the game so openly. We're not trying to take anything away from each other. We're trying to help each other and to just share our love of the game. Winning matters hugely, but I want the game of rugby to grow and to be truly great.

Some coaches and leaders prefer to run their lives in a more secretive way. But I have found that if you're open and you're sharing then, generally, you get more back than you give. I wouldn't have it any other way because, to me, it's stimulating and refreshing and rewarding.

I went to Argentina before the last World Cup to help their coaches set up a local club competition. I did it out of a genuine love for the game rather than because I was letting slip any A1 secrets – not that we really have any. We shared information, and when I got there I learnt some new ideas which have been of benefit to me and my team. I might have helped them think about the game in a different way, too, and how can that be anything but good for rugby?

When working with Beauden, I have learnt more about his humility and the way he keeps working at his game. He has twice been the IRB's World Rugby Player of the Year but, with Suntory, which is supposedly meant to be an easy gig for him, he comes out every morning for training with the vim and enthusiasm of an 18-year-old. One week, even when there was no game on the weekend and he had a crook neck and had to wear a medical bib, Beauden was at it with so much purpose and intent. He loves practising and training and playing, and I savour that undying passion that surges through him.

I've spoken about Beauden to my players in England. Over here, considering the length of the season and the environment, some players tend to go through the motions in training. But you need to find a way to retain that boyish love and enthusiasm for the game. On one of my trips to Japan in 2020, I had lunch with Ange Postecoglou. We had no idea that, a year down the track, he would be in Glasgow, managing Celtic. Instead we just spoke about coaching as, then, he was in charge of Yokohama. Ange had told his players the same thing that morning: 'Remember when you were a schoolboy? Remember that love of the game then? Try not to play any differently now.'

It is hard to do this in England. I find that players over here can age quicker than elsewhere because of the volume of rugby they play. When they age, desire fades fastest. But I also know there is great resilience among my best players, and so I don't want to make decisions until they are back in camp after the Lions tour. We will soon find out if they have found a way to refresh themselves; whether they can rekindle their desire to work hard for a team that has the vision of playing the greatest rugby ever seen. We have a long way to go before we reach that point, but the cycle continues and we have time over the next two years to make considerable progress.

I was asked the other day if the way we defeated France in the Six Nations might be a blueprint for our style of play in the World Cup? My answer was an emphatic 'no' because we don't know how the game will evolve. The ruck speed is increasing and referees are being highly inconsistent. Who knows what will happen in the scrum before the World Cup? The game could be completely different in late 2023. It is very important for us to be perceptive and adaptable.

Looking further ahead is more clouded. If you consider how leadership and coaching has changed over the last 20 years, we have an indication that there might be further seismic shifts during the next five years. Different athletes are emerging, and we will need different skill sets to get the best out of them. Players are more inclined to be vulnerable now because the pressures are greater and there is an accompanying culture to be more open. Naomi Osaka spoke about her mental health when dealing with the media as she pulled out of the French Open and withdrew from Wimbledon in the summer of 2021. Could you imagine Rod Laver, 50 years ago, saying, 'I can't do a press conference after a game'?

Media conferences and social media are often hostile places today but, back in Laver's era, the idea of expressing vulnerability was unacceptable. Players can be more honest now and, as a result, this affects the way you coach and lead them. In the coming years, I expect a head coach to become even more like a manager of resources. The players will need larger and more specialized coaching teams around them. Even now, to provide the best high-performance environment, you need to offer expert sports psychology, sports science, sports medicine, sports recovery, sports data analysis, as well as so many specialist skills coaches. The head coach will become even more of a facilitator as he or she strives to find the right balance for each player. I expect that the preparation of the players will become more individualistic. There'll be less team training and more individual preparation. Players may have their own group around them, managing their own preparation. We're already seeing examples of this in football because players have so much more influence than previously.

Data-driven analysis will remain integral because that provides your performance base. But the psychology of sport will become more important as the head coach and leader manage a wider range of emotions amongst the playing group. You have to react with real sensitivity. If you had been Naomi Osaka's coach 20 years ago, you might have said: 'If you don't want to be a professional tennis player then do something different.' But it would be totally wrong to say that today. You need to make sure you look after her in the right way. Most teams don't include a clinical psychologist on their staff. In five years we might need one, so that we can offer that level of psychological support to our players. The world is changing and leaders need to change even faster.

I am focused on the here-and-now and this explains why I really have no interest in the concept of legacy. I don't control it and I don't care what people might say I have offered to English rugby. I know I have poured everything of myself into trying to help and improve the players. That's all that matters. In the same way, while sharing information, I am committed to passing as much knowledge as I can to the next generation. It explains why, when I finally finish coaching Test match rugby, I would like to give something more back to the game. I would love to be involved in coaching coaches.

I remember the immense satisfaction whenever I have done this in the past. In South Africa, Jake White and I gave coaching clinics to schoolboy coaches. We met 400 coaches in two weeks as we went to all the rugby-playing schools in each of the major cities. It was all about giving back to the game through them. In Japan, I run a coaches' clinic for university and high school coaches. That runs every year – apart from this past year when Covid got in the way. Now, if a junior club asks me to look at what they're doing and to talk to their coaches in the North or the South of England, I'll do my best to help out. As long as it's done outside the international calendar, I am thrilled to offer support. It gives me so much satisfaction and pleasure and, yes, it is another opportunity to practise my coaching and my leadership.

I always want to be a servant to the players, and a servant to the game of rugby.

The last two years have been the most challenging and interesting of my coaching career. I have been tested and examined as a leader like never before. But it's all part of the ceaseless cycle of leadership. I believe I have grown and matured as a coach while relying on the building blocks of:

- Strategy

- People

- Operation

- Management

We have been through five stages of the leadership cycle:

1. Vision

2. Build

3. Experiment

4. Win [Overcome Failure]

5. Rebuild

I am ready to go again because the cycle has not paused – let alone ended. It has continued turning and whirring. So we will carry on as well, building, experimenting, winning and rebuilding, while managing the players and their behaviour, mining for the conflict which is always there and mapping our current place in the cycle.

I have improved as a coach and as a leader and I am confident that the next stages of the cycle will show the benefits of all we have learnt in these testing times. The work will continue, as always, alongside the sheer pleasure of coaching and the enduring honour of leadership.

MANAGE BEHAVIOUR, MINE FOR CONFLICT, MAP YOUR PLACE IN THE CYCLE

- Decide your scale of change. Refresh or rebuild

- Align resources

- Deliver quick wins and fundamental changes

- Rebuild–Experiment–Win [Overcome Failure] again at a tactical level

- Focus

- Resolve the areas that are sub-optimal

- Evolve and improve constantly, as demanded by a high-performance environment

- Make time to reflect, review and plan. Apportion time to professional development. Ask yourself what areas do you need to improve in? How can you facilitate that improvement?

- Drive for growth. You cannot stand still, or ever consider the cycle to be complete

- The pursuit of perfection, at least in the leadership cycle, is a dangerous illusion

- Practise, perform, listen, then learn and practise some more

ACKNOWLEDGEMENTS

I have been fortunate to have been educated in leadership by the great players I have coached, the coaches I have met and worked alongside and by various business acquaintances. They have all contributed to my views and understanding of how to lead and influence others.

In Australia, David Pembroke and Neil Craig have been great influences on me. Masa Mochida of Goldman Sachs and Masato Tsuchida and Junichi Inagaki of Suntory have provided guidance in Japan. Meanwhile, the opportunities in England to meet some of the greatest football coaches in the world have been exceptional.

Thanks to my agent Craig Livingstone for all his help and support as we developed this idea for a book about leadership. Neil Craig and Will Carling were good enough to share their thoughts with us on leadership. They helped a great deal.

All the staff at Pan Macmillan have been excellent as we prepared for publication. Thanks especially to Samantha Fletcher for making sure we got everything done and to Robin Harvie for his vision and editorial expertise. Robin worked closely with Don McRae and me as the three of us explored the themes and memories in this book in detailed discussions. Thanks again to Don for helping me write this book and telling the stories which frame these ideas of leadership.

PICTURE ACKNOWLEDGEMENTS

Will Genia, 2009: Ross Land, Getty Images Sport
Ayumu Goromaru, 2018: Koki Nagahama/Getty Images
James Haskell, 2016: David Rogers/Getty Images Sport
Eddie Jones in Australia, 2016: David Rogers/Getty Images Sport
England training session, 2016: David Rogers/Getty Images Sport
Jonny May, 2014: Phil Walter/Getty Images Sport
England v. Scotland, 2021 Six Nations: Adrian Dennis/AFP
Billy Vunipola, 2021 Six Nations: David Rogers/RFU, The RFU Collection
George Ford tackles Josh Adams: Michael Steele/Getty Images Sport
England win against France, 2021 Six Nations: Craig Mercer/ MB Media/Getty Images Sport
Kyle Sinckler, May 2021: Bob Bradford, CameraSport/ CameraSport
Steve Kerr and Ron Adams: Noah Graham/National Basketball Association
Arsène Wenger: Adrian Dennis/AFP
Pep Guardiola with FC Bayern Munich: A Beier/FC Bayern
Neil Craig and Eddie Jones, 2019: David Rogers/Getty Images Sport
Sean Dyche: Anadolu Agency
Billy Beane, Curt Young and Mike Aldrete: Michael Zagaris/ Getty Images Sport
2021 debut England players: Alex Davidson/The RFU Collection

INDEX

EJ indicates Eddie Jones.

access point, finding the 97, 118, 155–71
ACT Brumbies 1, 32, 37, 61, 72, 85, 91,
    112, 222, 224–5, 228–30, 239,
    274–6
acting lessons 74, 235
Adams, Josh 184
Adams, Ron 3, 34–5, 41, 213, 214–15,
    216, 217, 218, 219, 321
Adelaide Crows 41
adversity, response to 2, 87, 111, 152,
    177, 191–208, 266, 328, 329
Ajax Amsterdam 94–5, 221
Alexander, Lisa 305
alignment
    align resources to the changes
        required 97, 117, 120–33, 134, 135,
        313, 332–4, 335
    align the overall vision to individual
        journeys 5, 94–5, 96
Alldritt, Grégory 131
Al-Qaeda 262
America's Cup 200
Amor, Simon 55, 57, 302
Andrew, Rob 47
Apple 29, 262
Applied Cognitive Neuroscience Group,
    UCL 251
Argentina
    EJ helps coaches set up local club
        competition in 331

England rugby team tour of (2017)
    120, 126, 271, 297, 310
Argentina (national rugby union
    team) 10
Arnold, Rory 282
Arsenal FC 220–1
assessment
    clarity and 4, 5, 53–76
    transformation delivery versus goals in
        value terms, assessing 191–208
    management style, outside assessment
        of 321–2
Australia
    British and Irish Lions tour of
        (2013) 32
    England rugby team tour of (2004)
        280–1
    England rugby team tour of (2016)
        123–5, 164, 236, 277–80, 281–6,
        290–1, 298–9
Australia (national basketball team)
    (Boomers) 322–4
Australia (national cricket team) 73,
    228, 280, 319–20
Australia (national football team)
    (Socceroos) 324
Australia (national rugby union team) 8,
    10, 11, 15, 26, 63, 161–2, 170, 224
    British and Irish Lions tour to
        Australia (2013) and 32

Australia (rugby union team) (*Cont'd.*)
  Deans as coach of 31–2, 33, 34
  EJ as coach of 1, 8, 15, 26–7, 31, 32–3,
    34, 35, 37, 73, 85, 100, 112, 132, 147,
    161–2, 176, 213, 235, 253, 256,
    275–6, 280–1, 286–7, 292, 327–8
  EJ fired as coach of 176, 213, 235–6
  EJ's playing career and 213
  England rugby team tour of Australia
    (2004) and 280–1
  England rugby team tour of Australia
    (2016) and 11, 63, 123–5, 164, 236,
    277–86, 290–1, 298–9
  Tri-Nations (2001) 32–3, 34
  World Cup (1991) 44
  World Cup (1999) 31
  World Cup (2003) 1, 15, 26–7, 132,
    147, 236, 292, 327–8
  World Cup (2007) 26–7
  World Cup (2015) 284
  World Cup (2019) 10, 122
Australian Rules Football 41, 322
Austrian Bundesliga 182
authenticity 223–4
Autumn Nations Cup
  (2020) 2, 51, 56, 58, 63, 65, 69, 99, 200,
    201, 316
Autumn Nations Series (2021) 269, 318

Bancroft, Cameron 320
Barcelona FC 143, 221, 325–6
Barnes, Wayne 197
Barrett, Beauden 84–5, 93, 127, 130,
  270, 330, 331
Bath Rugby 121, 123, 127, 164, 239, 270
Battersea Ironsides 123
Bayern Munich 143–4
Beane, Billy 118–20
Becker, Boris 265
Benetton 38
Bennett, Wayne 67, 222–3, 225, 275
best players, secret of the 93

Beveridge, Luke 322, 323
big ball rugby 56–7
bin Laden, Osama 262
Blackadder, Todd 229
Blackberry 198–9
Blamire, Jamie 298, 308, 310
Bodyline 280, 281
Borthwick, Steve 37, 38, 231, 239
Boston Celtics 216
Botham, Ian 228
BP 265
Brace, Andrew 203
Bracken, Kieran 271
Bradman, Don 280
Brailsford, Dave 199, 213, 219
Brearley, Mike 160, 228–9
breathing lessons 69
Brisbane Broncos 222, 240, 275
Bristol Bears 121, 123, 125, 126, 295, 297
British and Irish Lions
  Australia tour (2013) 32
  Living with Lions video 289
  New Zealand tour (2017) 120, 271–2
  South Africa tour (1997) 289–90
  South Africa tour (2021) 56, 114,
    120–3, 125, 126, 131, 185–6, 196,
    234, 269, 270, 297, 299, 308–9, 331
Brown, Mike 126, 132, 268, 273, 279, 297
Brumbies *see* ACT Brumbies
Build (Stage 2 – leadership cycle) *viii*, 3,
  97–171
  access point, finding the 97, 155–71
  conflict, healthy 97, 137–53
  disciplined thinking and emotional
    journeys 97, 117–35
  Growth Mondays 97, 99–116
Burnley FC 144–6
Burrell, Luther 11, 282

Campese, David 92–3
Canada (national rugby union team) 120,
  296–8, 304–5, 306, 307, 308, 319

Cantona, Eric 126
captaincy
  Australia cricket team 73, 320
  Brumbies 228–30
  England cricket team 160, 228, 280
  England rugby union team 37, 39, 43–4,
    45, 46–7, 95, 107, 196–7, 230–4,
    234–5, 273–4, 278, 279, 282, 284, 286,
    295–6, 300–1, 304–5, 307, 319
  Japan rugby union team 158–60, 255
  South Africa rugby union team 9
Care, Danny 126, 132, 268, 297
Carling, Will 43–7, 68, 107, 108,
    231, 277, 295–6, 300–1, 304,
    319, 321, 322
Carter, Dan 91, 130, 270, 328
Cats (Super 12 team) 229
Catt, Mike 38
Celtic, Glasgow 323, 324–5, 331
certainty, psychology of 111–16
Champions League 23, 141, 324
Championship, Football League 144
Championship, Rugby 58
character, selection and ('character over
    cover drive') 31–52
Charlesworth, Ric 91
Cheika, Michael 279, 281–2
Chelsea FC 141, 258
chemistry, diversity and 4, 245, 278,
    295–311, 319, 320
Chicago Bulls 93, 111, 215, 222–3
CIA 262
Cipriani, Danny 93, 122
circumstantial success 117–35
clarity
  assessment and providing 4, 5,
    53–76
  conflict and sense of 140, 153
  of direction, supporting change with
    97, 99–108, 110, 116
climate
  reviewing the 245, 254, 259

understanding the 5, 18, 22, 25,
    146–7, 258, 318
coaches
  assistant 3, 11, 12, 17, 31–2, 33,
    34–5, 37, 38, 40, 41–2, 55, 58,
    71, 86–8, 103, 104–5, 106–8,
    109, 139–41, 146–9, 164–6, 177,
    193, 196, 198, 214, 215–16, 223,
    231, 232, 270, 277, 290, 300, 321,
    322, 325, 329
  'coach', etymology of 22
  coaching of 11, 333–4
  conflict among 86–8, 138–40
  consultancies 27, 32, 118,
    127, 219
  criticism, response to 31–4
  engagement with other 2, 3, 25,
    34–5, 36–7, 41, 90, 117–18,
    125–6, 141–6, 173, 209–25, 237–8,
    250, 258–9, 305–6, 320, 321,
    322–4, 329
  loneliness of/solitary nature of life
    31–6, 41, 183, 209–25, 253
  performance relationships rather
    than great friendships among
    36–7
  personal identity and 81–2
  recruitment/examination of 37–9,
    133, 240–4, 301–2
  'truth-teller' and 3, 35, 41–7, 216,
    252, 321
  See also individual coaches and team
    names
Cokanasiga, Joe 298, 308
conflict
  creating 12, 263–4
  mining for 4, 11, 12, 14, 58–9, 61,
    85–9, 252, 315, 317–18, 322,
    329, 335
  healthy 11, 12, 97, 137–53, 177–8,
    194, 239, 263
context, providing 97, 108–110, 116

continuous improvement *viii*, 16, 245, 249–50, 293, 329
core values 81, 93–4, 113, 199
Corry, Martin 44
COTE (Confidence, Optimism, Tenacity and Enthusiasm) 206–8
courage
  ambition and 150, 284
  core values and *ix*, 94
  emotional journeys and 118, 126
  leadership value *ix*
  mistakes and 90
  selection and 39
  setting the vision and 19–23, 29
  transformation and 261–76
Covid-19 3, 53–9, 62, 63, 66, 72, 74–5, 99, 102, 129, 177, 178, 182, 192, 195, 201, 213, 219, 254, 269, 286, 297, 307, 315–16, 334
Cowan-Dickie, Luke 124, 199
Craig, Bruce 270
Craig, Neil 11, 12, 41–2, 55, 58, 71, 86–8, 104–5, 106–8, 109, 139–41, 146–9, 164–6, 177, 223, 231, 232, 277, 300, 321, 322
Crusaders 31, 32, 229
curiosity *ix*, 19, 22, 129, 250
  be curious and open to new ideas 97, 99–108
Curry, Tom 49–50, 82, 90, 106, 115, 120, 131, 132, 180, 195, 197, 202, 203, 233, 255, 277, 297, 310, 328
cycle of success, five stages of the leadership *viii*
  See also Vision; Build; Experiment; Win; Rebuild

Daily Mail 60, 242
Dallaglio, Lawrence 304
Daly, Elliot 59, 199, 254, 277
data analytics 119, 133, 189, 217–18, 288, 332

Dawson, Matt 304
Deans, Robbie 31–2, 33, 34, 229
Dein, David 220–1
Deloitte 319
Dick, Frank 265
discipline
  leadership value *ix*, 22
  maintaining 175–90, 196, 202, 219, 222, 326
  tactical periodization and 57–8
  thinking, disciplined 97, 117–35, 145, 166
discretionary effort 18–19, 78, 114, 227
diversity, importance of 92, 117, 128, 229–30, 240, 245, 265, 279, 295–311, 319, 320–1, 322
Donald, Stephen 113
dressing room 289–93
drip-feed ideas/test reaction 24–5
Dupont, Antoine 202
du Preez, Fourie 91, 328
Dwyer, Bob 44, 70–1, 100, 106, 177, 180, 213, 330
Dyche, Sean 144–6

Eales, John 286–7
Edwards, Shaun 42
80:20 philosophy/rule 75, 148
Ella, Gary 43
Ella, Glen 43, 223, 224
Ella, Gordon 43
Ella, Mark 43, 223
Ella, May 43
end in mind, always start with the 7–30
engaged leaders and entitled leaders, difference between 319
England (national cricket team) 228, 269–70, 280
England (national football team) 213, 237–8, 305–6, 320

England (national rugby union team)
  acting lessons arranged for players 74, 235
  aligning vision of the team to path of a specific player 95
  Argentina tour (2017) 120, 126, 271, 297, 310
  Australia tour (2004) 280–1
  Australia tour (2016) 11, 63, 123–5, 164, 236, 277–86, 290–1, 298–9
  Autumn Nations Cup and *see* Autumn Nations Cup
  Autumn Nations Series and *see* Autumn Nations Series
  breathing lessons for players 69
  captaincy 37, 39, 43–4, 45, 46–7, 95, 107, 196–7, 230–4, 234–5, 273–4, 278, 279, 282, 284, 286, 295–6, 300–1, 304–5, 307, 319
  Carling role in 43–7, 68, 107, 108, 231, 277, 295–6, 300–1, 304, 319, 321, 322
  club–country dynamic and 25–6, 129, 269–70, 286–7
  coaching group recruitment/ examination 37–9, 240–4, 301–2. *See also individual coach names*
  core values 81, 93–4, 113, 199
  Covid-19 and *see* Covid-19
  dressing room 289–93
  EJ's arrival as coach (2015) 25, 37
  EJ's contract with 15
  EJ describes difficulty of coaching 78–9
  entitlement, sense of and 4, 59, 84–5, 113–16, 139, 234, 263, 275, 305, 319
  failure to utilize talent within 93
  four groups, break up of squad into 105–6, 134
  Fresh Eyes project 302
  glue players 47–50, 52, 72, 169, 304

Hill becomes team manager 47
hybrid style of rugby, creation of 201, 202, 203, 279
kicking game 56, 57, 200–1, 202
leadership group 2, 9, 45–6, 58–9, 70, 86, 107–8, 167, 181, 194, 228–34, 235, 251, 254–5, 277–9, 284, 286, 295–311, 318–21, 322
legacy, creation of 29
media and 60, 63–5, 72, 73, 84–5, 92, 113, 127, 128–9, 130, 159, 164, 167, 168, 175–6, 193, 204–6, 219, 240, 254, 267–8, 274, 282, 284, 295, 306–7, 309, 332
popularity of 200
pre-mortem concept and 59–61
red teaming strategies 262–76
rivalries between players from different clubs 58–9, 62, 64, 86, 139, 194, 254, 301, 320
Saracens debacle and 58–9, 62, 64, 86, 139, 194, 254, 301, 320
selection process 24, 55, 104–5, 108, 111, 120, 128–9, 131–2, 156, 160, 162–3, 179–80, 206, 237, 238–9, 240, 273, 297–8, 307–8, 318–19, 320–1
servant to the players, EJ as 23, 83–4, 128, 334
setting the tone and 104, 266, 277, 303
Six Nations and *see* Six Nations
sports psychology and 11, 85–9, 160, 290, 332
tactical periodization and 57–8, 325–7
USA and Canada tour (2021) 120, 296–8, 304–5, 306, 307–9, 319
winning ratio 21, 176
winning streak, 18-Test 16, 268
World Cup and *see* World Cup

England (national rugby union team)
(*Cont'd.*)
world's greatest team, goal of
becoming 21–2, 23–4, 51, 110
World XV, players left out of
selection 24
entitlement, sense of 4, 59, 84–5,
113–16, 139, 234, 263, 275,
305, 319
environment
knowing the 5, 11–12, 18, 20, 25, 30,
66, 146–7, 258, 310, 318
reviewing the 245, 248–52, 254,
259, 265
Erasmus, Rassie 9, 185, 186
European Champions Cup 131
Euro 2020 237–8, 305–6, 308
Ewels, Charlie 199, 297–8, 305
examination, close 173, 227–44
Exeter Chiefs 131, 178, 254, 297
Experiment (Stage 3 – leadership cycle)
viii, 3, 173–244
a close examination 173, 227–44
other voices 173, 209–25
review constantly 173, 175–90
3 Per Cent Reminder 173,
191–208

face to face meetings 54–5, 74,
163–4, 178–9
family, leadership and 35–6, 210–12
Farr-Jones, Nick 291
Farrell, Andy 38, 86
Farrell, Owen 9, 48, 59, 82, 86, 93, 105,
115, 184, 194, 195, 196–7, 202, 203,
230–3, 254, 255, 277, 278, 279, 282,
284, 283, 286, 300, 301, 318
Fast Retailing 19
Federal Aviation Administration
(FAA) 262
female staff 240–1
Ferdinand, Rio 141, 142

Ferguson, Sir Alex 2, 25, 36–7, 126,
142–3, 146, 221
Few, Mark 101, 102
Fickou, Gaël 202, 203
Finegan, Owen 132
finishers, substitutes referred to as
306–7
FitzSimons, Peter 291
Foley, Bernard 282
Ford, George 130, 202, 233, 263, 277,
283, 297, 298
Formula One 200
Frade, Vitor 326
France (national rugby union team)
42, 65
Autumn Nations Cup (2020)
and 201
Six Nations (2020) 40–1, 51, 202
Six Nations (2021) 180, 188, 189,
191–2, 194, 196, 197–8, 199, 201–5,
207, 332
Francis, Piers 309
Frazier, Denarius 248–9
French Barbarians 159
Fresno University 214, 215
fundamental changes, deliver 97, 133–4,
135, 313, 335
Furbank, George 298
Furst, Dr Andrea 88

Galthié, Fabien 191, 192
Gatland, Warren 121, 125, 187
Gaüzère, Pascal 184
General Electric 302
Genge, Ellis 123–4, 125, 281, 295, 296,
298, 299, 303–4, 305, 310
Genia, Will 169–70
George, Jamie 59, 106, 199, 233,
254, 277
Germany (national rugby union
team) 78
Ghosn, Carlos 79–81, 83, 302

Gibson, Daryl 229
Gleeson, Martin 302
Gloucester Rugby 3–7
glue players 47–50, 52, 72, 169, 304
goals
    assessing transformation delivery
        versus goals in value terms 191–208
    emotional connection helps
        individuals achieve their 155–71
    highlighting 97, 150–3
    translating the vision into achievable
        goals 65–6, 76
Golden State Warriors 3, 34–5, 214–16,
    217, 321
Goldman Sachs 1–2, 19, 50, 158, 256–8
Gonzaga Bulldogs 3, 99, 100–4, 145
Goorjian Brian 322, 323–4
Goromaru, Ayumu 155–8, 159, 161, 162
Gould, Phil 224, 225
Greenwood, Will 304
Gregan, George 90, 229, 230, 275
Growth Mondays 97, 99–116, 134
Guardiola, Pep 2, 141–4, 146, 250
Gustard, Paul 37–8

half-time 292–3
Hansen, Steve 15, 33, 113, 115, 229
hard work/graft *ix*, 8, 22, 39, 95, 97,
    114–15, 131, 150–3, 169, 251, 275,
    285, 303
Hardy, Kieran 184
Harlequins 38, 44, 123, 125, 129, 297
Hartley, Dylan 39, 95, 131–2, 230,
    268, 273–4, 278, 279, 282, 284,
    297, 318
Haskell, James 95, 132, 161–4, 268, 279,
    283, 284
Hatley, Neal 38, 239
Heinz, Willi 106
Henderson, Jordan 48
Henry, Graham 33, 113, 115
Hiddink, Guus 57, 258

Hill, Cory 184
Hill, Jonny 132, 199
Hill, Paul 298
Hill, Richard 47, 304
Hill, Ted 298
Hirose, Toshiaki 158–60
Hodgson, Brett 117–18
Hogg, Rodney 228
home life, settled 35–6
honesty 300, 322, 332
    ambitions, expressing 283
    coaching group/fellow leaders and
        210, 214
    conflict and 85–9
    delivering news to a player and 72–3
    honest conversations to improve
        performance, create a space for
        85–9, 96, 107, 109, 146
    mental health and 280
    mistakes, admitting 40–1
    referees and 197
    'truth-teller' 3, 35, 41–7, 216,
        252, 321
horizon, setting the 97, 110–16
Hull FC 117–18, 120

'ideas thief' 250, 259
individual journeys, aligning overall
    vision to 5, 94–5, 96
Ineos 200
International Grammar School,
    Sydney 179
iPad 29
iPhone 29
Ireland
    Six Nations (2019) 60
    Six Nations (2021) 175, 180, 188, 191,
        204–7
Italy
    Six Nations (2016) 167
    Six Nations (2021) 131, 181, 182,
        191, 199

Itoje, Maro 10, 59, 82, 115, 167–8, 184, 187, 195–6, 197, 199, 203, 233, 234–5, 255, 277

Jackman, Hugh 241
Jackson, Glen 271
Jackson, Phil 215, 222–3
Jalibert, Matthieu 203
Japan
 club rugby in 32, 50, 78, 84, 127, 162, 196, 254, 270
 corporate leaders in 1–2, 19–21, 25, 50, 79–81, 250, 256–8, 273
 EJ coaches club rugby in 127, 219, 255, 330
 EJ's coaches' clinic for university and high school coaches in 333–4
 EJ's family and 211–12
 Japanese 'yes' 109, 110, 288–9
Japan (national rugby union team) 8, 10, 27–9, 68, 79, 147, 150–2, 155–60, 213
 EJ as coach of 1, 8, 10, 27–8, 38, 45, 68, 79, 90, 129, 143, 147, 150–2, 155–60, 213, 236, 240–1, 255–6, 288–9, 292, 325–6, 327
 World Cup (2015) 7, 10, 27, 28, 29, 129, 147, 150–2, 155, 292, 327
 World Cup (2019) 163–4
 World Cup (2023) 219
Japanese internment camps, US 211–12, 214
Japanese Rugby Union 127
Jardine, Douglas 280, 283
Johns, Andrew 285
Johnson, Martin 44, 47, 296, 304
Jones, Adam 125
Jones, Alun Wyn 196–7, 234–5
Jones, Chelsea (daughter of EJ) 34

Jones, Eddie
 anger, sparing use of 89
 assessment of management style, outside (Simon Scott) 321–2
 assistant coaches, relationship with see individual coach names
 Australia head coach 1, 8, 15, 26–7, 31, 32–3, 34, 35, 37, 73, 85, 100, 112, 132, 147, 161–2, 176, 213, 235–6, 253, 256, 275–6, 280–1, 286–7, 292, 327–8
 Brumbies head coach 1, 32, 37, 72, 85, 91, 112, 222, 224–5, 228–30, 240, 274–6
 childhood 43, 44
 coaches, engagement with other 2, 3, 25, 34–5, 36–7, 41, 90, 117–18, 125–6, 141–6, 173, 209–25, 237–8, 250, 258–9, 305–6, 320, 321, 322–4, 329
 coaching consultancies 27, 32, 118, 127, 219
 coaching of coaches 11, 333–4
 coaching sessions, attends additional (outside England rugby union set-up) 117–18
 Covid-19 and see Covid-19
 cycle of leadership, four words that define 317
 England head coach see England (national rugby union team) and individual competitions and players
 face to face meetings, preference for 54–5, 74, 163–4, 178–9
 family and see individual family member names
 future ambitions 78–9
 Japan head coach 1, 8, 10, 27–8, 38, 45, 68, 79, 90, 129, 143, 147, 150–2, 155–60, 213, 236, 240–1, 255–6, 288–9, 292, 325–6, 327
 loneliness/solitary nature of leadership and 31, 34–6, 41, 183, 209–25, 253

Jones, Eddie (*Cont'd.*)
  mistakes, admitting 61, 178–80
  noise, external (criticism and doubt)
    and 34, 64–5, 76, 175, 176, 186,
    187, 189, 220, 274, 306 *see also*
    media
  outsider 127–8, 213, 282
  players, relationship with *see*
    individual player names
  purpose in life 79
  reading list 117
  refereeing mistakes and 183–6, 187,
    195, 196–8, 203, 231, 233, 332
  rugby playing career 213
  Saracens coach 217, 271
  servant to the players 23, 83–4,
    128, 334
  South Africa assistant coach 1, 2, 27,
    147, 254–5, 290
  Suntory, roles with 27, 32, 84, 127–8,
    219, 250, 255–6, 270, 330, 331
  teaching career 89, 179, 254
  WhatsApp communication, preference
    for hard documents over 71–2
  work–life balance 210–12
Jones, Hiroko (wife of EJ) 34, 35, 127
Jones, Nell (mother of EJ) 211–12
Jones, Ted (father of EJ) v, 89, 211, 212
Jordan, Michael 93, 111, 215, 222

Kafer, Rod 90, 230, 275
Kaizen ('continuous improvement' or
  'change for the better') 249–50
Kearns, Phil 213
Keating, Paul 24
Kefu, Toutai 33
Kerr, Steve 3, 35, 214, 215, 216,
  217, 321
Kipchoge, Eliud 200
Kirwan, John 156, 157
Klopp, Jürgen 22–3
Knight, Travis 100–1, 102, 103–4

knowledge, glue of 5, 77–96
  know yourself, know your players
    77–9, 96
  understand the gaps – in capability,
    values and belief 92–5, 96
  understand the groups, understand
    the individuals 79–91, 96
Kolisi, Siya 9, 255
Kruis, George 50, 115, 196, 254

Lam, Pat 125
Lancaster, Stuart 38–9
Langdon, Curtis 298
Langer, Justin 39–40
Larkham, Stephen 26–7, 90, 230, 275
La Rochelle 131
Larwood, Harold 280
Last Dance, The (documentary) 93, 111,
  222
Launchbury, Joe 115, 126, 196, 254
Laver, Rod 332
Lawes, Courtney 49, 254, 297
Lawrence, Ollie 84–5, 132, 298, 308
leadership *see individual areas of*
  leadership
leadership group 2, 9, 45–6
  conflict in 58–62, 64, 85–9, 139, 194,
    254, 301, 320
  examining/changing 107–8, 181,
    194, 228–34, 235, 254–5, 277–9,
    295–311, 318–21, 322
  fluid entity, making 318–19
  setting the vision and 70
  wider well-being of the squad and 68
learning
  remaining open to 173, 209–25
  science of 245, 247–59
Leicester Tigers 44, 239, 254, 295, 299
Leitch, Michael 152, 159–60
Lemov, Doug 247–9
Lensbury Hotel, Teddington 54–5
Lewis, Michael: *Moneyball* 118–20

Liverpool FC 22–3, 48
Living with Lions video 289
Lomu, Jonah 32–3, 44
loneliness/solitary nature of leadership
31, 34–6, 41, 183, 209–25, 253
Ludlam, Lewis 298, 309
Ludlow, Lewis 304, 307

MacDonald, Leon 229
Macqueen, Rod 31, 253, 274, 275
Malins, Max 199, 202, 297
Management phases 3, 27, 28
Vision stage (the glue of knowledge)
5, 77–96
Build stage (finding the access point)
97, 155–71
Experiment stage (a close
examination) 173, 227–44
Win stage (chemistry and diversity)
245, 295–311
Rebuild stage 313
manage up 216–18
managing behaviour 4, 315–35
Manchester City 141–2
Manchester United 25, 37, 141, 142,
146, 221
Mapimpi, Makazole 10
mapping where we are in the cycle
4, 315–35
March Madness 101, 102
Marchand, Julien 203
Marchant, Joe 298
marginal improvements 245,
252–3, 311
Marler, Joe 124, 280
Martin, George 180
May, Jonny 48, 90–1, 169, 187, 202,
298, 328
McCaw, Richie 49, 91, 115, 196, 234,
270, 328
McConnochie, Ruaridh 309
McKenzie, Ewen 37

media 35, 254
EJ as Australia coach and 74
EJ's coaching consultancies, criticism
of 127–8, 219
EJ's coaching philosophy and 83
England rugby team, conflict in and 86
England rugby team, criticism of 60,
63–5, 175–6, 103, 204–6, 219, 267–8
England rugby team selection and 84,
92, 128–9, 130, 167–8, 204–6, 307,
309
England rugby team sense of
entitlement and 113
England rugby team tour of Australia
(2016) and 282, 284
mental health and 332
Southgate and 306–7
Will Carling and 295
Mehrtens, Andrew 229
Melbourne Storm 231
mentors 43–7, 55, 95–6, 107, 108, 121,
122, 125, 212–13, 231, 277, 295–6,
300–1, 304, 319, 321, 322
Mercedes F1 team 200
Microsoft 262
Mills, Patty 323, 324
Mitchell, Alex 298
Mitchell, John 38, 55, 277, 302
Mochida, Masanori 256–8
motivation 17, 78, 94–5, 160, 171, 205,
242, 319
Moyes, David 199, 213, 219–20
Ms, three (Manage people, Mine for
conflict, Map where you are in the
cycle) 4, 315–35
Müller, Thomas 143
Murray, Conor 205

Nance, Steve 275
National Basketball Association (NBA)
189, 214–15, 216, 217, 219,
288, 321, 323

National Collegiate Athletic Association
(NCAA) 101–2
National Football League (NFL) 81
National Rugby League (NRL)
Premiership 117–18, 231
neuroticism 47, 92
Neville, Joy 203
Neville, Tracey 305
New Zealand, British and Irish Lions
tour of (2017) 120, 271–2
New Zealand (national rugby union
team) (All Blacks) 26, 31–2, 156,
200, 229
Autumn Internationals (2018) 46
British and Irish Lions New Zealand
tour (2017) and 120, 271–2
coaches *see individual coach names*
legacy and ambition, connection
between 45
player contracts 269, 270
six-month sabbaticals, player 270
Super Rugby and 269, 270
Tri-Nations (2001) 32–3
winning ratio 115
winning streak, 18-Test 16, 268
World Cup (1995) 27, 44
World Cup (2003) 38, 292
World Cup (2011) 33, 113
World Cup (2015) 33, 113, 285–6,
327–8
World Cup (2019) 7–9, 10, 11, 12, 13,
14, 28, 63, 202, 292, 293
World Rankings 279
Nice, OGC 200
9/11 261, 262
Nissan 79–81, 250, 302
noise, external (criticism and doubt) 34,
64–5, 76, 175, 176, 186, 187, 189,
220, 274, 306
Nokia 198
Nowell, Jack 178, 254
Number 10s 130

Oakland Athletics 118–20
Obano, Beno 164–6, 298, 304
O'Connor, James 122
Oghre, Gabriel 298, 310
Olympics 91, 265
(2016) 88
(2021) 323–4
Operation phases *viii*, 3
Vision stage (clarity is the new clever)
5, 53–76
Build stage (conflict is healthy) 97,
137–53
Experiment stage (other voices) 173,
209–25
Win stage (a clean sweep) 245,
277–93
Rebuild stage 313
Osaka, Naomi 332, 333

Paine, Tim 320
Panasonic Wild Knights 32
Paulson, Hank 257
Penaud, Damian 203
People phases *viii*, 3
Vision stage (character over cover
drive) 31–52
Build stage (disciplined thinking and
emotional journeys) 97, 117–35
Experiment stage (3 per cent
reminder) 173, 191–208
Win stage (red teaming
transformation) 245, 261–76
Rebuild stage 313
perfection, pursuit of 7–8, 326–8, 336
performance relationships 36–7
personal animosities 270–3
picking battles 288–9
Pietersen, Kevin 47
Pippin, Scottie 222
Pivac, Wayne 187
Pocock, David 164, 283
Ponting, Ricky 73

Postecoglou, Ange 323, 324, 331
Premiership, English 1, 25–6, 130–1, 275,
    281, 286, 297, 307, 310, 316, 320
pre-mortem 59–61
presentations/team talks, younger
    generation and 69–70
principles, setting 5, 16, 22–3, 30, 39,
    95–6, 113, 147, 175, 232, 251,
    259, 325
Proudfoot, Matt 55
Pryce-Tidd, Ollie 122
Pryor, John 325
psychological safety 138
psychometric testing, leaders and
    319–20

Queensland Reds 169–70
quick wins
    deliver the 97, 133–4, 135, 335
    identify the quick wins and the big
        changes required 5, 50, 51, 52

racism 214, 306, 320–1
Radwan, Adam 308, 310
RAF 265
Randall, Harry 132, 297, 308, 310
Randwick 1, 37, 68, 71, 92, 213, 223–4,
    256, 264, 274, 279, 285, 291–2, 327
Ratcliffe, Jim 199–200
Rebuild (Stage 5 – leadership cycle)
    313–35
    coaches, regular engagement with
        other 322–4
    core truths 328–9
    diversity and 320–1
    engaged leaders and entitled leaders,
        difference between 319
    fractured chemistry, repair the or
        rebuild the entire entity 320
    leadership group a fluid entity, making
        the 318–19
    perfection, pursuit of 327–8

psychometric testing of leaders
    319–20
    Simon Scott assesses EJ's management
        style 321–2
    tactical periodization and 325–6
red teaming transformation 245, 261–76
Rees-Zammit, Louis 184, 188
refereeing 34, 114, 183–6, 187, 195,
    196–8, 203, 231, 233, 332
Reid, Corinne 11, 85–6, 88
Renault 79–80, 81
resources, aligning to the changes
    required 97, 117, 120–33, 134, 135,
    313, 332–4, 335
review, constant 173, 175–90
Ricoh Black Rams 162
Ritchie, Ian 44
rivals, working with 100
Robinson, Andy 55
Robinson, Brett 228–9
Robinson, Ed 55, 302
Robinson, Jason 296
Robshaw, Chris 39, 95, 126, 132, 258,
    268, 279, 284, 297
Robson, Bobby 187
Robson, Dan 298, 304, 305
Rodman, Dennis 222
Roff, Joe 230
Rowntree, Graham 38
Rugby Football Union (RFU) 15, 44, 45,
    64, 128, 144, 176, 204, 214, 216, 217,
    218, 219, 316
Ruiz, Alex 184
Ryan, Peter 240
Ryles, Jason 55, 302

sabermetric approach 119
Sailor, Wendell 161–2, 327–8
salary cap 58, 320
Sale Sharks 125, 255
Saracens 58–9, 62, 64, 86, 139, 194, 217,
    254, 271, 301, 320

Saviour World 121–2, 125

Sayle, Jeff 213, 285, 291

Schweitzer, Louis 79

Scotland

  Six Nations (2019) 86, 263, 264

  Six Nations (2021) 34, 55, 59–62, 164, 175, 178–82, 183–4, 188, 192, 194, 195, 198, 199, 201, 204

Scott, Simon 321–2

Second World War (1939–45) 211–12

selection process

  access points, finding and 97, 118, 155–71

  aligning resources to the changes required 120, 128–33

  captain *see* captaincy

  character and ('character over cover drive') 31–52

  chemistry and diversity and 295–311, 320–1

  coaching staff 240–3, 301–2

  disruption and 132–3

  dropping players 131–2, 163–4, 237–8

  entitlement/complacency and 24, 111, 113–16, 120, 128–9, 234

  leadership group *see* leadership group

  mistakes in 179–80, 272–3

  player bust-ups and 272–3

  substitutes 237–8, 306–7

  Southgate and 237–8, 306–7

  winning and 104–5

self-knowledge 77–9, 81, 96

set the tone 104, 266, 277, 303

Sevens rugby 57

Sexton, Johnny 205

Sharks (Super 12 team) 112, 230, 255

Sheedy, Callum 184

Simmonds, Sam 131

Sinckler, Kyle 10, 120–8, 195, 203, 281, 297, 298–9

Six Nations

  (2015) 63, 124, 279, 281, 286

  (2016) 95, 162, 236

  (2017) 236

  (2018) 63

  (2019) 60, 86, 263, 264

  (2020) 2, 40–1, 51, 56, 65, 71–2, 99, 176, 195, 200, 201, 315–16

  (2021) 2, 33–4, 36, 55–62, 63, 75, 84, 113–14, 120, 139, 164, 175–6, 177–90, 191–2, 195, 200–8, 214, 218–19, 231, 232, 254, 277–8, 286, 287, 295, 298, 303, 316, 319, 332

Slade, Henry 202, 203, 298, 304, 305, 310

Smit, John 255

Smith, Cameron 231–2

Smith, George 49, 85, 90, 196, 229, 230

Smith, Marcus 128–30, 297, 307–8, 310

Smith, Steve 319–20

Smith, Wayne 32–3, 34, 38, 41

soft skills 231, 234

Solomona, Denny 272

Somerville, Greg 229

South Africa

  British and Irish Lions tour of (1997) 289–90

  British and Irish Lions tour of (2021) 56, 114, 120–3, 125, 126, 131, 185–6, 196, 234, 269, 270, 297, 308–9

  coaching clinics to schoolboy coaches, EJ gives 333–4

  England tour of (2018) 263

South Africa (national rugby union team) 100

  British and Irish Lions tour of South Africa (1997) and 289–90

  British and Irish Lions tour of South Africa (2021) and 56, 185

  EJ assistant coach 1, 2, 27, 147, 254–5, 290

  England tour of South Africa (2018) and 263

South Africa (national rugby union team)
    (*Cont'd.*)
  Tri-Nations (2001) 33
  World Cup (2007) 26–7, 254–5, 290
  World Cup (2015) 28, 152, 292,
    327, 328
  World Cup (2019) 7, 8, 9–13, 14, 15,
    16, 28, 64, 110, 255, 321
Southgate, Gareth 2, 213, 219, 237–8,
    305–6, 320
South Sydney Roosters 224
sports administrators 287–8
sports psychology 11, 85–9, 160,
    290, 332
Steward, Freddie 308, 310
St George's Park 54
Stoke City 205
Strategy phases 3
  Vision stage (setting the vision) 3, 5,
    7–30
  Build stage (growth Mondays) 97,
    99–116
  Experiment stage (review constantly)
    173, 175–90
  Win stage (science of learning) 245,
    247–59
  Rebuild stage 313
stress, managing 54, 241, 292–3, 310
Stuart, Will 132, 161
substitutes 237–8, 283, 306–7
Suntory 27, 32, 84, 127–8, 219, 250,
    255–6, 270, 330, 331
Super Rugby 1, 31, 169, 269
Super 12 32, 112, 228, 229,
    230, 276
Sweeney, Bill 216–17, 218
Sydney University 291–2

tactical periodization 57–8, 325–7
talent, failure to utilize 93
Team Sky (cycling) 199–200
Telfer, Jim 290

temperature of the room, testing the
    82–91, 96, 324
Te'o, Ben 273
Thomas, Teddy 202, 203
Thompson, Daley 265
Thorne, Reuben 229
3 Per Cent Reminder, The 173,
    191–208
TMO 46, 184, 185, 203, 282
togetherness with the right people
    around you, building 31–52
tone, setting the 104, 266, 277, 303
Torres, Ferran 142
Toshiba 158, 255
Toyota 249–50
transformation
  fresh eyes and 297–311
  join the vision to the 108–10,
    116, 297
  plan the 50, 51, 52, 80, 107, 108–9
  red teaming 261–76
Tri-Nations (2001) 32–3
'truth-teller' 3, 35, 41–7, 216, 252, 321
Tuilagi, Manu 48–9, 272, 298

UK Athletics 265
Underhill, Sam 46, 115, 120, 131, 132,
    180, 297, 298, 304, 305, 308, 310
Uniqlo 1–2, 19–21, 25, 250, 273
USA (national rugby union team) 78–9,
    120, 296–8, 304–5, 307, 308, 319

Vakatawa, Virimi 202
values
  core *ix*, 81, 93–4, 113, 199
  establishing the 5, 16, 22–3, 26, 30,
    39, 73, 81, 93–4, 96, 113, 125, 323
  gaps in, understanding 92–5, 96
  leadership *ix*
van Gaal, Louis 221–2
Verheijen, Raymond 57, 326–7
Vickery, Phil 296–7, 304

Vision (Stage 1 – leadership cycle) *viii*, 3, 5–96, 329
  character over cover drive 31–52
  clarity is the new clever 5, 53–76
  setting the vision 5–30
  the glue of knowledge 5, 77–96
voices, other 173, 209–25
vulnerability 32–3, 40–1, 88, 123, 126, 161, 214, 216, 332–3
Vunipola, Billy 59, 254, 298
Vunipola, Mako 49, 59, 106, 233, 254, 277

Wales 42
  Six Nations (2021) 33–4, 114–15, 175, 182–9, 191, 192, 194, 195–8, 199, 201
  World Cup (2015) 284
  World Cup (2019) 10, 15, 187
  World Cup (2023) 188
Walker, Andrew 223–5, 230
walking the floor/close observation 18, 25, 146–7, 258, 318
Walsh, Bill: *Finding the Winning Edge* 81
Walsh, Vincent 251
Warne, Shane 47
Warner, David 319–20
Wasps 130, 254, 302, 310
Watson, Anthony 106, 202, 203, 270
Welch, Jack 302
Wenger, Arsène 2, 90, 220–1, 258–9
Western Bulldogs 322
West Ham United 220
Wests Tigers 117
WhatsApp communication 71–2
White, Jake 16, 100, 290, 333
Wilkinson, Jonny 15
Williams, Liam 184
Willis, Jack 130–1
Wilson, Mark 47, 202, 298, 309
Win [Overcome Failure] (Stage 4 – leadership cycle) *viii*, 3, 245–311
  a clean sweep 245, 277–93

  chemistry and diversity 245, 295–311
  red teaming transformation 245, 261–76
  the science of learning 245, 247–59
Winter, Tex 215
Wisemantel, Scott 'Wisey' 38, 240
Witt, Katarina 265
Woki, Cameron 203
Woodward, Clive 38, 60, 219, 242
World Cup
  (1991) 44, 100
  (1995) 27, 44, 45
  (1999) 31
  (2003) 15, 26–7, 38, 47, 132, 147, 236, 254, 292, 304, 327–8
  (2007) 16, 26–7, 254–5, 290
  (2011) 33, 113, 156
  (2015) 25, 27, 28–9, 33, 39, 86, 93, 113, 129, 130, 147, 150–2, 155, 160, 169, 236, 241, 279, 284, 285–6, 292, 326, 327, 328
  (2019) 2, 4, 7–16, 23, 26, 28–9, 38, 51, 57, 58, 59, 63–4, 78, 85–8, 110, 112, 120, 125, 132, 133, 134, 147, 163, 176, 187, 196, 202, 221, 238, 240, 255, 264, 273, 292, 293, 309, 319, 327, 328
  (2023) 4, 8, 15, 19, 23, 51, 56, 120, 132–3, 177, 188, 189, 219, 240, 255, 267, 297, 299, 309, 318, 321, 332
World Rugby 185, 331
Wray, Nigel 217

Yanai, Tadashi 1–2, 19–21, 23, 25, 250, 273
Yokohama F. Marinos 324, 331
Youngs, Ben 184, 187, 298

Zimbabwe (national rugby union team) 27
Zoom 34, 55, 74–5, 100, 102, 117, 178, 199, 214, 219, 223, 232, 247, 248, 249, 250, 323